The Geopolitics of East Asia

The search for equilibrium

Robyn Lim

Routledge
Taylor & Francis Group

LONDON AND NEW YORK

First published in hardback 2003
by Routledge
first published in paperback 2005 by Routledge
2 Park Square, Milton Park, Abingdon, Oxon, OX14 4RN

Simultaneously published in the USA and Canada
by Routledge
270 Madison Ave, New York, NY 10016

Routledge is an imprint of the Taylor & Francis Group
First published in paperback in 2005

Typeset in Times by Routledge
Printed and bound in by

British Library Cataloguing in Publication Data
A catalogue record for this book is available from the British Library

Library of Congress Cataloging-in-Publication Division

Lim, Robyn, 1947-
The geopolitics of East Asia: search for equilibrium/Robyn Lim.
        p.cm.
Includes bibliographical references and index.
ISBN 0–415–36030–7 (pbk)
ISBN 0–415–29717–6 (hbk)
1. East Asia--Politics and government--20th centruy. 2. Geopolitics--
East Asia. I Title.
DS518.1.L49 2003
950.4--dc21
                2002036964

For my parents, Roy and Majory Abell

Contents

Acknowledgements

This book is a consequence of a suggestion by the former deputy director general of the Office of National Assessments in Canberra, A.D. 'Tim' McLennan. His constant support and encouragement was invaluable. Another large debt of gratitude is owed to Professor James Auer (USN ret.), director of the Centre for U.S. Japan Studies and Cooperation at Vanderbilt University's Institute for Public Policy Studies. Jim Auer opened many doors for me, and introduced me to a flotilla of his American and Japanese navy friends. I am also especially grateful for the encouragement of the veteran Australian journalist Denis Warner, who linked me up with his old friend Sol Sanders ('Ye Olde Crabbe'). Thanks are also due to Tim Huxley, Senior Fellow for Asia Pacific Security at the Institute of Strategic and International Studies in London, for his encouragement from the outset.

I am also indebted to friends and colleagues who read parts of the text. These include Thomas Bartlett, Edward Dreyer, June Teufel Dreyer, Bruce Ellemann, Edward Griffin, Ingolf Kiesow, Hisahiko Okazaki, Richard Parker, David Potter, Sueo Sudo, Stanley Weeks, Martin Weinstein and Kenneth Weisbrode.

Special thanks are also due to my spouse Lim Soo Khiam (Simon) for all kinds of support, especially with logistics. I am grateful to Simon Nevitt for the maps.

I also gratefully acknowledge Nanzan University's financial support in the form of a Pache 1-A research grant for the years 2000 to 2002.

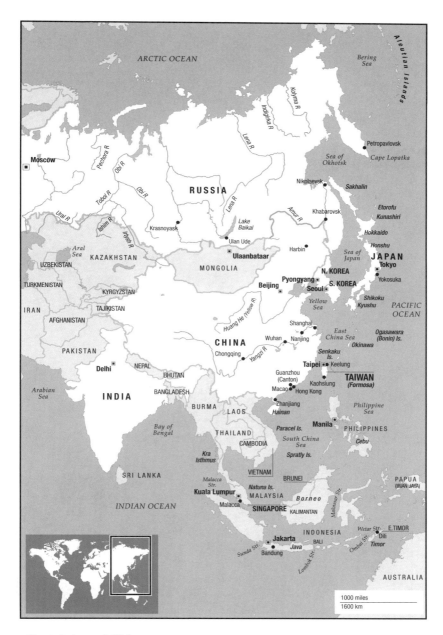

East Asia and China

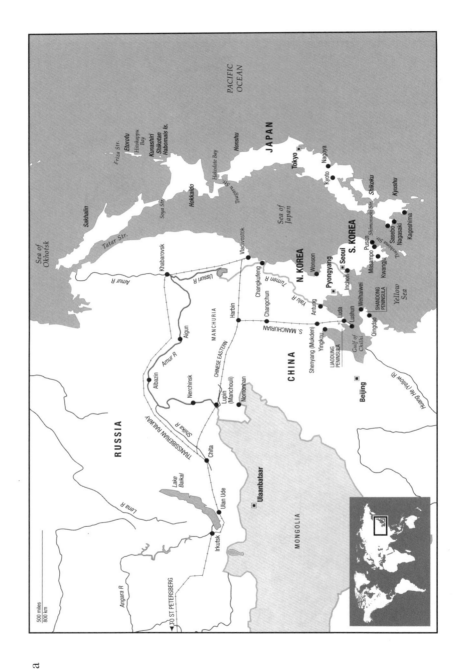

Korea

Introduction

More than a decade ago, the winning of the Cold War saw East Asia become the global focus of unresolved great-power strategic tension. That was because the collapse of Soviet power saw equilibrium restored to the western end of the Eurasian landmass, but not to its eastern edge. In Europe, strategic security is now settled in the broad.[1] Another European great-power war is highly unlikely, as shown for example by Russia's edging ever closer towards NATO.[2] When a German-speaking Russian president can address the parliament of a reunified Germany in Berlin, as Vladimir Putin did in mid-2002, we can be confident that the historic contest between Russia and Germany for hegemony over Eurasia is truly past.

But in East Asia, the end of the Cold War saw no such resolution of great-power strategic tension. There the East Asian quadrilateral – the United States, China, Japan and Russia – continues, albeit on the basis of new configurations of strategic interest. The quadrilateral, which never really disappeared under the overlay of the Cold War, resurfaced with a vengeance in 1991. Since the end of the Cold War, strategic tensions in East Asia have arisen solely as a consequence of fluctuations in strategic interests within the quadrilateral – they are no longer mostly reflections of strategic tensions that have their roots in collisions of great-power interest in Europe, as they had been since the quadrilateral assembled in 1905.

In East Asia, although great-power war is far from inevitable, it remains thinkable – not only between the United States and China, but over the longer term between China and Japan, the two great powers of East Asia that have never previously been strong at the same time. As America makes war in Afghanistan, in response to the terrorist attacks on the United States in September 2001, it cannot afford to neglect the problems of East Asian security. That's particular so because the region is now the focus of global economic growth, fuelled in large part by the burgeoning Chinese economy.[3]

Regional tensions focus on the Korean peninsula, the Taiwan Strait and the East and South China Seas – a half-island, a strait and two semi-enclosed seas. That all points to the maritime dimension of the region's security. Maritime tensions are bound to engage the strategic interest of the United States, because of the maritime basis of America's own security. The theme of this book is how East Asia's strategic geography bears on the interests of the United States as the dominant maritime power.

Since 1905, America's essential strategic interest in East Asia has been to see established a balance of power on the opposite shore of the vast Pacific Ocean. Throughout all the gyrations of the East Asian quadrilateral, the United States has pursued this goal with remarkable tenacity. It was the pursuit of equilibrium that led President Theodore Roosevelt to broker the peace at Portsmouth in 1905, after Russia and Japan had fought each other to exhaustion. Subsequently, America's interest in maintaining a balance of power in East Asia led into all its wars there – the war against Japan, the Korean war and the Vietnam war.

The essential American interest does not lie in any particular configuration of strategic interest within the quadrilateral. Rather, America's overriding concern is with the balance of power. The East Asian quadrilateral has fluctuated constantly over time, and is likely to continue to do so. Since 1991, the most serious tensions have been between the United States and China. But this was not the case in the past, and might not always be so in future.

Currently, however, America's search for equilibrium is at the heart of the growing collision of interest between the United States and China. Because of the maritime basis of its own security, the United States cannot tolerate the assertion of hegemony over Eurasia, or any of its vital parts, and China is the current chief candidate. China now represents the chief challenge to the balance of power in East Asia because it possesses the motive, will and opportunity to seek dominance there. If China were to become dominant in East Asia, that would detract from American security directly by excluding US military power from the area, or by seeking to do so; and indirectly by its effects on Japan. Currently, the US–Japan security treaty provides strategic security for Japan in ways that do not disturb its neighbours. But Japan, if faced with the prospect of Chinese hegemony, would either knuckle under – to America's detriment – or, more likely, would resist. If Japan were to do so unilaterally, that would inflame regional tensions.

In East Asia, America's essential task is to help integrate a rising China peacefully into the global and regional order, while reassuring Japan. Thus the most important decisions about East Asia's strategic future are likely to be made in Washington rather than in Beijing or Tokyo. Thus it is critical that the United States thinks and acts strategically. This book adopts an historical approach because that is the only way to comprehend how and why the East Asian quadrilateral assembled by 1905, and the role it subsequently played in the global balance. History may not repeat itself, but certain patterns are too striking to ignore. Moreover, the East Asian states are highly attuned to history and to its contemporary political uses – even if Americans often are not.

The Western Pacific is mostly a maritime theatre because the Pacific is the largest of the world's oceans, larger than the Indian and Atlantic Oceans combined. In order to maintain a balance of power on the opposite shore of the Pacific, the United States must project power over enormous distances. Thus an appreciation of the importance of maritime power is a theme of this book. Maritime power provides the means to bring military power to bear decisively – ranging from the transport of troops across water, through blockade, to securing airfields and bases in order to strike at the enemy's vitals. Strategic flexibility is also greatly enhanced by maritime power, as shown for example by General MacArthur's landing behind enemy lines at Inchon during the Korean war.

Exploiting the flexibility and mobility that sea power confers, the maritime powers have won all the great global strategic contests of recent history. As leaders of mixed maritime–continental coalitions, they defeated in turn Napoleon, Hitler and the Soviet Union, who all strove mightily for hegemony over Eurasia. If China, a rising continental power, is indeed seeking domination over East Asia and its contiguous waters, this pattern of conflict is set to continue – because the United States, with its own maritime security at stake, is bound to stand in China's way.

East Asia's strategic geography: the two 'core areas'

Strategic geography is the relationship between power in the international system and the geographical setting.[4] Geography doesn't change, but the interests of states do, and so does technology. East Asia's strategic geography will be defined as those parts of the Eurasian landmass adjoining the Pacific Ocean, their hinterlands, and the offshore islands. Large landmasses further afield, notably the Indian subcontinent and the island continent of Australia (with its strategic dependency of New Zealand) are also relevant to East Asia's strategic geography because they affect the regional balance.

East Asia possesses two 'core areas', China and Japan.[5] China is a mostly self-sufficient continent-sized land power which occupies the central geographical position on the eastern edge of the Eurasian landmass. For its part, Japan is a resource-poor but populous archipelago barely off the littoral.

China: Middle Kingdom

China dominates East Asia for reasons of size, centrality and demographic weight.[6] It also represents the world's longest continuous civilization, and thus exerts immense cultural influence in its region. China, from its hydrographical centre based upon the three main rivers flowing into the East and South China Seas, developed extensive irrigation that permitted farming and dense populations. To the north, the nomads were kept at bay, most of the time at least, by the Great Wall. Behind the wall, China developed its distinctive hierarchical civilization of strict Confucianism mitigated by the gentler teachings of Buddhism and Taoism.[7]

With its 8,700-mile-long coastline and great navigable rivers draining eastwards to the Pacific, China always had the potential to become a sea power of the first rank. Indeed, for a time it seemed that it might do so. China showed a serious interest in maritime power from the time of the collapse of the Northern Song dynasty in 1127 through the Mongol (Yuan) dynasty and until the Mings (1368–1644). The Mongols or Tartars, although horsemen of the steppes, proved surprisingly adept at developing maritime power. Between 1274 and 1294, they launched unsuccessful invasions of Japan, amphibious assaults against northern Vietnam, a seaborne invasion of southern Vietnam and an invasion of the Majapahit empire on the distant island of Java.[8] They also tried without much success to capture all of peninsular Southeast Asia, with attacks through China's back door in Burma intended to link up with the amphibious attacks into Vietnam.[9] Even further afield, Mongol ships arrived at the Indian Ocean island of Ceylon in 1291, in vain demanding the holy relic of Lord Buddha's Tooth. After the restoration of Han rule by the Ming dynasty, China's interest in maritime expansion accelerated.

In 1405, the Ming emperor Yongle (Yung Lo) dispatched the Muslim eunuch official Zheng He (Cheng Ho) on the first of seven great ocean-going expeditions. Large armed Chinese junks were deployed into the Indian Ocean, sailing as far west as the Persian Gulf. Subsidiary expeditions went as far as the Red Sea and the Mozambique Channel between Madagascar and the African mainland. That was at a time when the much smaller Portuguese caravels, pushing eastwards, were still clinging to the West African coast.

Zheng He, in pursuit of political objectives as well as treasure, secured the allegiance to China of many of the kingdoms and sultanates of maritime Southeast Asia. A notable new vassal was the sultan of Malacca, astride the vital strait of the same name that links the Indian and Pacific Oceans. In 1405, the sultan of Bengal sent an envoy to the Chinese court, so becoming a vassal in Chinese eyes. Further afield, in 1409 in Ceylon, where the current king still refused to hand over Lord Buddha's Tooth, Ming forces fought their way to the royal mountain redoubt at Kandy. Soon both king and Tooth were on their way to Beijing.[10] Thus, under the early Mings, China's maritime periphery extended far into the Indian Ocean. Although the Ming voyages were mostly peaceful, the junks were heavily armed, and the Mings did not shrink from the use of force, as shown by the Kandy expedition for example.

But the Ming voyages proved short-lived. In 1433, they were terminated because officials had become concerned at their high cost and poor returns. More broadly, China could pursue maritime ambition only if its land frontiers were secure. That was rarely the case because of the constant pressure from armed nomads on the vast steppes. Thus in 1525 an imperial edict ordered the destruction of all large seagoing vessels and the arrest of their crews. Moreover, in 1644 another northern dynasty, the Manchus, ousted the Mings. Unlike the Mongols, the Qing (Ching) dynasty showed little interest in maritime expansion. Thus China turned away from the sea just as the Western maritime powers were beginning to push their way into Asia. China's turning inwards at this critical juncture was to have fateful strategic consequences.

Japan: subtle defiance on China's maritime periphery

Typically, states surrounded by sea are more secure than those facing enemies across land boundaries. Water provides a more effective barrier than rivers, or even high mountains. Thus, in 1274 and 1281, the Tsushima Strait between Japan and South Korea protected Japan from the Mongols, who had occupied the southern part of the Korean peninsula. With their talent for warfare, the Mongols might have invaded Japan if the 'divine winds' or *kamikaze* had not scattered Kublai Khan's invasion fleets off Kyushu. Still, the Mongol invasions were a rarity. For centuries, China's lack of maritime ambition protected Japan. China saw itself as a self-contained civilization rather than a nation-state, and was not generally interested in trying to invade Japan. So Japan's history did not much resemble that of England, that other small island barely offshore at the opposite end of Eurasia. There, large continental states with hegemonic ambitions tried quite often to invade England across its 'narrow seas'.

Thus Japan, a homogeneous country like China, long pursued an independent existence on the margins of the Chinese world. The Japanese did not contest China's cultural superiority. To the contrary, Japan derived from the Middle Kingdom much of its culture, including its written language, its administrative system, Buddhism and Confucianism. But while borrowing much from China, the Japanese retained their own traditions. They kept their spoken language, their *samurai* warrior culture and their pantheistic Shinto religion, the 'way of the gods'.

Moreover, the Japanese rejected Chinese concepts that did not mesh with their own traditions. For example, China's notion of the 'mandate of heaven', the source of the emperor's authority, did not suit the Japanese. It implied that the mandate might be withdrawn, and that would undermine the belief that Japan's emperor was descended in an unbroken line from the gods. Nor did the Japanese adopt, as the Koreans did, some key elements of Chinese Confucianism such as the imperial examination system. Notably, Japan's *samurai* also possessed much greater prestige than did warriors in China, where scholar-bureaucrats disdained the profession of arms.

Despite having adopted so much from the mainland, the Japanese subtly defied China in myriad ways, notably by insisting on calling their own king 'heavenly emperor' or ('*tenno*'). Which implied a higher status than that of a mere 'son of heaven'. One of the earliest documents in Sino–Japanese diplomacy shows that the Japanese asserted the parity of their emperor with the Chinese ruler. The letter was addressed 'from the Son of Heaven in the land where the sun rises to the Son of Heaven in the land where the sun sets'. Naturally, that did not please the Chinese.[11] Japan also became notorious as the home of pirates, whom the Chinese called 'wako' or 'dwarf pirates', who frequently raided far into inland areas of China and Korea.

Japanese tribute missions to China ended in the ninth century, and were taken up again only briefly in the fifteenth century. In 1401, the shogun ('barbarian-suppressing generalissimo') Ashikaga Yoshimitsu reopened diplomatic relations with China. He accepted the status of vassal to the Ming emperors in order to obtain control over Japanese trade with China. The economic benefits of this trade enabled Yoshimitsu to stabilize his shaky rule, and to bypass the authority of the emperor in Kyoto.

But that period of vassalage did not last long. Japan's trading rights in China lapsed in 1547, after which Japanese were excluded from China. Not long after that, the shogun Toyotomi Hideyoshi, having unified Japan, tried twice to invade China via Korea. Moreover, the succeeding Tokugawa shogunate (1603–1868) did not enter into formal relations with China because it refused to accept the subordinate status demanded by the Mings. And when the Manchus took power in Beijing in 1644, the Japanese called them 'Tartars' – 'northern barbarians' no better than the Mongols. China, they said, had again succumbed to barbarian rule, while the land of the gods remained inviolate. There was more than a hint here of a willingness to overturn the Confucian world order of the Middle Kingdom.

The Tokugawas also defied China by seeking the subordination of other kingdoms. They succeeded with the Ryukyus (Okinawa), which they invaded in 1609 and made vassal to the Satsuma clan in Kyushu. (Because the China trade conducted via the Ryukyus was lucrative for all concerned, the Ryukyu king remained a vassal of China as well.) But the Tokugawas proved unable to make vassals of the flinty Koreans.

For most of their history, Japanese–Korean relations consisted of peaceful trade conducted via the Inland Sea. The Koreans often sent emissaries to Japan. But they did so on the basis of exquisitely careful assertions of equality. While the Koreans had been forced to acknowledge the suzerainty of China, a powerful empire with which they shared a long border, they did not see themselves as subordinate to the Japanese across the Tsushima Strait. Moreover, the Koreans naturally found it hard to overlook Hideyoshi's occupation of Korea. The continuing legacy of that invasion was the mound of some 10,000 Korean and Chinese ears and noses that Hideyoshi sent to a temple in Kyoto, where they remain to this day.[12]

Still, those acts of aggression were aberrations in the long and generally peaceful shared history of China, Japan and Korea. So were the attempted Mongol invasions of Japan three centuries before. Sino–Japanese relations might have been less irenic if the rulers in Beijing had felt more confident about their land frontiers. The Manchus, had they felt as secure on their northern borders as the Mongols had been, might possibly have developed maritime power which would have threatened the Japanese in their island redoubt. But by the time the Manchu dynasty took power, the Russians had almost reached the Pacific. For two centuries they represented an incipient rather than a palpable threat. Still, the Manchus now had a new kind of 'northern barbarian' to contend with, and these were unlikely to prove assimilable.

Moreover, by the time the Russians had reached the Pacific overland, the 'southern barbarians' of the Western maritime powers were pushing their way into the region. For centuries, China, two oceans away from Europe, was able to resist encroachment on its sovereignty. But resistance became more difficult as the Western maritime powers developed longer maritime reach, as well as technologies apposite to naval warfare. And as they reached the China Seas, their stepping stones to both China and Japan were on the long island chain that runs down the East Asian littoral.

The offshore island chain

Because the Pacific is so large, its numerous islands are an especially important feature of its strategic geography.[13] The most strategically significant of these islands is the chain that runs just off the littoral, from the Aleutians down to the south island of New Zealand. The offshore island chain thus creates a series of marginal seas – the Sea of Okhotsk, the Japan Sea, the Yellow Sea, the East China Sea and the South China Sea.

The tiny island of Singapore at the tip of the Malay peninsula holds the key to the crossroads between East Asia's marginal seas and the Indian Ocean. It has done so since 1819, when an expanding British maritime empire established a strategic foothold there. That bolted the door to the Indian Ocean from the east, thus protecting India, the 'jewel in the crown' of the British empire. Britain's possession of Singapore also provided a jumping-off point for penetration of the China Seas. Singapore's importance as the 'Gibraltar of the East' did not diminish over the succeeding centuries.[14] Thus, in 1941, as we shall see, the defence of Singapore against Japanese ambition became a vital interest of the United States. Currently, the security of this island redoubt continues to engage the vital interest of the maritime powers, and all those who rely on them for protection.

In strategic terms, the island chain that runs down the East Asian littoral is a two-edged sword. For the land powers, it constitutes a barrier against potentially hostile maritime powers. During the Cold War, for example, the Soviet Union turned the Sea of Okhotsk, behind the barrier of the long curve of the Kuril island chain, into a bastion for its ballistic missile submarines. (At the opposite end of Eurasia, its counterpoint was the Soviet bastion in the White Sea.)

But the East Asian island chain, while protecting the land powers, also blocks their egress to the open ocean. For centuries the Russian empire, expanding across the top of Eurasia, sought a warm-water port on the Pacific. That brought Russia into collision with the expanding empire of

Japan, leading to war in 1904–1905, when Japan defeated Russia. By 1905, Japan, enjoying the advantages of proximity, and allied with Britain – then the dominant maritime power – had closed to Russia all the marginal seas of North Asia.

Because of the imperatives of strategic geography, strategic history tends to impose similar patterns. During the Cold War, for example, Japan played the same role in blocking Soviet egress to the open sea as it had against Russia earlier in the century. Moreover, Japan did so in alliance with the United States as the dominant maritime power. Because of the great curve of the Japanese archipelago, in wartime the American and Japanese navies would have been able to close off the vital straits – Soya (La Perouse), Tsugaru and Tsushima – which provide egress from the main Russian base at Vladivostok.

With the end of the Cold War, strategic tensions have moved down the island chain because of the collapse of Russian power. China, enjoying the advantages of proximity, seems intent on turning the South China Sea into a Chinese lake. Because of the vastness of the Pacific Ocean, China can do so without developing maritime power commensurate with that of the United States. But China, like Russia before it, is a continental power which must contend with the fact that Japan is an island state that lives on the chain, and is allied with the dominant maritime power.

Even though Japan has chosen not to develop long- range maritime power projection capabilities, it possesses by far the most powerful navy in north Asia. Moreover, Japan's alliance with America affords the United States access to bases on strategically vital parts of the chain, not least the outlying island of Okinawa, where 75 per cent of US bases in Japan are concentrated. Okinawa, taken by the United States at huge cost in lives in 1945, remains the key to US strategy in the Western Pacific. The island became even more important after the US navy was required by the Philippine government to leave its base at Subic Bay in 1991. That stretched US maritime capabilities in the vast distance between Japan and the Persian Gulf, which is the responsibility of the US Pacific Command.

A little further down the chain, the island of Taiwan occupies a critical position because it screens the maritime approaches to both China and Japan from the west. That's why Taiwan (Formosa) attracted the attention of the maritime powers when they first began to push into East Asia. In 1895, Japan registered its appreciation of Taiwan's importance when it took the island as a spoil of its naval war with China. Since 1949, when the defeated remnants of the armies of Jiang Jieshi (Chiang Kai-shek) fled to Taiwan after China's civil war, the island has been a bone in the throat of the rulers of Beijing – not least because the United States insists that China does not have the right to use force to reintegrate Taiwan.

The plan of the book

This book consists of six chapters, laying out the process by which East Asia became the global focus of unresolved great-power strategic tension, and how that attracted the interests of the United States because of the maritime basis of American security. Chapter 1 examines how, by 1905, all the elements of the East Asian quadrilateral had been assembled. The chapter analyses how the European powers brought strategic competition to East Asia. For several centuries, strategic tensions in East Asia were manifestations of the clash of great-power interests in Europe. That process began when the European maritime powers fought one another in eastern waters in pursuit of spices, tea and religious converts. Then a rapidly industrializing Japan entered the great-power game late in the nineteenth century. Japan did so in order to escape the fate of China, upon whose sovereignty the European powers had increasingly encroached. At the same time, the United States became an actor in East Asian security when it took the Philippines in 1898 as a spoil of the naval war with Spain, and took Hawaii as well.

By 1905 Japan and Russia had clashed in Manchuria, the 'cockpit of Asia'. That led into the Russo–Japanese war, the first defeat of a European power by an Asian one and thus a milestone in global strategic history. Thus, by that time, China, Russia, Japan and the United States had all been brought into the great-power game in East Asia, establishing the quadrilateral. In order to establish equilibrium on the far side of the Pacific Ocean, the United States was willing to broker the peace between Japan and Russia.

Chapter 2 is the first of two chapters examining the effects of the First and Second World Wars on East Asian security. In essence, the strategic history of the first half of the twentieth century was a contest between Germany and Russia, two continental powers, for hegemony over Europe/Eurasia. The United States intervened in the two world wars in the interests of its own security, in order to prevent an expansionist Germany from dominating all of Eurasia. The First World War was essentially a blockade of Germany, achieved at very high cost. Unresolved great-power tensions arising from that war then laid the basis for the Second World War, whose European dimensions replicated those of the previous war. But the Pacific theatre of the Second World War saw conflict raging over more than half the globe. That gave great-power war a truly global dimension for the first time.

The chapter examines the collisions of interest in East Asia from 1905 to 1935, when the Soviet dictator Josif Stalin formed 'united fronts' at both ends of Eurasia. He did so in order to counter the growing threat of two-front war, as an increasingly militarist Japan aligned itself with Hitler's Germany. In East Asia, as Japan encroached further on China's sovereignty, the United States stood in its path. America had striven mightily to strike and maintain a stable balance of power, including via the 1921–1922 Washington naval arms control agreements. But the equilibrium thus established was not proof against changing times – especially the onset of the

Great Depression and the rise of Chinese nationalism, which undermined the moderates in Japan and fostered militarism there.

Chapter 3 looks at the growing collision of interest between Japan and the United States after 1935. It examines how developments in Europe impinged on the East Asia balance, as Stalin subtly encouraged Japan into war with China, and then with the United States. Although the United States sought to deter Japan from further aggression in China, it saw no interest there that justified the risk of war. But then Japan in 1940 sought to exploit opportunities created by Hitler's victories in Western Europe by moving into Indochina, thus threatening Singapore. So the United States grew more willing to risk war in order to deter Japan from seizing the vital pivot between the Indian and Pacific Oceans.

Chapter 4 is the first of two chapters on the Cold War. The outcome of the Second World War established the foundations of the Cold War, which had a distinctly Eurasian cast. Neither of the principals, the United States and the Soviet Union, was a West–Central European power, even though Western Europe was at the heart of their strategic contest.

By 1949, the United States had decided that, in the interests of its own security, it must contain Soviet efforts to dominate Europe. Then Stalin brought the Cold War to East Asia when he made an alliance with the victorious Chinese communists, and gave communist North Korea a green light to invade South Korea. The Korean war widened the terms of engagement of the Cold War, making it a global strategic contest whose strategic geography essentially replicated that of the Second World War. But by 1971, Russia and China had fallen out, and the United States was anxious to find an exit from the quagmire of its war in Vietnam. Those imperatives drew the United States and China into an unlikely strategic alignment which soon presented the Soviet Union with the credible threat of two-front war.

Chapter 5 examines the last stage of the Cold War. Exploiting America's strategic paralysis resulting from Vietnam and the Watergate scandal that destroyed the Nixon presidency, the Soviet Union went for broke, thinking it could win. All over the globe, American allies wobbled. But when president Ronald Reagan determined that the United States must reverse these dangerous trends, America was able to bring down the overextended Soviet empire. Both China and Japan, in their separate ways, contributed to the winning of the Cold War. Thus, in the Cold War, America's success proved definitive. Soviet power collapsed, while Britain, France, Germany and Japan all continued to depend on the United States for their ultimate security.

The final chapter looks at what happened in East Asia when the overlay of the Cold War melted. The East Asian quadrilateral, which had been subsumed under the frost, soon resurfaced, although the constellations of power within it had radically altered. Moreover, problems on the Korean peninsula and in relation to Taiwan had not been resolved.

   With the end of the Cold War, security in Western Europe is not only settled, but largely disconnected from the problems of East Asia. Now the empires of the European maritime powers have finally dissolved. The end of that long process, which began at the time of the First World War, was marked when Britain returned Hong Kong to China in 1997 and Portugal gave back Macao in 1999. Because the Western Europeans no longer have problems of territorial security in East Asia, they now focus almost exclusively on trade and economics.

   Moreover, with European security now settled in the broad, strategic tensions in Europe no longer flow over into the equations of power at the opposite end of Eurasia. Thus, for the first time since the East Asian quadrilateral assembled in 1905, the balance of power in the region is being determined solely by fluctuations among the four powers, though Russia is little more than an interested bystander. Still, America's vital interest remains the same as it was when the quadrilateral was assembled in 1905 – the search for equilibrium on the far shore of the Pacific Ocean.

1 East Asia to 1905

The European ascendancy

In geostrategic terms, Europe is a small peninsula on the western edge of Eurasia. Yet it dominated the global order after Columbus discovered America in 1492. China and Japan, East Asia's two core areas, were not drawn into the world order until the mid-nineteenth century. That was mostly because they were an ocean further away from India and Southeast Asia, to which the Europeans were initially drawn in their efforts to wrest the lucrative spice trade from the Arabs.

China and Japan responded in different ways to Europe's encroachment. In trying to resist, China lost much of its sovereignty. Japan, alarmed at China's fate, abandoned its efforts to seek security in isolation. From 1868, Japan entered the international system, while seeking as much as possible to set the terms of its engagement. Thus, by 1905, when Japan defeated Russia, all the elements had been assembled in East Asia that were to play themselves out until 1991.

Europeans by sea...

'Globalization' began in 1492. Europe's unprecedented domination of the global order after the age of Columbus was a strategic consequence of the Renaissance, especially the development of technology apposite to maritime power. Until then, Europe had been subject to constant invasions from Asia and Arabia. Indeed, in the thirteenth and fourteenth centuries, the Mongol empire was the largest the world had ever seen, larger even than that of Rome. At its apogee, the empire of the Mongols stretched from Korea to Hungary, incorporating most of Asia and much of eastern Europe. Yet, unlike the Roman empire, the Mongol empire vanished almost without trace. Despite their military proficiency and superior tactics, the horsemen of the steppes lacked higher technology, science or culture.

The Mongols had an especially devastating impact on Russia, wrenching it away from Europe for centuries, with long-term consequences. Kievan Rus, where the first Russian state had been established in 862 at the confluence of river systems, had been converted to Christianity by Byzantine missionaries in 988. Then, in 1240, the Mongols of the 'Golden Horde' sacked Kiev, the 'mother of cities'. For four hundred years thereafter Russia languished under the 'Tatar yoke'. And it was a Muslim yoke, the Khan of the Golden Horde having being converted to Islam in 1252.

When the Venetian adventurer Marco Polo reached China ('Cathay') overland in the era of Kublai Khan, he whetted Europe's appetite for the riches of Asia. Soon the development of maritime transport in Europe, initially based on the ocean-going sailing ship, shrank distance far more quickly and effectively than could be done on land. On land, mechanical means of transport were a precondition of mobility that took several centuries to develop, their first manifestation being the railways. So, for centuries, sea transport had the edge because of its ability to harness natural phenomena such as wind and ocean currents to the movement of ships.[1]

Sailing around Africa, the Portuguese Vasco da Gama reached India in 1498. Soon the Spaniards entered the Pacific from the west. Gradually the sea routes eclipsed the ancient caravan routes, including the famed Silk Road, which had carried Asia's luxury goods to the Levant. Thus Europe's economic centre of gravity slowly moved from the Mediterranean to the Atlantic ports. Then the rivalries of a fractured Europe, compounded by the religious hatreds of the Reformation, fuelled the competition of nascent European states in distant waters. Early imperial contest saw Portugal, Spain, Holland and England struggling in Southeast Asia, mainly to wrest control of the spice trade from Muslim traders. The ambitions of the Iberian powers had a particular religious edge, since in 1492 the long struggle for the reconquest of Spain from the Muslims had succeeded after almost eight centuries of occupation by the 'Moors'. Thus, wresting the spice routes from the Arabs represented revenge as well as profit.

Portugal, intent on establishing control of the eastward bound sea routes from Europe, took Goa in India, and then Malacca in 1511. Consequently the Dutch, in their struggle for liberation against Spain (united with Portugal in 1580), carried the fight to the Spanish and Portuguese in the east, capturing Malacca in 1641. As we have seen, two centuries previously the Chinese admiral Zheng He had also appreciated the significance of the control of the Malacca Strait. Meanwhile, Britain's attention was focused on India. In 1699, the British East India Company established itself in Calcutta, at one of the mouths of the Ganges.

During the eighteenth century, on a scale and in places that would have been impossible on land, Britain and France fought a series of global wars. France, partly because of its continental distractions, proved unable to translate its dominant position in Europe into global maritime supremacy. As a consequence of the Seven Years War (1756–1763) – which ranged from India to North America, the Philippines and Cuba – France lost its grip on North America and India. For its part, Britain lost its American colonies when they rebelled. Still, Britain emerged from these global wars as the pre-eminent maritime and commercial power.

The British, then as later, were conscious of the risks of overextension. When France overran Holland during the Napoleonic wars, Britain took the Dutch empire into 'protective custody'. The British could have kept all the Dutch possessions. They chose not to, partly because British security required that the Low Countries be strengthened lest they again fall under French domination. Britain also sought to avoid the risk of imperial over-stretch. So it retained only those Dutch colonies that were of strategic value to the sea route to the east – the Cape of Good Hope, Ceylon and Malacca.

Although British possession of Malacca helped screen the maritime approaches to India from the east, it was the tip of the Malay peninsula that dominated the crossroads of the Indian Ocean and the China Seas. Thus, in 1819, Sir Stamford Raffles, then lieutenant-governor of Java, founded a settlement at Singapore. Singapore was founded mostly with an eye to promotion of British trade with China, centred on the tea trade. But until the mid-nineteenth century, China largely escaped encroachment by the Western maritime powers, mainly because it was an ocean further away. Moreover, Spain's Asian empire, based in the Philippines, faced eastwards, oriented towards the lucrative galleon trade with Mexico. As long as the Spaniards could exchange Mexican silver for Chinese luxury goods in Manila, they had neither the urge nor the means to encroach upon China's sovereignty.

It was not only for reasons of distance that China was better able to resist European encroachment than were India's princely states, or the kingdoms and sultanates of maritime Southeast Asia. That was because China was more organized and centralized. Indeed, at about the same time as the Dutch took Malacca, a vigorous new dynasty, the Manchus, captured Beijing. For two centuries, the Qing dynasty remained strong enough to fend off European encroachment. Self-sufficient and confident of their cultural superiority, the Manchus had little interest in the outside world.

Thus the Qing dynasty tightly controlled the conditions under which foreign traders were allowed to operate in China's ports. In 1699, the British East India Company was permitted to establish a trading post in Quangzhou (Canton), forty miles up the Pearl river from the Portuguese enclave of Macao. On their way up-river, British ships had to pay dues at the fortified *Bocca Tigris* (Tiger's Mouth). While at anchor in Whampoa, they lay under the guns of the forts. China thus held the upper hand, but the imbalance of trade portended trouble. From China, British East India Company ships transported tea and other luxury products to Europe. But there was little that the Chinese empire wished to import, so the trade imbalance had to be made up in Mexican silver. The drain on British coffers was not likely to prove sustainable for long.

...and by land

While the maritime powers were encroaching on China from the sea, Russia – having thrown off the Tartar yoke – was expanding rapidly overland. Under Ivan the Great (1462–1505), Duke of Moscow, who took the title of tsar (Caesar), Moscow assumed the mantle of the 'Third Rome', after the Turks sacked Byzantium (Constantinople) in 1453.[2] Now Moscow became the guardian of Orthodox Christianity. The Russian state, still bearing the imprint of the Mongols, was centralized and authoritarian. But there were some free spirits. In pursuit of furs, the 'soft gold' of the north, Cossack adventurers began to move across the vast steppes and taiga, filling the vacuum created by the disintegration of the Mongol empire. In 1607, the same year the English founded Jamestown, Cossacks reached the Yenisey river.[3]

The Cossacks' highway to the Far East was the Amur, the 'Black Dragon' river, so named by the Chinese because of the silt that it carries down from the mountains. The Amur, which flows 2,700 miles to the Sea of Okhotsk, is the only major Siberian river to flow eastwards to the Pacific Ocean. Navigable for a thousand miles, the Amur is longer than the Danube. It beckoned the Russians towards Manchuria, that vast, sparsely populated but potentially rich expanse of China's northeast which is larger than Germany and France combined. But until Britain's victories in the Opium Wars in the mid-nineteenth century revealed the extent of the rot within their empire, the Manchus remained strong enough to keep the Russians north of the Amur.

For centuries, the landlocked Russian empire had been seeking to break through to the open oceans. After Peter the Great (1689–1725) defeated Sweden, thus giving him a window on the Baltic, he organized a victory parade through Moscow with warships mounted on sleds. Peter forsook Moscow when he sited his new capital of St Petersburg on the Baltic, thus orienting Russia towards the West. Still, Russia's vast spaces, and the lack of natural barriers, made for geostrategic thinking on a grand scale. The tsar believed that there were three points of primary strategic importance to Russia – the mouths of the Neva, the Don and the Amur. In the Far East, Russia broke out to the sea via the Amur even before it reached the Baltic and the Black Seas. Cossack adventurers founded Okhotsk on the Sea of Okhotsk in 1647. Distant and bleak though it was, Okhotsk was to be the base for Russian exploration of the northern Pacific.

In 1651, the Russians founded Irkutsk, where the Angara flows into Lake Baikal. Then they made a settlement at Nerchinsk, on a tributary of the Amur about 400 miles east of Lake Baikal. Nerchinsk became the jumping-off point for the Russian penetration of Manchuria. In 1651 the Russians built a fort at Albazin further downstream from Nerchinsk. Soon Russia's chain of forts became a continental counterpoint to Britain's network of naval bases. Although distances in both empires were immense, until the development of the railways Britain's maritime imperium had the edge. That was because land transport could not compete with ocean-going ships.

The Manchus, alive to the threat to their ancestral homelands, razed Albazin in 1685. With a delegation complete with 10,000 bannermen, artillery and Jesuit interpreters, they parleyed with the Russians at Nerchinsk in 1689. The Treaty of Nerchinsk was the first and last treaty China made with a European power on the basis of equality. By means of this treaty, the Manchus kept the Russians north of the Amur from a point just east of Albazin.

Denied access to the Amur, the Russians then made a flanking movement from Okhotsk down the Pacific coast. In 1707 they seized the Kamchatka peninsula, which juts out into the Pacific from northeastern Siberia. There they established the settlement at Petropavlovsk na Kamchatke in 1740. Petropavlovsk was not the ice-free port that the Russians craved. But it provided a base for probes towards Hokkaido, the northernmost of the four main Japanese islands, where the Russians discovered the splendid bay of Hakodate.[4]

Petropavlovsk also provided a base for expansion across the Aleutian island chain to the North American continent in Alaska, and then down the Californian coast. In 1811 – ignoring Spanish protests – the Russians established Fort Ross north of San Francisco. But Russia, lacking a secure base on the Amur, was overextended, so it opted for retreat. Like the British, the Russians were aware of the risks of imperial overstretch. So they sold Alaska, including the Aleutian chain, to the United States in 1867, in order to provide a buffer between themselves and British maritime power based in Canada. Besides, by that time, Britain's assault on China's sovereignty had created new opportunities for Russia on the Amur.

The nineteenth century: the assault on China's sovereignty

As so often in its later history, China was partly the architect of its own misfortune. The Manchus, incapable of dealing with others on the basis of reciprocity, ignored the growing military capabilities of the European maritime powers. By the late eighteenth century, the Manchu empire was the largest in Chinese history. But its successes had been achieved against enemies far less formidable than the Europeans.

Britain, in search of trade rather than territory, was not seeking to carve up China. Having learned from its mistakes when it lost its first empire after the American colonies rebelled, Britain now preferred a free-trading global system which strengthened the sinews of its industrial, commercial and maritime power. Thus Britain saw China mainly as a market for its industrial products, and a destination for British investment. The British East India Company sought to remind its employees (not always with success) that their business was trade, not war.

But Britain, at the height of imperial power after the great series of wars of the eighteenth century, chafed at the lowly status of its merchants at Canton. Whereas Britain was proud of its reputation as a nation of shop-keepers, merchants were at the bottom of the Confucian hierarchy, with traders from 'barbarian' nations the lowest of the low. Unlike the Japanese, the Chinese had a similar disdain for soldiers. Such contempt was now dangerous. After the abolition of the East India Company's monopoly in 1834, which signaled Britain's switch from mercantilism to free trade, China found itself dealing not with 'John Company', but with the victors of Trafalgar and Waterloo. While the British government preferred peaceful trade, it was not squeamish about using force.

In their inland redoubts, the Manchus remained oblivious to the growing peril from the sea. Meanwhile, the military and technological consequences of Europe's industrial revolution, especially the ironclad steamship, were making China increasingly vulnerable. And by now, British merchants had discovered one product that was in demand in China, and was thus able to stem the outflow of silver into China's coffers – opium, grown in India and Persia. In 1841, the Chinese government's efforts to confiscate opium stock-piles triggered the so-called Opium War, the first assault on China's sovereignty.

British naval superiority routed the Chinese, and the vast manpower of India, once harnessed, proved a valuable adjunct to British military capabilities in the Far East. After 1841, British punitive expeditions in China had large sepoy contingents. Under the terms of the 1842 Treaty of Nanking, Britain acquired Hong Kong, opposite Macao at the entrance to the Pearl river. Five other ports were opened to foreign trade. The monopoly in Canton was abolished, and foreigners gained extraterritorial rights. That meant that they were subject to their own legal arrangements, and not left to the tender mercies of Chinese law. China also lost control of its tariffs, and was made to pay a large indemnity. Moreover, the breach in China's sovereignty now provided the opportunity that Russia had long been seeking on the Amur.

Accelerated Russian penetration of China

The appointment in 1847 of General Nikolai Muraviev ('Amurski') at the age of thirty-nine as governor general of Siberia marked a new stage in Russian expansion. Muraviev enjoyed the strong support of tsar Nicholas 1 (1825–1855). As soon as the Opium War had revealed the extent of the decay within the Chinese empire, Russia began a new forward policy on the lower Amur. In July 1850, Fort Nikolaevsk was founded a short distance from the mouth of the river, and the Russian flag was raised on Sakhalin. Russian expeditions sailed down the Amur, in violation of the Treaty of Nerchinsk. Muraviev himself travelled down the river with a force of eight hundred men.

The Crimean War (1854–1855) then made acquisition of a secure base on the Amur seem even more imperative for Russia. In Europe, Russia had been seeking to exploit the decline of the Turkish empire in order to gain control of Constantinople (Istanbul). That would give Russia the keys to the Turkish straits, which blocked its egress to the Mediterranean from the Black Sea. Determined to contain Russian power, Britain and France declared war. In the Far East, an Anglo–French force bombarded Petropavlovsk. Although an attempted landing failed, the remoteness of Petropavlovsk showed its deficiencies as Russia's main Far Eastern base, because it could not be supported by land forces.

So the Russians transferred their main base to Nikolaevsk at the mouth of the Amur. In developing the new base, the Russians demonstrated that they understood that they would need maritime as well as land power in order to secure their interests in the East. The Crimean War had also closed the sea route by which supplies could be sent to Siberia from southern Russia. But Nikolaevsk had its limits because the mouth of the Amur and most of the Tartar Strait freezes in winter, due to the enormous flow of fresh water. Russia had still not found a warm-water port on the Pacific coast.

Having consolidated their grip on the mouth of the Amur, the Russians renewed their encroachment on its lower reaches. In 1858, under duress, China signed the Treaty of Aigun. The treaty ceded Russia the left bank of the Amur, as well as rights to vast territories between the Ussuri river and the sea. Both the great Manchurian branches of the Amur, the Sungari and the Ussuri, were to be used only by Chinese and Russian vessels. Since the Sungari is the hydrographical axis of the Manchurian plain, Russian access to it portended ambition south towards the Liao valley, and hence control of the whole of Manchuria.[5]

By that time, new opportunities were emerging for Russia as the Anglo–French powers renewed their assault on China's sovereignty. In 1856, continued Chinese resistance to foreigners saw Britain and France again resorting to force in the Arrow War. In retaliation for the murder of members of the captured party of the British consul in Canton, Anglo–French forces looted and burned the Summer Palace. The Treaty of Peking forced China to pay another large indemnity, and to concede Kowloon to Britain. Ten more treaty ports were opened on the coast and on the Yangzi. One of these was Newchwang (Yingkou) at the estuary of the Liao river. That paved the way for British commercial penetration of southern Manchuria. It thus represented a palpable threat to Russian ambitions there.

Russia had been playing a double game, pretending to support the Chinese against the British and French while pursuing ambition on the Amur. The Russians were quick to benefit from China's troubles. China conceded to Russia both sides of the lower course of the Amur, as well as land stretching down the coast to Korea. In 1860, the Russians transferred their naval headquarters from remote Nikolaevsk south to Vladivostok, 'Ruler of the East', where Muraviev had discovered a fine harbour. But Vladivostok, although not as isolated at Petropavlosk or Nikolaevsk, was not an ice-free port – its harbour froze from Christmas until March. So the Russians kept pressing for access to a warm-water port on the eastern side of the Korean peninsula, with Wonsan especially in mind.

Russian ambition in Manchuria and Korea then brought it into collision with Japan. By that time, the Japanese were beginning to realize that they would share China's fate if they allowed the European powers to trample on their sovereignty. The Japanese, unlike the Chinese, had been long ruled by military governments. Thus they were attuned to the utility of force, and rightly concluded that resistance was futile. So Japan decided to join the great-power game, on the basis of its own choosing as much as possible. The European powers, as a consequence of their encroachments on China, had opened the way for the first non-European power to join the international system.

Enter Japan

Although Marco Polo reported on his return from China news of 'Cipangu', the first known Western discovers of Japan were Portuguese sailors ship-wrecked in 1542. Portuguese traders from Macao and Goa followed, and in 1549 the missionary Francis Xavier arrived from Goa. European weapons such as cannon and muskets proved useful in the efforts of Japan's shoguns to unify the country after a series of disastrous civil wars, and then to support a foreign expedition.

After 1592 the shogun Hideyoshi Toyotomi, having brought most of Japan under centralized control, sought twice to conquer China via Korea. The Mings responded by sending an army across the Yalu river. Korean and Chinese bows and arrows proved useless against the musketry which Japan had copied from the Western powers. But the Korean Admiral Yi Sun Sin and his armoured 'turtle ships' played havoc with the Japanese transports, creating the first Korean anti-Japanese hero. Although Hideyoshi did not leave Japan, his forces held Seoul for seven years. But they were overex-tended, and forced to withdraw before his death in 1598. Hideyoshi's grandiose dreams of invading China succeeded only in earning the enduring resentment of the Koreans.

In opting for retreat, Hideyoshi may have also feared the growing power of Spain in the Philippines, where the Spaniards had moved their capital northwards to Manila in 1571 after their initial settlement in Cebu in the central part of the archipelago. Indeed, at one time Hideyoshi entertained ambitions of invading the Philippines. In 1591, he sent the Spanish governor-general a demand that he should become a Japanese vassal. Similar missives were sent to Taiwan and Goa. But the shogun's ambition had outrun his capabilities, and his successors were more cautious.

In 1600 the shogun Tokugawa Ieyasu won the decisive battle of Sekigahara near present-day Nagoya. Having completed the unification of Japan, he established his capital on the coast at Edo, 'Gate of the Waters'. The Tokugawas, who were to rule Japan with an iron fist until the 1868 Meiji Restoration, sought security in isolation from 1636 onwards. Since Iberian colonialism had been fuelled partly by a drive for Catholic converts, the Tokugawas grew anxious about this alien influence. The Philippines was an example of what might happen to a divided archipelago which let in the Catholics. In Kyushu, many *daimyos* (feudal lords) had been converted, and Christianity was growing rapidly. So the Tokugawas perceived a palpable threat to their authority, and to the national unity that had been hard won after years of civil wars. They ruthlessly stamped out all manifestations of Catholic Christianity.

The Protestant Dutch were still permitted to trade, but only via the tiny island of Deshima in Nagasaki harbour, which was rigidly controlled. All other foreigners were expelled – except for the Chinese, who were also confined to Nagasaki, and the Koreans, who were allowed to continue to trade via the Tsushima islands in the Tsushima (Korea) Strait. Japanese were forbidden to travel overseas, and ships authorized for coastal trading were required to display the seal of the shogunate. Thus Japan sought security in isolation. But by the mid-nineteenth century, outsiders were again knocking loudly at the door. This time the Americans were in the van.

Knocking at Japan's door

By now Europe's encroachment on China had drawn the United States, a second extra-European power, into the global order. Indeed, much of Russia's forward movement on the Amur had been designed to keep the Americans at bay. American whalers and sealers had long roamed the Pacific, founding many a New England fortune. By mid-century, the acquisition of California had given the United States a Pacific as well as Atlantic coastline. A rising America wanted its share of the China trade, and the advent of the steamship was driving the US Navy's search for coaling and bunkering facilities on the other side of the Pacific. Moreover, American sailing ships using the great circle route between California and China sought ports and facilities in Japan.

Thus in July 1853 Commodore Matthew Perry, USN, bearing a letter from President Millard Fillmore, arrived off the entrance to Edo Bay. Perry wanted trade with Japan, better treatment for shipwrecked American sailors, as well as coaling and bunkering facilities. Although America came in pursuit of trade rather than territorial conquest, it was, like Britain, willing to use gunboat diplomacy. Among Perry's 'black ships' were two steamers and two men-of-war sailing ships. The firepower commanded by even this small force produced panic in Edo, now a city of some three million, whose coastal batteries were known to be outdated and of little use.

Seven centuries before, Japan had been saved by 'divine winds' when the Mongols sought to invade Kyushu. But in 1853, the gods failed to scatter Perry's fleet. He delivered his letter and left, saying with polite menace that he would come back in the spring. When Perry returned in February 1854 with a larger force, Japan took the point, knowing that the European maritime powers would not be far behind. By means of the Treaty of Kanagawa, Japan agreed to bunkering facilities at the ports of Shimoda and Hakodate, as well as better treatment for shipwrecked sailors. In accordance with the 'treaty port' system that had been imposed on China, these privileges were extended to other countries which made similar agreements with Japan. In 1856, Townsend Harris took up his lonely post in the fishing port of Shimoda, south of Tokyo, as the first American consul to Japan.

In August 1853, four Russian warships under the command of Admiral Putiatin arrived in Nagasaki. Ostensibly friendlier than Perry, Putiatin took advantage of the Americans' success in opening Japan. In February 1855, he signed the treaty of Shimoda, by which the Russians gained access to Shimoda and Hakodate, the freedom to visit Nagasaki, and extraterritorial privileges. By means of this treaty, the Russians and Japanese divided the Kuril archipelago, the boundary being made to run through the Friza strait. Thus the southern islands of Itorofu (Iturup) and Kunashiri (Kunashir) became Japanese, while the islands from Urup northwards belonged to Russia.

Japan was being opened up, but not easily. In reprisal for attacks on foreigners, in 1863 British warships bombarded Kagoshima in southeastern Kyushu, the seat of the Satsuma *daimyo*.[6] The British also opened the Inland Sea, the maritime heart of Japan, by forcing the Shimonoseki Strait between Honshu and Kyushu. In 1864, in retaliation for attacks on foreign ships, eighteen foreign steamships led by British warships bombarded the town of Shimonoseki, bastion of the Choshu clan. By now it was apparent that Japan's isolation had caused it to lag dangerously in the technology of maritime warfare. No Japanese resented these humiliations more bitterly than the young samurai of the Choshu and Satsuma clans.

While these outlying clans were not well disposed to each another, they were both traditional enemies of the Tokugawa, having fought on the wrong side at Sekigahara. Unlike the Manchus, a northern dynasty closeted in its inland capitals, these samurai lived by the sea. For that reason, they had no difficulty in comprehending the nature of the threat presented by the Western maritime powers. They also burned with resentment because the European powers had imposed the China treaty port system on the 'land of the gods'. Moreover, they were in a position to do something about it.

Thus in 1868 the Meiji Restoration came about when the lower-ranking samurai of the Satsuma and Choshu clans sank their differences in order to bring down the shogunate. To provide a focus for national unity, they brought the fifteen-year-old emperor Meiji ('Enlightened Government') out of seclusion in the imperial capital of Kyoto to Edo, now renamed Tokyo

('Eastern Capital'). He was duly installed as the head of a new emperor-worshipping state cult, based on Shinto.

In 1889, Ito Hirobumi, a Choshu who became one of the *genro* ('original elders'), drew up a constitution modelled on that of Bismarck's Germany. Those arrangements ensured that the emperor, rather than parliament, remained the locus of sovereignty. Then the Japanese lost little time in industrializing and modernizing in order to escape China's fate. They saw an urgent need to develop a modern conscript army and a navy, under the slogan of 'rich country, strong army'. After Prussia defeated France in 1870, Germany became the model for the new Japanese army, replacing the earlier French model. Britain, naturally, served as the model for the navy. The Satsumas provided the nucleus of Japan's modern navy, and the Choshus its army.

The Japanese were fortunate in the calibre of the leaders who composed the *genro*. They were also lucky that during the critical years between 1853 and 1868, when they were struggling to respond to the foreign threat, much European and American energy was diverted by the Crimean War, the American Civil War and the 1857 rebellion against British rule in India.

Japan's geostrategic situation

In geostrategic terms, Japan's position seemed to resemble that of Britain. The hydrographic centre of both countries faced the continent opposite – the Thames valley in the case of Britain, the Inland Sea in the case of Japan. But there the similarities ended.

By the late nineteenth century, the British had accumulated four hundred years' experience as the 'offshore balancer' in Europe. Because Britain had faced recurrent threats of invasion, its strategy focused on control of the English Channel and the river mouths opposite. England had stood at greatest risk of invasion, in 1588 and 1805, when a European hegemon occupied the Low Countries and threatened the British across their 'narrow seas'. But since 1066, no invader had managed to cross the Channel.

For the British, survival meant keeping the world's sea lanes open to trade and commerce. But the Royal Navy could operate in distant waters only if the Continent were in balance. For that reason, the British had long maintained equilibrium on the Continent opposite by astute diplomacy, and by switching allegiances when necessary – the classic reversal of alliances which earned Britain the sobriquet 'Perfidious Albion'. As required, when the balance of power broke down in Europe, the British inserted their small professional army at the right time and place. They also used their financial power to fund continental allies that undertook the brunt of the fighting.

Nothing in Japan's past resembled this history of the British way of diplomacy and warfare. As we have noted, China was not in the habit of trying to invade Japan. Japan's relations with Korea, at least until the time of Hideyoshi, had consisted mostly of peaceful trade. Apart from the Korean peninsula, where the resilience of the Koreans had long helped to protect Japan, the continent opposite Japan consisted of the sparsely populated expanses of Manchuria and the trackless wastes of Siberia. These represented no threat. So Japan had not needed to develop a large navy, or Britain's diplomatic skills and modes of strategic thought.

But by the late nineteenth century, Japan's geostrategic situation was becoming more like Britain's. Because of the Russian threat to Manchuria and Korea, for the first time since the Mongols Japan was facing a hostile power on the littoral. Like Britain in Europe, Japan's security required keeping the mouths of the rivers opposite out of hostile hands. The mouth of the Amur was already in Russia's control, while the mouth of the Tumen was within striking distance of Vladivostok. A struggle was looming for the control of the mouths of the Yalu and of the Liao, which flow to the Yellow Sea on either side of the Liaodong (Liaotung) peninsula which juts out from South Manchuria.[7] A strong Korea, able to resist the Russians, as it had done so often in the past against threats from the north, would have best suited Japan's interests. But the Korean peninsula was weak and divided.

With Russian and Japanese interests clashing in Manchuria, it was Japan that 'opened' Korea, the 'hermit kingdom'. The Koreans, abandoning the careful diplomatic courtesies they had observed under the Tokugawas, had made no secret of their contempt for what they saw as Japan's spinelessness in opening itself up to foreigners. Thus in 1868 Korea snubbed the Meiji Restoration ceremonies in Tokyo. Instead of an ambassador bearing gifts, the Koreans sent a letter accusing Japan of kowtowing to the southern barbarians. Not surprisingly, the letter was long kept secret.[8] But it was not forgotten or forgiven.[9]

In 1876, Japan used gunboat diplomacy to force on Korea the Treaty of Kangwha, by which Japan obtained trading concessions and extraterritorial privileges. Japan thus imposed on the Koreans the kind of humiliation that the Western maritime powers had imposed on Japan. Japan also interpreted the treaty as evidence that Korea was no longer a vassal of China, and saw that as the first step in asserting Japanese hegemony over Korea. But there was a setback in 1884, when a Japanese-sponsored coup failed and the Chinese reasserted their authority. With China and Japan now beginning to clash in Korea, a naval arms race began.

China was encouraged by its 'self-strengthening' movement, which included an effort to develop a modern army and navy. So it believed it could bring to heel the insolent land of the 'dwarf pirates' across the waters. In 1891, China sought to intimidate Japan with a visit by its two German-built warships. These were larger and more heavily armed than the British-built cruisers of the Japanese navy. But Commander Togo Heihachiro, a Satsuma who had fought the British as a young samurai in Kagoshima in 1863, was unimpressed. Having been trained in the exacting standards of the British Navy (where he had complained about the food), Togo was disgusted by the garbage on the decks of the Chinese warships, and the laundry hanging from their guns.[10] The Chinese, as was their wont, had allowed hubris to lull them into complacency.

By this time, Japan had built a protective screen in the islands which guarded its maritime approaches from the southwest. In 1861, the shogunate had taken the Bonin (Ogasawara) islands. Perry subsequently wanted to claim these islands for the United States, but his claim was disavowed. With American support, Japan's claims to the Bonins were recognized in 1875. In the previous year, the Meiji government had sent a punitive expedition to Formosa (Taiwan) because local aborigines had slaughtered and eaten stranded Okinawan fishermen. These expeditions also provided an outlet for underemployed Japanese samurai. China was unable to resist. Japan gained an indemnity, as well as tacit recognition of its claims to the extensive Ryukyu island chain, including Okinawa, which China had previously claimed as tributary. (As we have seen, the Ryukyu king since 1609 had been a vassal of both Japan and China.) But for now at least, Taiwan lay beyond Japan's grasp.

Japan: checkmating Russia, enclosing the Sea of Okhotsk

On the northern front, where Russia was operating at long distances from its main base at Vladivostok, Japan proved able to checkmate the Russian advance. In an agreement in 1875, Japan acquired the whole of the Kuril island chain. As we have seen, the Kurils had been first divided in the 1855 Treaty of Shimoda which had split the chain at the Friza Strait, thus awarding nearly all of the islands to Russia. Now, by means of the Treaty of St Petersburg, the boundary was made to run between Cape Lopatka on the Kamchatka peninsula and Shumshu (Paramushir), the first Kuril island (as measured from the Kamchatka peninsula). In return, Japan recognized Russia's sovereignty over the large island of Sakhalin, and the boundary between Japan and Russia was made to run through the Soya Strait. Thus, after 1875, the most northerly of East Asia's marginal seas, the Sea of Okhotsk, was in effect closed. But it was closed not by Russia, but by Japan, which had exploited the advantages of proximity.

Still, Russia had retrenched in the foggy and distant Kurils in order to concentrate on the cornucopia of Manchuria. Thus the threat to Japan via Manchuria and Korea continued to grow, with the new technology of the railways adding to the sinews of Russian power. In 1891, Russia began to build the Trans-Siberian railway. In 1886, the completion of the Canadian Pacific railway had proved that railways could indeed be built in high latitudes. Like most Russian railways, the Trans-Siberian was built on the wide five-feet-one-inch gauge, meant as a deterrent against invasion. (European railways had a narrower gauge.) In Vladivostok in 1890, the future tsar Nicholas II wheeled the first barrow of soil for the construction of the railway, after which he traveled 1,500 miles by boat up the Amur. He was returning to Russia from a visit to Japan, where he had been attacked by a deranged samurai. That did little to improve his attitude towards the Japanese. By building the Trans-Siberian railway, Russia sought to shorten its lines of communication – in the same way that the arrival of the steamship and the construction of the Suez canal in 1869 had shortened the maritime lines of communication of the British empire.

But the Trans-Siberian's section from the eastern shores of Lake Baikal along the great northeastward curve of the Shilka and Amur rivers presented huge problems of climate and terrain. It would be much cheaper and convenient to cut across Manchuria to Vladivostok. Thus, by means of a treaty with China in which Russia promised not to violate China's sovereignty, and to help defend China against Japan, Russia obtained the right to build the Chinese Eastern railway from Chita to Vladivostok. (A bribe to the Chinese negotiator also helped.) The Chinese Eastern railway, completed in 1903, was tantamount to a Russian bid for hegemony over all of Manchuria. Thus in 1894–1895 Japan fought a war with China in order to prevent Russian control of Korea. Both Japan and Russia saw this war as a curtainraiser for their eventual showdown.

Japan's defeat of China

The immediate cause of the war was an anti-foreign revolt in Korea. As both China and Japan moved troops into Korea following disorders in Seoul, the Japanese fleet left its base at Sasebo in western Kyushu. In London, the betting was 7:3 on China.[11] The Chinese fleet seemed superior. Moreover, in the Yellow Sea, the Chinese had the advantage of proximity, operating from their bases at Lushun (Port Arthur) at the tip of the Liaodong peninsula, and Weihaiwei on the Shandong peninsula.

A week before the declaration of war, Japanese vessels sank a Chinese troop convoy off Chemulpo (Inchon) in a surprise attack that was to become Japan's hallmark. Japan, wishing to win the war before any other power could intervene, sank most of the Chinese fleet outside the mouth of the Yalu, then finished if off outside its base of Weihaiwei. After Japanese armies won the Battle of Pyongyang, they crossed the Yalu and drove into Manchuria. The Liaodong peninsula, the key to Manchuria, was the main battleground of the ground war. Port Arthur fell in November, after the Japanese navy landed troops on the eastern side of the peninsula. Having captured the peninsula, Japan was able to cut China off from Korea. Japanese forces then took Weihaiwei from the rear in February 1895. Now Japan controlled both the vital Liaodong and Shandong peninsulas. That laid open the approaches to Beijing, so China had to sue for peace.

The Treaty of Shimonoseki forced China to recognize the independence of Korea and to cede the Liaodong peninsula to Japan. Six months after the treaty was signed, Japanese freelancers in Seoul engineered the murder of the Korean queen, whom they suspected of secret dealings with Russia and China. Japan thus moved a step closer towards making Korea a protectorate. Divided against itself, Korea was unable to resist Japanese encroachment. But in murdering Queen Min, the Japanese stoked the fires of a fierce anti-Japanese nationalism which had been first lit by Hideyoshi.

Under the terms of the Treaty of Shimonoseki, China was required to pay a huge indemnity. Japan used this money to buy warships from Britain, and to build a large iron and steel works at Yawata in Kyushu, which relied on Chinese coal and iron. During the war, Japan had also occupied Taiwan and the Pescadore islands in the Taiwan strait, which it kept under the terms of the Shimonoseki treaty. Japan's navy soon established a base at Makung (Bako) in the Pescadores. Thus Japan's acquisition of these subtropical areas suggested ambition much wider than Manchuria – directed towards the South China Sea and beyond.

Japan had now established itself as the dominant Asian power, and ended its period of humiliation by forcing the foreign powers to renounce their rights of extraterritoriality. But for the moment at least, Japan's reach exceeded its grasp. The European powers were alarmed at Japan's seizing of Port Arthur, which allowed the Japanese to control Manchuria's outlet to the sea, as well as the seaward approaches to Beijing. They had warned Japan's government that they would not permit Japan to stay in Port Arthur, but the military refused to listen. So France, Germany and Russia jointly intervened, while Britain looked on with interest. Under threat of war by this 'Triple Intervention', Japan was forced to return the Liaodong peninsula to China. To rub salt into Japan's wounded pride, Russia's own designs on the strategic peninsula soon became manifest. Moreover, the tsar was being urged into war with Japan by his cousin, the German emperor.

Enter Germany

The 1894 Triple Intervention marked Germany's entry into the equations of power in the Far East. In 1871, the emergence at the centre of Europe of a unified German empire, with a militarized Prussia at its core, was to prove highly destabilizing for world peace. Milestones in the consolidation of Prussian power included the conquest of Denmark, by which Prussia obtained the territory necessary for the Kiel Canal, completed in 1895. The canal enabled Prussia to move ships between its Baltic ports and the North Sea, thus avoiding the chokepoint of the Kattegat at the entrance to the Baltic, which the British Navy had long been able to control in time of war. In 1866, Prussia's defeat of Austria gave it the dominant position among the German states. Four years later, by defeating France, Prussia acquired the provinces of Alsace and Lorraine, together with their rich iron ore deposits. By the end of the century, the iron and steel industry of the Ruhr valley had made Germany Europe's leading industrial power.

Bismarck, Germany's long-serving 'Iron Chancellor', comprehended that France could never be reconciled to Germany after the loss of Alsace-

Lorraine. So he conducted an intricate balancing act whose centrepiece was alliance with Russia. This protected Germany against the threat of a Franco–Russian alliance, and hence the threat of two-front war to which its central position in Europe rendered it vulnerable. Aware of the risks of overextension, Bismarck restrained German ambitions overseas and in the Balkans. But after Wilhelm II became emperor (kaiser) in 1888, he dismissed Bismarck and refused to renew the 'reinsurance' treaty with Russia. The kaiser's ambitions soon put Germany on a collision course with the Russian empire. This had repercussions in the Far East which fed back into the European balance.

Kaiser 'Willy' pretended to be on good terms with his cousin 'Nicky', who as Nicholas II became tsar in 1894. Their absurd pretensions even led them to address each other as the Admiral of the Atlantic (Willy) and the Admiral of the Pacific (Nicky). But in reality they shared little more than hatred of their British royal cousins whose Navy did rule the waves in both oceans – and the Indian Ocean as well. In the Triple Intervention, Germany supported Russia because the kaiser sought the freer hand in eastern Europe which seemed in prospect if Russia came into collision with Japan, as Willy so ardently hoped. Blocked in the west by the rise of Germany, why should not the tsar be tempted towards eastward expansion?

The kaiser, much influenced by Alfred Mahan, the American apostle of naval expansion, had his own ambitions in the Far East. By this time, the advent of the steamship meant that the race was on for coaling stations and ports around the globe. In 1885, Germany secured islands off New Guinea in the South Pacific, and in the following year a colony in the northeast quarter of that island. The Germans also acquired the Marshall Islands in the mid-Pacific, and Nauru in the southwest Pacific. But these were mere scraps of empire, because Germany had arrived too late on the scene. The kaiser wanted more, and new opportunities soon presented themselves in China after Japan's victory in 1895 revealed the weakness of the Manchus.

The scramble for territory in China

In November 1897, two German Jesuit priests were murdered on the Shandong peninsula. Even though their order was banned in Germany, the kaiser saw his chance. He ordered his Far Eastern naval squadron to seize the Shandong port of Jiaozhou (Kiaochow), one of the best harbours on the China coast. Germany soon also gained the nearby port of Qingdao (Tsingtao). Like Russia, Germany saw the need for maritime power to protect its interests in the east.

With this move, the kaiser acquired his coveted port on the China coast, and also encouraged Russia into war with Japan. As he anticipated, Germany's move into Shandong led Russia to seize Port Arthur. The Russian finance minister, Count Sergei Witte, tried in vain to warn the tsar that taking Port Arthur would lead to war with Japan.[12] But the tsar would not listen. Port Arthur was especially alluring to Russian expansionists because it was a warm-water port, as well as the best harbour on the south Manchurian coast. Russia thus proceeded to make Port Arthur the main base of its Far Eastern fleet. A year later, Russia also gained control of the port of Dairen (Dalny). Both Port Arthur and Dairen were then closed, in keeping with Russia's autarkic practices. Now Russia controlled the strategic Liaodung Peninsula, and this threatened both Japan and China. Thus, only a few years after Japan had defeated China, the two East Asian powers sank their differences in order to combine against Russia.

Russia, in order to consolidate its grip on Manchuria, began to build a railway down the Liaodong Peninsula to its new ports. This South Manchurian railway linked up with the Chinese Eastern railway at Harbin on the Sungari River, thus making Harbin the strategic pivot of Manchuria. When the South Manchurian and the Chinese Eastern railways were completed, Port Arthur would be a mere fifteen days' journey from St Petersburg. Moreover, the creation of the Russo–Chinese bank, with French financing, gave Russia the right to build railways anywhere on Chinese territory. These new manifestations of Russian ambition in China made war with Japan ever more likely.

The scramble for territory in China also accelerated the decay of the Manchu empire. This did not suit Britain. Unlike Russia, Britain was more interested in keeping what it already had in China than in acquiring more. Britain was also anxious to uphold the treaty system on which its privileges depended. In China, Britain's main interest was the preservation of its vast sphere of influence in the Yangzi valley, amounting to nearly one third of China.

Still, Britain could not ignore the Russian and German land grabs in China. In particular, the Russian base at Port Arthur threatened not only Beijing, but the entire British position in China. On the China coast, Britain was already squeezed between the Russians in the north and Russia's ally France in the south. (In 1891 France and Russia had set aside their differences in order to counter the growing German threat in Europe.) France, having sunk the Chinese fleet in 1884 in a surprise attack while it lay at anchor, was ensconced in Kwangchow Bay (Zhanjiang), as well as in the splendid harbour of Cam Ranh Bay on the coast of Vietnam, now a French colony.

Thus Britain, in order to protect its interests in the Yangzi valley and on the China coast, took control of the former Chinese naval base of Weihaiwei opposite Port Arthur, only eighty miles distant. That was at the invitation of the Chinese, who were anxious to counter the Russians at Port Arthur. From Weihaiwei, the Royal Navy could guard the seaward approaches to Beijing. To shore up the arrangement, China in 1897 leased to Britain the New Territories opposite Hong Kong.

Globally, Britain built up its naval strength to match that of Russia and France combined. Despite the growth of the navies of its potential enemies, maritime geography still favoured Britain. Inferior to the Royal Navy and lacking a global network of bases, the fleets of France, Russia and Germany in the Far East were all vulnerable to a British fleet placed between them and Europe.

Then the rebellion of the Society of the Harmonious Fists, known in the West as the Boxers, created new opportunities in China for both Russia and Japan. The rebellion broke out in the Shandong Peninsula, and then spread to Beijing in June 1900. When the Dowager Empress, a doughty opponent of reform, threw in her lot with the Boxers, a siege of the foreign legations began.

The Japanese, with 10,000 men, provided most of the foreign forces that relieved the legations. For their part, the Russians did not miss the opportunity to move into Manchuria. They expelled the Chinese from the northern bank of the Amur, drowning thousands in the process. Russian forces then crossed the Amur, and occupied all three provinces of Manchuria. The tsar ignored warnings that this meant war with Japan. But Japan was not ready yet. First it needed to protect its back against France, Russia's ally. Thus an alliance with Britain had much to recommend it.

The German threat to global British interests

By now, it suited Britain to enlist Japan's help in checking Russian expansion in the Far East. The Boer war (1899–1902) had revealed Britain's overextension and international isolation. Moreover, Germany was increasingly willing to challenge Britain. German influence, hostile to both Britain and Russia, was becoming preponderant in Constantinople and the Middle East – Germany's 'push to the east' being marked by the intention to build the Berlin–Baghdad railway. Moreover, in 1898 and 1900, naval bills passed the German parliament, laying down a challenge to British naval supremacy in the North Sea. That also meant a threat to Britain's role as dominant maritime power.

If Britain could no longer play its traditional role as offshore balancer, hegemony over Europe would be within the kaiser's grasp. By now, the development of its highly efficient railways was giving Germany the ability to swing its forces rapidly from one front to another. In fact, the German high command had made railway timetables into a new military art form. The capabilities of its railway system raised the prospect that Germany might be able to defeat France, then turn on Russia before the vast Russian armies could properly mobilize. Thus Germany hoped to overcome the threat of two-front war to which the abandonment of Bismarck's balancing policies had made it vulnerable.

But by threatening vital British interests, the kaiser was attracting new enemies without acquiring new allies. Moreover, the ally that he did have, Austria–Hungary, was more of a liability than an asset. This was mostly because it was a ramshackle polyglot empire that threatened to embroil

Germany in its own collision of interest with Russia in the Balkans. Not without reason had the Iron Chancellor warned that the Balkans were not worth the bones of a single Pomeranian grenadier.

Britain responded to the German challenge in several ways – by a vigorous naval building programme; by retrenchment from overextended positions in order to meet the German threat in Europe; by global rapprochement with Russia and France; and by turning over to Japan the task of containing Russia in the Far East. In 1905, Britain laid down the keel of a revolutionary new capital ship, the *Dreadnought*. It also pursued global retrenchment. In order to conciliate the United States, Britain backed down in a dispute in 1895 over the border between Venezuela and British Guiana. It also reduced its West Indies fleet, thus giving the United States a free hand in the Caribbean. During the 1898 Spanish–American War, Britain gave the United States moral support, and diplomatic help in Europe when some of the European powers threatened intervention. And by means of the 1902 Hay–Pauncefote treaty, Britain conceded to the United States the right to build a canal through Panama to link America's Pacific and Atlantic coasts.

Having appeased a rising America, Britain moved to settle outstanding colonial issues with France. That led to the *Entente Cordiale* of 1904. With Russia and France already allies, the kaiser's minatory and erratic behaviour had now provoked the formation of the very coalition that Bismarck had so feared. In the Far East, Britain also sought to reduce tensions with Russia. In 1899 Britain renounced its interest in railway concessions north of the Great Wall, in exchange for Russia's doing so in the Yangzi valley. The area between them became a neutral zone. With its position in the Yangzi secured, Britain then delegated to Japan the task of containing Russian ambition in the Far East.

The precursor to the Russo–Japanese War, the alliance between Britain and Japan, was signed in 1902. Each power agreed to remain neutral in case the other were attacked by a single power, but would come to the assistance of the other if it were attacked by a third power. Thus Britain protected Japan against Russia's ally, France. The alliance of the two maritime powers at opposite ends of Eurasia was meant to confine Russia within its continental imperium. Britain was to guard against Russia's break-out to the Black Sea, the Atlantic and the Indian Oceans, while Japan would close Russia's exits to the Pacific. Despite the growing German threat, Britain had not yet abandoned its traditional role of blocking Russia's ambitions to break out to the open oceans.

The treaty with Japan was the only long-term alliance Britain entered into between 1815 and 1914. For Japan, because of the maritime basis of its security, alliance with the dominant maritime power represented optimal security. The younger elements of the Meiji élite had won out in arguments with the older leaders, who preferred entente with Russia. After all, the older leaders had thrust Japan out of its self-imposed isolation because they saw Britain as the main threat. But the younger generation perceived that Britain was now a sated power, while Russia burned with ambition.

Still, the Japanese government was not thirsting for war. The *genro* sought an agreement that would have given Russia a free hand in Manchuria and northern Korea in return for giving Japan *carte blanche* in southern Korea. In 1894, Field Marshall Yamagata Aritomo, a Choshu and founder of the modern Japanese army, visited Russia for the coronation of Nicholas II. Yamagata offered to divide the Korean Peninsula at the 38th parallel. That would have given Russia the warm-water port of Wonsan on Korea's northeast coast that it had long coveted. In conjunction with Port Arthur, possession of Wonsan would have given Russia *de facto* control of all of Manchuria and much of Korea – except the southern half of the peninsula, which had been vital to Japan's security since the days of the Mongols.

But the tsar spurned the offer because he wanted more. Thus he failed to honour undertakings, to Japan and the Western powers, that Russia would withdraw from Manchuria. And in 1902 a Russian company began to cut timber on the banks of the Yalu. Soon large numbers of Russian troops, thinly disguised as lumberjacks, were pouring into Korea. The tsar ignored warnings that this would lead to a war that Russia might not win. But for Nicholas II, his forehead still slightly scarred by the samurai sword attack during his visit to Japan as a young man, this was also a matter of revenge. Besides, how could mere Asian 'monkeys' defeat a European power of the first rank?

The Russo–Japanese War

Japan, much weaker than Russia in terms of manpower and industry, struck pre-emptively, before the Trans-Siberian railway could be completed in the most difficult section around Lake Baikal.[13] This helped Japan exploit Russia's disadvantages in terms of the vast distances from Europe.

Although Russia's Far Eastern Fleet possessed more battleships than Japan's, maritime geography favoured Japan. Russia's Far Eastern Fleet was separated from its other fleets, the Baltic and Black Sea Fleets, by the vast Eurasian landmass. The Far Eastern Fleet was also divided between its squadrons based at Port Arthur and Vladivostok. These were 1,200 miles apart and separated by the Tsushima Strait, now under Japanese control. Thus Japan was able to concentrate its naval forces, while Russia's were divided. On 8 February, the Imperial Navy landed troops at Chemulpo, after sinking a Russian cruiser and gunboat there. Repeating the pattern of surprise attack that Japan had employed in the war against China, Admiral Togo Heihachiro then ordered a torpedo attack on the unsuspecting Russian fleet at Port Arthur.

To his chagrin, Togo did not succeed in bottling up the Russian squadrons at Port Arthur and Vladivostok, and had to resort to distant blockade. He also knew that the Russian Baltic Fleet was being sent under the command of Admiral Rozhdestvenski to reinforce the Port Arthur squadron.[14] (The Black Sea Fleet, weak in any case, was unable to help because of the treaty following the Crimean War, which prohibited Russia from taking warships out of the Black Sea without the permission of Turkey.) Togo was also embarrassed by the break-out of the Vladivostok squadron. These warships passed through the Tsugaru Strait and sailed down Japan's east coast, causing panic in its coastal cities. Then they sank Japanese transports reinforcing Korea.[15]

Still, Togo did gain enough sea control to support the army in the first stage of the ground war, the capture of Korea. The second stage of the war was the attack on the Russian forces in Manchuria. There, Japan met its major military objectives, including the great battle before Mukden in early 1905, where the fighting was on a larger scale even than in the American Civil War. At Mukden more half a million men took the field. New weapons such as long-range automatic machine guns were greatly increasing the carnage of war, although the European powers did not seem to take much notice. They had, after all, been at peace since 1815, except for the brief period of the Crimean War.

Japan took Port Arthur from the rear in January 1905 after a costly five-month siege. This made the three-ocean transit of the Russian Baltic Fleet a 20,000-mile journey to nowhere. Fearing an attack by shadowing British warships, most of the fleet avoided the Mediterranean, where Britain had so many bases. The Suez Canal was also a dangerous bottleneck. So the main elements of the fleet took the much longer route around the Cape of Good Hope. At Cam Ranh Bay, in French Indochina, the fleet was reinforced by the elements which had come through Suez. But the Combined Fleet knew it was doomed. With Port Arthur now in Japanese hands, the fleet had no option but to make a run for Vladivostok. That meant passing through one of the straits through the Japanese archipelago. Admiral Rozhdestvenski's only hope was to try to slip through in the fog that often shrouds those waters. Togo guessed correctly that the Russians, low on coal, would opt for the shortest route through the Tsushima Strait. So he planned his ambush from his base in Masampo on the southern tip of Korea.

The engagement turned into a rout as Togo, in his flagship *Mikasa*, famously 'crossed the T', thus enabling his modern battleships to cripple the lead elements of the Russian columns. Almost six thousand Russian sailors were captured, and 4,830 killed. Japanese losses were insignificant. Tsushima was the most momentous naval engagement since Trafalgar. But for Japan, there was no accompanying Waterloo. This was because victory at Tsushima could not bring Japan the decisive victory in the ground war.

Japan had sought to fight a limited war to prevent Russian control of Korea and southern Manchuria. In doing so, it had become bogged down. The more progress Japan achieved against Russia, the more it became enmeshed. Military success enlarged the victor's area of occupation and extended his lines of communication. Moreover, Japan was unable to attack Russia's centre of gravity, which lay on the far side of the Urals, while Russia possessed enormous manpower reserves. It was only temporarily exhausted and would soon regroup. For Japan, the war was, or should have been, a lesson for the future about the perils of war on the Asian continent.

But Russia, its fleets sunk, also lacked the means of bringing the war home to Japan. In addition, the flames of revolution (fanned by Japanese agents) were flickering at home. Moreover, Japan had captured the large island of Sakhalin, increasing the threat to the Siberian seaboard. So Russia also needed peace, and agreed to US President Theodore Roosevelt's brokering a settlement at Portsmouth in New Hampshire. Sergei Witte, who had tried in vain to warn the tsar of the risks of war, was called upon to salvage as much as he could for Russia.

A brokered peace at Portsmouth

Russia kept the northern half of Sakhalin, and refused to pay an indemnity. But otherwise, the treaty favoured Japan, because Japan had won the war. Russia agreed to transfer to Japan its lease on Port Arthur and Dairen, China's nominal consent having been attained. Thus Japan reversed the effects of the 1895 Triple Intervention. Russia also ceded to Japan most of the South Manchurian railway. In addition, Japan retained the southern half of Sakhalin, the partition being made along the fiftieth parallel. This kept the two large bays in Japanese hands.

Not for the last time, Japan had benefited from the internecine struggles of the Europeans. Britain, with an eye mostly on the growing German threat in Europe, had been willing to let Japan play the key role in blocking Russian ambition in the Far East. After the war, Britain turned over to Japan the task of protecting Britain's position in the Far East. By the end of 1905, Britain had closed its China station, transferring its battleships to the Channel Fleet. Now Japan had not only established itself as the dominant naval power in the north Pacific, but had virtually enclosed the Yellow Sea and the Sea of Japan. As we have noted, it had already enclosed the Sea of Okhotsk. Thus, half a century after Perry had sailed into Edo Bay, Japan had already enclosed three of East Asia's marginal seas.

This did not suit the interests of the rising maritime power on the opposite side of the Pacific, the United States, despite the fact that America had backed Japan against Russia. Russia had a bad press in America, not least because of recurring pogroms against the Jews. When the war broke out, President Roosevelt warned France and Germany that if they again ganged up with Russia against Japan, as they had in 1895, the United States would 'promptly side with Japan and proceed to whatever length was necessary on her behalf'.[16] But the dimensions of the Japanese victory at Tsushima worried Washington, because of America's obligations to the security of the Philippines, and its pursuit of the Open Door in China.

Enter America: the Open Door to China

The United States pursued the Open Door with remarkable tenacity from the mid-nineteenth century onwards. This was because the policy reflected both American economic interests and its values, especially its missionary instincts towards China. A commercial republic rather than an imperial power, the United States did not seek the territorial concessions on the China coast which might have underpinned its growing maritime reach. At the end of the century, with the European powers scrambling for territory and coaling stations in China, the US State Department ruled out the Navy's attempts to secure for itself a port on the China coast.

Still, by this time America was the world's leading manufacturing power. With growing commercial interests in the Pacific, it did not want to be squeezed out of the China market by the creation of further European and Japanese exclusive zones there. Thus US policy towards China was set out in the two Open Door Notes by Secretary of State John Hay, on 6 September 1899 and 3 July 1900. Their purpose was to ensure that European spheres of influence in China did not become colonial possessions, as the international force prepared to relieve the siege of the legations in Beijing during the Boxer Rebellion. Then America's concerns were heightened after the rebellion gave the Europeans further excuses for establishing enclaves in coastal China.

So the second Hay Note spelled out not only the principle of equal opportunity, but also the territorial integrity of China. With allied forces poised to march on Beijing, the second Open Door Note said that 'the policy of the United States is to seek a solution which may bring about permanent safety and peace to China, preserve Chinese territorial integrity and administrative entity, protect all rights guaranteed to friendly powers by treaty and international law and safeguard trade with all parts of China'. The second Open Door Note prevented further landgrabbing in China – though not the looting of Beijing, or successful demands by the European powers for another large indemnity.

For its part, Britain supported the Open Door policy because its interests were congruent with those of the United States. Dominating the China trade by virtue of its commanding position in the Yangzi valley, Britain also had a vested interest in maintaining China's integrity, and thus equality of opportunity there. And although America's Open Door policy was initially inspired by commercial motives, by 1900 it had acquired a strategic dimension. This was a consequence of America's having acquired island territories in the Pacific that lay between it and Japan.

Problems of Philippine security

For America, East Asia was only one ocean away, not two, as it was for the European maritime powers. So events in East Asia drew in the United States, which became a Pacific power when it took the Philippines in 1898 as a spoil of the naval war with Spain. In 1868, the United States Navy had occupied Midway Island, with a view to making a naval station there on the route to China. Then the 1898 war with Spain demonstrated America's growing maritime reach.

After considerable debate, the United States decided to keep the Philippines, largely in order to prevent Germany or Japan from taking possession of these islands. The United States also kept Guam as a spoil of the war with Spain because the island was well located to serve as a coaling station between Hawaii and Asia. In addition, in 1899 the United States took eastern Samoa in the South Pacific and annexed Wake Island. Shortly after taking the Philippines, America also annexed the Hawaiian Islands, not least to forestall Japanese ambition there. But it did not take the Caroline and Mariana Islands from Spain. Rather, it allowed them to go to Germany, which already possessed the Marshall Islands. So Germany was permitted to occupy these 'stepping stones on the Royal Road to Manila'. America was later to have cause to regret this decision, when the Japanese seized the opportunities presented by the First World War to occupy these islands.

The Philippine archipelago, located on a central point in the chain of islands down the East Asian littoral, is only six hundred miles from the Chinese coast. Acquisition of these islands could constitute a strategic asset only if America enjoyed maritime supremacy in the Western Pacific. Their outlying northern islands were almost within sight of Taiwan, which Japan had taken as a spoil of the naval war with China in 1895. But the Philippines were 5,000 miles from Hawaii. Hawaii itself was 2,000 miles from San Francisco. And after 1905, Japan was the dominant maritime power in North Asia.

Japan had a battle fleet in the Western Pacific, while the United States did not. America's battleships were permanently based in the Atlantic, and the Panama Canal was not opened until 1914. (Moreover, Mahanian doctrine decreed that the battle fleet not be divided.) In the Russo–Japanese War, Japan's navy had proved that it could convey in secret 100,000 soldiers to Korea and Manchuria. Theodore Roosevelt, much influenced by Mahan, had urged the taking and retention of the Philippines. But after Tsushima, he realized that the islands were an Achilles' heel. They were simply too close to Japan, and too far from America. That fuelled the president's interest in brokering the peace at Portsmouth.

The balance of power in East Asia in 1905

Thus, by 1905, the East Asian quadrilateral had assembled. China and Japan, the two core states of East Asia, had been brought into strategic collision as the consequence of the push of the European powers into East Asia. Japan had defeated China, after which a greatly weakened China had moved into alignment with Japan in order to oppose the growing Russian power that threatened them both. The United States had supported Japan against Russia. But soon America saw a potential threat from the victors of Tsushima, and so tried to strike a balance of power between the expanding Russian and Japanese empires that would preserve America's essential interest in achieving equilibrium on the far shore of the Pacific Ocean.

The entry into the East Asian power game of Japan and the United States, two extra-European powers, thus created a world order that was much more than the European concert extended by geography. And, while Europe remained the global focus of great-power strategic tensions, fluctuations in the East Asian quadrilateral fed back into the global balance. For example, after Russia was thwarted in its ambitions to reach a warm-water port in the Far East, it returned with renewed energy to old ambitions in the Balkans and the Turkish straits. That heightened Russia's collision of interest with Germany's ally, the Austro–Hungarian empire. With the European powers no longer able to dissipate their energies in imperial expansion, dangerous tensions were building up in Europe. This had been predicted by the British geographer Sir Halford Mackinder, in a lecture in 1904. In 1914 these strategic tensions exploded into war, with a ferocity and on a scale than none had anticipated – few had noticed the carnage of the Russo–Japanese War.

By 1905, tensions were starting to rise between Japan and the United States, even though America had cheered on Japan in its war with Russia. Shortly after the battle of Tsushima, Admiral Togo visited Admiral Rozhdestvenski as he lay recovering in a Sasebo hospital. Togo's escort was a young lieutenant, Yamamoto Isoroku. In December 1941, Yamamoto, now an admiral himself, was to plan the surprise attack on the American fleet at Pearl Harbor. The roots of that attack were to be found in the hubris that overtook the Japanese military after it defeated Russia, and in the strategic miscalculation that Japan made when it sought, in collusion with Russia, to close the door to Manchuria in Washington's face.

2   Unstable balance 1905–1935

From 1905 to 1935, East Asia remained part of a global security system whose great-power tensions focused on Europe, but it was becoming a more important part of the global balance. By 1935, Russia – the only Eurasian power – was beginning to worry about the threat of two-front war, as an increasingly militaristic Japan began to align itself with Hitler's Germany.

But Russia did not seek, as America did, to maintain equilibrium in East Asia. To the contrary, after the 1917 Bolshevik revolution, Russia's main objective in Asia – as in Europe – was to pit the capitalist powers against one another. By encouraging inter-capitalist war, the Russians hoped to foster revolution. Thus Russia constantly undermined America's efforts to strike and maintain a balance of power in East Asia by means of the Washington treaty system. And by 1935 the Washington system was in tatters, as a consequence of the onset of the Great Depression and the rise of Chinese nationalism, both of which served to undermine the moderates in Japan and foster the rise of militarism there. The more ambition Japan showed in Manchuria, the more it collided with the American interest in maintaining the Open Door in China. The origin of this collision of interest was the fateful strategic error that Japan made in 1905, when it decided to collude with Russia in order to keep American economic interests out of Manchuria.

Japan: keeping America out of Manchuria

Immediately after the Portsmouth treaty, the American railway tycoon, Edward H. Harriman, visited Japan. He had close links with Jacob H. Schiff, who had helped finance Japan's war effort.[1] Harriman wanted to invest in railways in Manchuria, which he envisaged as part of a vast Eurasian railway network encircling the globe. Railways already linked the US east and west coasts. Characteristically, American railways had been developed mostly by private capital, with economic rather than strategic considerations uppermost. That was in contrast to the traditions of the continental powers, where railways were mainly instruments of state policy, even if they never turned a profit.[2]

Still, strategic considerations were not entirely absent from American thinking. Harriman enjoyed strong State Department support during the Taft administration. That was because America's interest in the Manchurian railways was not just commercial. The United States did not wish to see Russia knitting together vast expansions of Eurasia by means of its transcontinental railways. Naturally, the Chinese government liked Harriman's proposals. It recognized the benefits of American investment in Manchuria as a hedge against both Russian and Japanese ambition.

The more farsighted Japanese leaders also supported an American commercial presence in Manchuria. They saw that Japan's interests would be best served if Manchuria became a buffer between the Russian and Japanese empires. Besides, Manchuria – unlike Korea – was indisputably Chinese territory. These leaders recognized that the balance of power in East Asia remained unstable after 1905 because Japan had not been able to bring the war home to Russia. Japan's victory represented the power equation at the time, but that was not the end of their rivalry. Thus, after 1905, Japan faced two great strategic problems – Russian revanchism and Chinese nationalism.[3]

But Japan pursued narrow rather than enlightened self-interest, as it was to do from this point onwards, and opted to collude with Russia at China's expense. That was partly because Harriman's planned railway from Jinzhou (Chinchow) on the Gulf of Chihli to Aigun on the Amur would have sliced through Manchuria, competing with the South Manchurian railway. This threatened both Japanese and Russian interests. Thus the East Asian quadrilateral fluctuated again. When Japan had fought Russia, China and the United States had cheered Japan from the sidelines. Now Russia and Japan aligned themselves against China and the United States.

For Japan, colluding with Russia to keep American interests out of Manchuria proved to be a great mistake. By 1923, expansion into China had cost Japan its alliance with Britain, because the United States believed that the alliance was providing a screen for Japanese ambition in China. Then Japan, having set itself adrift, soon found itself on a collision course with the United States. To its existing problems with the land powers – Russian revanchism and Chinese nationalism – Japan thus added a third major strategic challenge, in the form of a growing clash of interest with the rising maritime power across the Pacific.

Japan colludes with Russia

Japan lost no time after the war in consolidating its grip on southern Manchuria. In December 1905, it concluded a treaty in which China acquiesced in the Portsmouth transfers of the southern Manchurian ports and railways. China also agreed not to build railways in competition with the South Manchurian railway. So the Portsmouth Treaty became the basis of Japan's rapidly expanding claims in Manchuria.[4]

In 1906, the transfer to Japan of the South Manchurian railway provided an opportunity for negotiations between Russia and Japan. In the following year, they exchanged public pledges to respect each other's territory and such rights as sprang from the treaties each had made with China, and from the Portsmouth Treaty. At the same time, they secretly partitioned Manchuria and Mongolia into spheres of influence.[5] Japan asserted its dominant interests in the Liao valley, plus exclusive interests in Korea. For its part, Russia retained most of the Manchurian plain, including the valley of the Sungari, as well as a free hand in Outer Mongolia. But there was still little trust between these two erstwhile enemies. As a hedge in case Japan ever interdicted the Chinese Eastern railway, which cut across Manchuria, in 1908 Russia began construction of the Amur railway from Chita to Vladivostok. This railway was built entirely on Russian territory.

Japan and Russia signed two further conventions in July 1910. Their collusion, leading to ever greater infringements on China's sovereignty, contributed to the mutiny that forced the abdication of the Manchu dynasty in February 1912. A provisional national assembly, meeting in Nanjing (Nanking), declared as provisional president Yuan Shih-kai, the chief military commander of the Manchus. The overthrow of the Manchus set off another round of competition between Russia and China for control over Mongolia, which had declared independence and looked to Japan for support. Russia, purporting to support Mongolian independence, had trained the Mongolian army and sought to make the territory a protectorate. But Japanese determination to contain the Russian advance was incorporated into the Russo–Japanese convention of July 1912, which partitioned Inner Mongolia. These efforts to carve up China were resisted by the United States, which continued to see itself as the protector of China's sovereignty – even though America had been willing to accommodate what it saw as legitimate Japanese interests in Korea.

Conciliating Japan: Korea

President Roosevelt recognized the legitimacy of Japan's concerns about Russia, and wanted a *quid pro quo* in relation to the security of the Philippines. So he was willing to recognize Japan's paramount interests in Korea. On the eve of the Portsmouth conference, the Korean nationalist leader Syngman Rhee came to America to plead his country's case. (Rhee, who had been educated in America, was to become South Korea's president after the Second World War.) But he met no success. In July 1905, by means of the Taft–Katsura agreement, Washington recognized Japan's suzerainty over Korea, in return for Japan's disavowal of aggressive intent towards the Philippines. By November of the same year, Japan had imposed a treaty on Korea which made the peninsula a Japanese protectorate.

The Korean king's appeal to the 'international community' fell on deaf ears. A secret appeal to the newly-established Permanent Court of

Arbitration in The Hague having failed, the king abdicated in favour of his son, who was more compliant towards Japanese interests. In 1910, Japan annexed the peninsula. Subsequently, Japan's colonial rule in Korea contributed greatly to the peninsula's economic development. But Japan ruled with an iron fist, provoking continued resistance. The flames lit by Hideyoshi and rekindled by the murder of Queen Min never died out.

The 1907 war scare

Despite America's efforts to conciliate Japan, by 1906 passions were running high on both sides of the Pacific. That was partly a consequence of a decision by the San Francisco school board to bar Japanese pupils, as had long been done with Chinese students. The decision reflected Californians' alarm at growing Asian immigration, as well as resentment at the Japanese public ill will directed towards President Roosevelt as a consequence of his having brokered the peace at Portsmouth. Because Russia had not paid the indemnity which the heavily-taxed Japanese populace had expected, Roosevelt was pilloried in Japan.

In opposing non-white immigration, the British dominions of Canada and Australia supported the Californians. President Roosevelt defused the crisis in 1908 via a so-called Gentlemen's Agreement, by which Japan agreed to prohibit the direct migration of labourers to the United States. But the immigration troubles in California fed into the war scare of 1907, fanned by the American press. The crisis passed, but in the following year concern for the security of the Philippines led Roosevelt to accommodate Japan in Manchuria. In an exchange of notes between Secretary of State Root and Japan's ambassador Takahira in November 1908, Roosevelt sought to ease tensions. The Root–Takahira agreement was suitably ambiguous, but could be read as Japan's having pledged to respect the integrity of the Philippines in return for a free hand in Manchuria.

Impressing Japan: the Great White Fleet

Having accommodated what he saw as legitimate Japanese security concerns, President Roosevelt hoped to impress Japan with the growing power and reach of the US Navy. Unlike some of his successors, Roosevelt never forgot the need to back diplomacy with a credible force balance.

By 1907, the US Navy had outbuilt Germany's, and moved into third place behind Britain and France. It had twenty-one battleships and cruisers, compared with Japan's fourteen.[6] The US Navy withdrew its European and South Atlantic squadrons and concentrated them to form the Atlantic Fleet, composed of sixteen modern battleships. And by building the Panama Canal, America was strengthening the sinews of its maritime geography in ways that could hardly escape notice in Japan. Shaving some 8,000 miles from the distance between the Atlantic and Pacific coasts of the United

States, the canal would make it possible to swing the US battle fleet much more quickly between the two oceans. And to impress upon Japan the growing strength of the US Navy, the president decided to send the Atlantic Squadron – 'the Great White Fleet' – around the world.

That was welcome news for the British dominions in the Pacific. After the battle of Tsushima, Australia and New Zealand worried whether the Royal Navy would be able to protect them against Japan. For its part, Canada fretted about the danger of finding itself on the wrong side of a war between Japan and America as a consequence of the Anglo–Japanese alliance. The new federation of Australia irritated London by pressing for the Great White Fleet to visit Sydney, where it was as rapturously received as it had been in British Columbia. The Japanese, in order to show that they had not been intimidated by this naval display, also issued an invitation to the fleet. When it arrived in Tokyo, its officers and men were lavishly entertained. But in the privacy of their tea houses, the victors of Tsushima scoffed at the 'pretty battleships' of the Americans and the 'men of pleasure' who manned them.[7]

The First World War: Japan shows ambition

In East Asia, the main consequence of the First World War was the increased strategic latitude of Japan. That fired Japan's ambitions, while the European powers were distracted by war.[8] And only America stood in Japan's path.

China, in turmoil after the 1911 revolution, was in no position to resist renewed assaults on its sovereignty. In Beijing, the weak government of Yuan Shih-kai was hard pressed to maintain order. Yuan's imperial ambitions also put him at odds with the champions of parliamentary government, led by Sun Yat-sen in Canton. Britain, fearing that Japan would exploit the Anglo–Japanese alliance as a cover for its territorial ambitions in China, would have preferred Japan to remain neutral. But when the German East Asiatic Squadron under Admiral Graf von Spee broke out into the Pacific, the British had to ask for Japanese help. Soon a Japanese fleet appeared off Quingdao (Tsingtao). Japanese troops, with grudging British support, took the German ports from the rear.

Japan also pursued ambition further afield. Japanese naval forces, ostensibly in pursuit of von Spee, occupied the German mid-Pacific islands of Micronesia – the Marianas, Carolines and Marshalls.[9] As we have seen, America had neglected to annex these Spanish possessions when it took the Philippines after the war with Spain. Now Japan's seizure of these islands gave it the central geographical position in the Western Pacific. The islands lay athwart the US Navy's line of advance to the Philippines, now surrounded on two sides by Japanese-controlled territory. That was a major reason for growing American hostility to the Anglo–Japanese alliance, which the US Navy believed was allowing Japan to threaten American sea lines of communication across the Western Pacific.

Japan, collecting further alliance dues, then concluded a secret treaty with Britain early in 1917. This treaty stipulated that Japan should retain Germany's rights on the Shandong peninsula and in the former German island territories that Japan now controlled. In return, Japan would support the British empire's claims to the former German islands south of the equator, which Australian and New Zealand forces had seized in order to forestall Japan.

In return for these gains, Japan made a modest contribution to the allied cause. Britain, hard pressed by Germany's submarine campaign in the Atlantic, needed Japan's support in the Pacific. By 1916, Japanese ships were guaranteeing the security of Singapore and other British possessions. After the threat of German raiders was removed, the Japanese Navy patrolled the Pacific sea lanes, and escorted troop convoys from Australia and New Zealand sailing to Europe across the Indian Ocean. Japan also sent destroyers to the Mediterranean, although it refused to send its heavier naval units.

Japan's 'twenty-one demands' on China

Japan was not the only power to seek gains in East Asia while the struggle in Europe diverted the attention of the Western maritime powers. In Mongolia, where proximity strengthened its hand, Russia continued its forward policy. By 1915 it had succeeded in detaching Outer Mongolia from China by means of a treaty. Moreover, much larger gains seemed in prospect elsewhere. In an admission of imperial weakness, Britain reversed its historic policy of blocking Russia in the Turkish Straits. By early 1915 it had promised Moscow the keys to Constantinople.

For its part, Japan sought nothing less than hegemony over China. In January 1915 Japan presented Yuan Shih-kai with the infamous 'twenty-one demands'. These amounted to demands for a protectorate over all of China, and were a blueprint for Japan's continental ambitions. The twenty-one demands struck at the heart of British commercial interests in the Yangzi valley. They also pledged China not to cede or lease 'to any power any harbour or bay or any island' along the China coast – a demand calculated to obtain international recognition of the maritime province of Fujian (Fukien), opposite Taiwan, as a Japanese sphere of interest.[10] That was of particular concern to the United States, since Japan already had naval bases in the Pescadores and Taiwan.

Japan's occupation of Fujian would have allowed it to control both sides of the Taiwan Strait, a major international waterway commanding the approaches to the China coast. Japan was already in control of the Liaodong peninsula, the Korean peninsula, the Shandong peninsula, the Okinawan island chain and the island of Taiwan. Control of the Taiwan

Strait would be another large step towards allowing Japan to enclose the East China Sea. With the Sea of Okhotsk, the Japan Sea and the Yellow Sea already virtually enclosed by Japan, that would make the East China Sea the fourth of East Asia's marginal seas to be enclosed by Japan. How long would it be before Japan pressed on the South China Sea as well? With the Japanese now also ensconced in the mid-Pacific islands, Japan's ambitions in China represented a palpable threat to American maritime interests, as well as to the security of the Philippines.

Yuan Shih-kai, with the support of Britain and the United States, resisted Japan's 'twenty-one demands'. Hitherto, the British had taken a relaxed view of Japanese ambition in Manchuria, since it did not impinge on their interests. But now, with their nerve centre in the Yangzi touched, the British supported the Americans and pressed moderation upon their Japanese ally. Although Japan greatly improved its leverage over China, the Sino–Japanese treaties of 25 May 1915 left China with enough legal loopholes that it was not reduced to a Japanese protectorate. Still, Japan had tightened its grip on Manchuria, extending the leases on the key strategic railways (South Manchurian and Antung–Mukden) from 1923 until far-distant 1997.

In 1916, Japan signed yet another secret convention with Russia which confirmed their previous arrangements over Manchuria and Mongolia. By means of this agreement, Japan gained the right to purchase part of the Chinese Eastern railway running north from Changchun to Harbin. The move was described by the Japanese foreign minister as designed to 'ensure that all the natural resources of the Kirin plain fall into our hands'.[11] Under the 1916 secret convention, Russia and Japan recognized that 'their vital interests demand that China not fall under the political domination of any third Power hostile to Russia or Japan'.[12] This was obviously pointed at the United States. The Japanese feared that in East Asia, apart from Japan itself, the United States would be the main beneficiary of the distraction of the European powers. But soon Russia was too weak to help Japan or anyone else, because the Bolshevik revolution knocked it out of the war.

America enters the war

In 1917, the United States intervened in Europe's struggles because of the maritime basis of its own security. With Russia prostrate, Germany was on the brink of winning the war. If it had done so, Germany would have commanded the vast resources of Russia, and would soon have developed the maritime power to threaten the United States in its own hemisphere.

March 1917 saw the overthrow of the tsar and the coming to power of the weak Kerensky government. Then the Bolshevik revolution in November led to Russia's accepting a punitive peace at Brest-Litovsk.[13] The Germans had helped engineer this outcome when they permitted the Bolshevik revolutionary Lenin, who was already in their pay, to travel across Germany by train from his Swiss exile 'to the Finland station' in St Petersburg, now

renamed Petrograd. Preaching 'bread and peace', Lenin undermined whatever resolve was left in Russia for prosecuting the war. In March 1918, with
German troops within four hundred miles of Petrograd, Germany imposed
a savage peace. The Brest-Litovsk treaty was an indication of the kind of
peace Germany would have imposed on the allies had they lost the war,
which they very nearly did. Russia was forced to surrender Poland, the
Baltic states and the Ukraine. This was a vast tract amounting to about half
of Russia's industrial and agricultural resources, as well as a third of its
population.

In March 1918, after having long fought a defensive war on the western
front, Germany launched an offensive in the west. With Ludendorf's great
push bringing Germany close to victory, the United States had to gear up to
redress the imbalance of power in the old world. American intervention was
made inevitable by Germany's resumption of unrestricted submarine
warfare in February 1917. The Germans had gone for broke, calculating that
they could win before US forces arrived to tip the balance. In the summer of
1918, the US Navy conveyed one-and-a-half million American soldiers
across the Atlantic to France. Thus Anglo–American control of the seas
proved the key to allied victory, not only in blockading Germany, but in
providing the means by which America could reinforce Europe.

But rather than admit the sound geostrategic calculations that had
informed American policy, President Woodrow Wilson preferred to talk in
idealistic terms about the 'war to end wars'. He refused even to refer to the
United States as an 'ally' of Britain and France, preferring the term 'associated power'. Thus, while the United States practised geopolitics, it talked in
language that was soon to be called 'Wilsonian'. And in proclaiming the
right to self-determination of all peoples, and the war to end all wars,
Wilson aroused expectations that proved impossible to fulfil.

Japan: reversal of alliances?

As the United States prepared to redress the imbalance of power in Europe,
danger loomed in the Far East. There the allies worried that Japan might be
making overtures to Germany. There was considerable sympathy for
Germany in Japan, especially in its German-trained army. General Karl
Haushofer, doyen of the German *Geopolitikers*, was also influential there.[14]

Haushofer had spent the years 1909 to 1912 in Japan as a captain on the
general staff of the Bavarian army, attached to the Japanese army as an
artillery officer. After learning Japanese and Chinese, in 1913 he wrote a
book entitled *Greater Japan*. Haushofer dreamed of a vast transcontinental
bloc 'from the Rhine to the Amur and the Yangzi'. This bloc, replicating the
dimensions of the Mongol empire, would be knitted together by the
transcontinental railways, and pointed at British sea power.

Afghanistan, because it guarded the landward approaches to India from
Persia and Central Asia, was an obvious target for the continental powers

seeking to attack the British Raj and break through to the Indian Ocean. Thus, while Haushofer was serving as a major-general on the western front, his protégé Oskar von Niedermayer was making his reputation as the 'German Lawrence' in Afghanistan. Without much success, Niedermayer sought to stir up the Afghans against the Raj, thus taking a leaf out of the Russian book. As part of the Great Game, the Russians had long sought to foment Afghan nationalism.

But now Russia was prostrate at the feet of Germany. Thus German ambition knew no bounds. In the spring of 1918, after General Ludendorf launched his great offensive on the western front, rumours reached British ears that Japan might be contemplating a reversal of alliances. In a dispatch to London on 18 March 1918, the assistant British military attaché in China warned that, if Japan were not given a free hand in some part of the Far East, it might go over to the enemy. With Russia out of the war, Japan and Germany would form a formidable combination which would threaten all of Britain's possessions in Asia and Australasia.[15] For the United States, the threat by a Europe–Asia combination, which first appeared at the time of President Monroe, had again manifested itself.[16] (During President Monroe's time, the challenge had been from Russian expansionism down the American west coast, combined with the threat that France intended to intervene in Latin America. That led in to the 1823 Monroe Doctrine.)

In 1917, in order to dissuade Japan from going over to Germany, the United States believed it was necessary to offer Japan some territorial concessions. In November 1917 the Lansing–Ishii agreement went further than any previous, or subsequent, American agreement in recognizing Japan's claims to Manchuria. The United States recognized that 'territorial propinquity creates special relations between countries, and consequently, the Government of the United States recognizes that Japan has special interests in China, particularly in the part to which her possessions are contiguous'.[17] Although the United States held its nose when it signed the Lansing–Ishii agreement, it was a necessary expedient at a dangerous juncture of the war.

But during this period at least, the United States recognized that force balances matter. Partly with Japan in mind, America decided to build a navy second to none. Congress had authorized the construction of ten battleships in August 1916. In the interests of maintaining a balance of power in East Asia, the United States also sought to deny Japan a free hand in the Russian Far East when a power vacuum emerged there as a consequence of the Bolshevik revolution.

Japan's Siberian intervention

By early 1918, the Bolshevik revolution had led to the collapse of Russian power in Siberia and northern Manchuria. Japan's opportunity came when Britain and France decided to send expeditionary forces to Murmansk, the

Black Sea and the Far East. The ostensible purpose of this intervention was to rally Russian forces against Germany, and to prevent allied stores from falling into enemy hands. The real mission was to strangle Bolshevism in its cradle.

Japan said it intended to occupy Vladivostok and operate the Chinese Eastern and Amur railways. Invoking treaties it signed with China, Japan marched into northern Manchuria in July 1918. Japanese forces also occupied north Sakhalin and Vladivostok. The United States had no love for the Bolsheviks, but even less wish to see Japan in control of all the territory east of Lake Baikal.

Differences among the allied powers hindered coordination of their policies. Britain and France, locked in mortal combat with Germany, were intent on appeasing Japan, hoping to deflect its ambition away from their possessions in China. Britain also saw Japan as a bulwark against the spread of communism in China and India. So the task of containing Japan was left to America. The United States prevented Japanese control of the Chinese Eastern railway, which was entrusted to an inter-allied commission headed by an American. Britain and France then sought American approval of Japan's occupation of Siberia along the Trans-Siberian railway, as far as the Urals. The United States, unwilling to see Japan expand in any direction, proposed instead a joint US–Japanese occupation of eastern Siberia.

Worried that Japan would cut the Trans-Siberian railway, the Bolshevik Commissar for Foreign Affairs, Leon Trotsky – who had founded the Red Army – now secretly called for American intervention.[18] Even at this desperate juncture, Lenin and the other Bolshevik leaders did not lose their nerve, and saw how they might exploit America's Open Door policy for their own ends. In bidding for American support, Trotsky pointed to the risk that Japan might cut the Trans-Siberian railway in cahoots with Germany. The risk that Germany and Japan then might meet in the Urals, over the corpse of a defeated Russia, was a threat that America could not ignore.

In the end, Japan contributed 72,000 of a total allied force of less than 100,000, ostensibly designed to rescue former Czech prisoners of war. Supporters of the allied cause, the Czechs were making their way eastwards on the Trans-Siberian railway, impeded by both Germans and Bolsheviks. US forces totalled 9,000 – barely enough to keep an eye on what the Japanese were up to. In order to prevent Japanese control of the Trans-Siberian railway, America had to keep its forces in Siberia long after the armistice on the western front. They were not fully withdrawn until April 1920. Japanese troops lingered until 1922, after Moscow's control over eastern Siberia had been firmly re-established.

Moreover, the often brutal behaviour of Japanese troops in Siberia, especially when in league with the Cossacks, contrasted sharply with the standards that Japanese forces had observed during the war with Russia. In the 1905 conflict, Japan had been anxious to show that it was a modern state capable of observing the rules of civilized warfare as laid down by the Western powers. At that time, the Anglo-Saxon powers had seen their Japanese allies as 'plucky little Japs'. By 1918, however, Japan's samurai tradition was being seen in a different light. Japan's repression in Korea also contributed to its growing image of being incorrigibly militaristic. On 1 March 1919, a peaceful independence demonstration led to the killing and wounding of a large number of protestors. Thereafter a Korean government in exile was set up, first in China and later in the United States. To this day, South Korea commemorates 1 March as a national holiday.

The Versailles peace conference

At the Versailles conference after the First World War, Japan reaped the rewards of its limited commitment to the conflict. It was ranked as one of the great powers and given one of the four permanent seats on the Council of the League of Nations. Nitobe Inazo, the Japanese educator and internationalist, was named as an under-secretary of the new League.[19] At Versailles, President Wilson, leading the American delegation in person, sought to draw Japan into a cooperative great-power order based on collective security. Acceptance at the top table bolstered the position of the moderates in Japan, whose influence had grown because the Western democracies had won the war. The moderate internationalists were strongly represented in court circles, big business, the navy and the foreign ministry.

But America remained unreconciled to the Anglo–Japanese secret agreement that had allowed Japan to take Germany's mid-Pacific islands. Moreover, Britain's Pacific dominions complicated matters. They had made great sacrifices during the war, so felt entitled to a strong voice in imperial councils and at Versailles. Fearing Japanese expansionism, they insisted on keeping the former German territories south of the equator. But Wilson could not insist that Japan give up the former German territories now under its control if the British dominions were determined to hang on to theirs. With difficulty, Wilson achieved consensus on a modified mandate system that gave Japan, Australia and New Zealand extensive rights in the former German colonies without permitting formal annexation.

The Australians, represented by their prime minister Billy Hughes, a feisty Welsh-born Labour prime minister who irritated almost everyone at Versailles, were not thinking strategically. They lacked the population and resources to be able to defend their island continent against a major strategic threat. But Hughes incurred Japan's enduring resentment when he led successful resistance to its quest for international recognition of the principle of racial equality. 'White Australia' was popular at home, but why poke a finger in the eyes of the victors of Tsushima? Australia could not be certain that the Anglo–American maritime powers would forever remain strong enough to keep Japan on leash.

And as noted, by insisting on retaining Australian control over former German New Guinea, Hughes made it impossible for President Wilson to evict Japan from the mid-Pacific islands. Japan's continued possession of these islands did much to impede America's ability to project maritime power across the vast reaches of the Pacific. Not for the last time, Australia refused to see that its security depended on the balance of power in North Asia rather than on the defence of the 'arc of islands' just off its northern shores.

The British dominions, in clinging to their territorial gains, also made it harder for Wilson to defend China from Japanese encroachment. Nor did the Chinese make his task easier. Yuan Shih-kai had died in 1916, to be replaced by a weak and divided leadership. China earned its place at Versailles by a belated entry into the war in August 1917. But the Beijing government, in return for Japanese loans, had signed yet another treaty with Japan immediately before the conference convened. Yet, just after China had signed this new treaty, the Chinese delegates at Versailles believed that they could insist upon the instant abandonment of the entire edifice of unequal treaties that had been imposed on China since the Opium Wars. Thus they threatened the interests of all the major powers, especially Japan. And because Japan enjoyed the advantages of proximity, the only safe way to keep the expansionists there under control was gradually to dismantle the treaty system, by general agreement among the powers. But the Chinese, focused on their grievances against all who had preyed on China since 1840, could not be made to see where their best interests lay.

Wilson, his hands tied by the 1918 Sino–Japanese treaty, was forced to agree to Japan's special rights in Shandong. Japan said it that intended to hand back the peninsula in full sovereignty to China, but it would retain the economic privileges granted to Germany and the right to establish a settlement at Qingdao. In theory, China retained sovereignty over Shandong. In practice, Japan now had a springboard for further penetration of China. When the news of the Shandong agreement reached China, it provoked widespread riots – the 'May fourth' movement – as well as anti-Japanese boycotts. Then Wilson's Republican opponents in the American senate seized on the Shandong issue as an excuse for rejecting both the League of Nations and the Versailles Treaty. Had Wilson not been both ill and stubborn, that unhappy outcome might have been averted. For now one of the most powerful states in the international system was unwilling to play an active part in its maintenance. Hence the League was fatally weakened even before it was born.

The United States thus washed its hands of recalcitrant Europeans, who seemed mired in old habits of secret treaties, territorial aggrandizement and alliances. Even though the United States had gone to war to redress the imbalance of power in the Old World, most Americans saw 'balance of power' in itself as a cause of war. And behind renewed American isolationism lay the assumption that the United States could continue to rely on the 'free security' provided, *de facto*, by the British Navy.

Still, America showed a more consistent interest in the balance of power in East Asia than in Europe. This was despite the fact that American economic and cultural interests were far greater in Europe. Part of the reason for this paradox was that Americans remained imbued with missionary instincts about China. Moreover, possession of the Philippines gave the United States a problem of territorial security in East Asia that could not be ignored. Thus the United States had reason to seek to enshrine the Open Door into international law, and to seek to strike a balance of power in North Asia by means of the Washington naval arms control arrangements.

The 1922 Washington agreements

At the Washington conference, held between November 1921 and February 1922, the United States fulfilled its three main objectives – to 'cap' the incipient naval arms race among America, Britain and Japan; to create a multilateral framework which would guarantee China's territorial integrity and work towards the gradual elimination of the unequal treaties; and to use these international agreements as a means of restraining Japan.

The arms control component of the Washington settlement was the first and last international arms agreement that called for the scrapping of armaments already in existence or being built. In terms of the ratios of naval tonnage, the agreement froze the existing 'correlation of forces'. The United States was permitted a battle fleet of 501,000 tons; Britain 580,000 and Japan 301,000, representing a 5:5:3 ratio. Corresponding ratios were to apply to aircraft carriers, submarines, destroyers and cruisers. There was to be a ten-year holiday on building capital ships.[20]

The *status quo* in the Pacific was also retained in relation to fortifications. Britain undertook not to fortify any of its possessions east of 110 degrees east, except those adjacent to the coasts of Canada, Australia and New Zealand. The United States agreed not to fortify any islands apart from those adjacent to the coasts of the United States, Alaska, the Panama Canal zone and Hawaii. This meant that America could not build new bases in the Aleutians, Guam, Pago-Pago or the Philippines. For its part, Japan promised not to establish new fortifications in the North Pacific islands under its control. The naval ratios and the non-fortification agreements were integrally linked. This was because the naval tonnage ratios reflected a calculation of each country's naval requirements in relation to its geographical position. A rule of thumb held that, for every thousand miles a fleet steamed from its base, it lost 10 per cent of its fighting efficiency.

At America's insistence, the Anglo–Japanese alliance was replaced *de facto* by a Four Power Treaty between the United States, Britain, Japan and France, which respected their rights over their island possessions. In relation to China, a Nine Power Treaty bound the parties to respect the sovereignty, independence and territorial integrity of China. The parties undertook not to support their nationals in seeking spheres of influence or 'mutually exclusive opportunities in designated parts of Chinese territory'. Japan also agreed to restore Shandong to China 'in full sovereignty', and to withdraw from Siberia and northern Sakhalin.

How did the Washington arrangements serve the interests of the major parties? The United States benefited because it was relieved of the expense of a naval arms race with Britain. Some in the US Navy had sought such an arms race, even though there was no collision of strategic interest between Britain and America. This is a good illustration of the fact that, if left to their own devices, militaries everywhere are tempted to create 'budgetary enemies' in order to justify defence spending and force structure.

The Washington agreements also enshrined the Open Door policy in international law, and helped underpin the security of the Philippines. In addition, the agreements helped preserve for the United States the geopolitical advantages conferred by the Panama Canal. If the United States had been forced to keep up with Japan in building huge battleships, its ships would have become too big to fit through the canal. The demise of the Anglo–Japanese alliance, which Britain agreed to let lapse in 1923, also removed the threat, however remote, of a two-ocean naval war in which Japan and Britain might be allied against the United States.

Japan also derived significant strategic benefit from the Washington arrangements. Like the US Navy, the Japanese Navy was inclined to create budgetary enemies. Yet its more moderate elements knew that Japan lacked the resources to win an arms race with America. Unlike China, Japan had refused to infringe its sovereignty by relying on foreign loans. But that meant it had to tax severely its already hard-pressed peasantry. The Japanese public was already becoming restive with high taxes, and frustrated with the poor returns of the Siberian intervention. Despite the inferiority of the naval ratios allocated to Japan, the Washington agreements underpinned Japan's security because they guaranteed Japan's maritime supremacy in the northwest Pacific.

The Japanese delegation at Washington included Admiral Kato Tomosaburo, a moderate. He secured Tokyo's agreement to the naval arms limitation agreements because there were significant benefits to Japan. The moderates saw that the non-fortification agreements gave Japan far more security than it could ever achieve by a naval arms race with the United States. Because of the non-fortification agreement, the Anglo–American battle fleets, even if they should combine against Japan, would have no bases closer than Singapore and Hawaii. Both islands were more than 3,000 miles distant, considered well beyond combat range. Moreover, Guam and the Philippines were removed as possible threats to Japanese security.

Despite all these gains, the Japanese compounded their problems by rampant factionalism. Also included in the Japanese delegation was the nationalist Admiral Kato Kanji, who railed against the alleged inferiority enshrined in the 5:5:3 naval ratios. The 'treaty faction' barely carried the day at Washington against Kato Kanji's militant 'fleet faction'. When Kato Tomosaburo, who had become prime minister, died prematurely in 1923, the 'fleet faction' started to get the upper hand.

At Washington, Britain was also spared the cost of a naval arms race with the United States, the last country Britain could afford to antagonize given imperial weakness. Drained by a continental commitment in the First World War far beyond anything previous contemplated, the United Kingdom was exhausted and mired in debt. By virtue of the Washington arrangements, Britain preserved its position in East Asia when it could no longer afford to maintain a battle fleet there. Admittedly, this was at the cost of the alliance with Japan. The alliance had afforded Britain leverage in Tokyo, and boosted the position of the moderates there. But the British Empire, with Canada in the lead, opposed the continuation of the alliance. In any case, Japan had done much to set itself adrift, because it had used its alliance with Britain as a screen for ambition in China. That was bound to raise American opposition.

Yet Britain could not afford to allow its position in the Far East to depend on Japan's goodwill. For that reason, Britain had decided before the Washington conference (without announcing it) to build a naval base at Singapore. The security of the Empire in the Far East would depend on the doctrine of 'Main Fleet to Singapore' – the doctrine that if a threat arose in the Far East, the main fleet would be sent to Singapore. The Japanese, of course, knew that the base was pointed at them. But they put a good face on things, as they had done with the visit of Roosevelt's Great White Fleet in 1907.

Still, there was much resentment in Japan at the apparent inferiority of Japan's naval tonnage ratios, the decision to build the Singapore base, and the refusal of the Western powers to grant Japan's wish for a clause on racial equality in the League of Nations charter. In 1924, new tensions arose at the exclusion of Japanese immigrants from America. High tariffs also restricted Japanese access to the US market. These festering resentments undermined what had been achieved at Washington. They thus provided opportunities for Russia, which had been excluded from the Washington conference, to drive a wedge between Japan and the Anglo-Saxon powers. For the last thing Moscow wanted to see was equilibrium in East Asia.

Russia redux: the Rapallo treaty

In 1924, the establishment of the Mongolian Peoples' Republic as a *de facto* Soviet protectorate marked the return of Russia to the equations of power in the Far East. China remained mired in warlordism, and with rival govern-ments in Beijing and Canton. Foreign powers recognized the Beijing government, but in Canton Sun Zhongshan (Sun Yat-sen) was mustering powerful nationalist forces. Western governments, resenting Sun's attempts to overturn the treaty system on which their privileges rested, declined to give him aid. The Bolsheviks were quick to seize the opportunity to under-mine the position of the Western powers in China. But for them, fomenting anti-Western nationalism in the Far East was a means to a wider end. Their main focus was on weakening the Western colonial powers in order to divert their resources and attention from the main game in Europe. Not for nothing had Lenin said that 'the road to Paris lay through Peking'.

The Bolsheviks were obsessed with Germany, seeing the success of the revolution there as vital to their own survival. Moreover, the failure of the German revolution was embarrassing for Marxist theory. Marx and Engels had both been German. The revolution was supposed to occur in advanced Germany, not backward Russia. But when the German revolution failed in 1919, the Bolsheviks were forced to make up with Germany as opportunity permitted. That chance soon presented itself in the resentment of Weimar Germany at what it saw as the harsh peace imposed at Versailles. Bolshevik Russia and Weimar Germany also resented the fact that Poland had been reborn at Versailles, carved out of territory that they believed was rightly theirs.

In the best traditions of *realpolitik*, that most reactionary of monocled Prussian generals Hans von Seeckt, head of the new German army or *Reichswehr*, was soon in unlikely collusion with Karl Radek. Radek, one of Lenin's companions on the famous train journey across wartorn Europe in 1917, was now the agent for Germany of the Communist International (Comintern). In Radek's dealings with von Seeckt, Lenin took a close personal interest. Seeckt's secret link to Radek was none other than Haushofer's protégé, Oskar von Niedermayer, now a colonel. This time the former 'German Lawrence' was calling himself 'Major Neumann'.[21] In 1922, the fruit of the Seeckt–Radek conspiracy was the Rapallo treaty between the Soviet Union and Weimar Germany.

By means of Rapallo, Russia and Germany renounced all claims to war indemnities, and Germany renounced all claim to properties expropriated by the Bolsheviks. The treaty's secret provisions allowed Germany to manufac-ture tanks, aircraft and chemical weapons in the vast expanses of the Ukraine, and to train its forces there. That allowed the *Reichswehr* to bypass the clauses of the Versailles Treaty that restricted the German army. The Rapallo Treaty is an illustration of the fact that it is impossible to disarm a defeated enemy unless it is occupied – a lesson that the United States had to relearn in relation to Iraq after the 1991 Gulf War. From 1921 to 1932, Niedermayer headed the Moscow office of this secret German army in Russia, the 'Black *Reichswehr*'. Meanwhile, the Bolsheviks, while making up with Germany as opportunity had permitted, did not overlook new possibilities in the Far East for fomenting anti-Western nationalism. Radek was in the thick of this as well.

Russia redux: the Far East

The elements of continuity in Russian foreign policy after the Bolshevik revolution are striking. Gregorii Chicherin, the Commissar for Foreign Affairs who succeeded Trotsky, was a former aristocrat who had served as an archivist in the Asiatic department of the tsarist foreign ministry. There he had absorbed all the Anglophobia associated with the Great Game.

The Bolsheviks now had at their disposal propaganda tools that the tsarist state would have envied. In 1919, the Karakhan Manifesto proclaimed that the USSR would abrogate all the 'unequal' tsarist treaties with China. Five years later, the Beijing government signed a treaty with Russia that ostensibly renounced all privileges enjoyed in China by the tsarist government, including Russia's share in the Boxer indemnity and the right of extraterritoriality. Russia also recognized Chinese sovereignty over Mongolia, and signed a provisional agreement for joint management of the Chinese Eastern railway. In reality, by means of the 1924 treaty, the Bolsheviks consolidated their grip on Outer Mongolia, while retaining all the tsarist properties.[22] But the professed renunciation of the 'unequal treaties' made for potent 'agit-prop' (agitation-propaganda) at the hands of skilful publicists such as Radek.

At the same time that the Bolsheviks were negotiating with Beijing to protect Russian interests inherited from the tsars, they also fomented revolution in Canton. There, Moscow's main agent was Mikhail Gruzenberg ('Mikhail Borodin'), who helped reorganize the *Guomindang* (Kuomintang) as a Leninist party with Sun Zhongshan (Sun Yat-sen) at its head. The Chinese Communist Party (CCP), founded in 1921, was ordered to cooperate with the *Guomindang* in a united front. A key role was played by A. Joffe, who, as Russian ambassador to Berlin, had done much to foment the failed German revolution of 1919.

In 1921, the Bolsheviks set up in Moscow the University of the Toilers of the East to train communist Asian workers in revolutionary theory and practice. During the 1920s, hundreds of Chinese studied there. Sun Zhongshan University of the Toilers of China was also established in Moscow in 1925, with Karl Radek as rector. Alumni of Sun Zhongshan University included the future Chinese communist leader Deng Xiaoping.

The Bolsheviks, having harnessed the forces of rising Chinese nationalism, then pointed them at British interests in China. In May 1925 the death of a striking Chinese worker in Shanghai riots sparked the 'May Thirtieth' movement in which a dozen Chinese were killed by British police in the International Settlement. The violence had been partly incited by cadets from the Whampoa military academy, which had been established in 1924. Its commandant was Jiang Jieshi (Chiang Kai-shek), who had been trained at a military academy in Japan. In 1925, Jiang sent his son Jiang Jingguo (Chiang Chingkuo) to study at Sun Zhongshan University in Moscow as soon as it opened. Zhou Enlai (Chou En-lai), who was to become Communist China's foreign minister after the 1949 revolution, was a political commissar at Whampoa.

After the disturbances in Shanghai, riots spread to Canton. In the autumn of 1926, *Guomindang* forces led by Jiang Jieshi, now Sun Zhongshan's successor, swept northwards into central China. Soviet general Vasilii Bliukher ('Galen'), who had commanded Bolshevik forces in the Far East from 1918 to 1922, was a key advisor to the nationalist armies. The British were unable to defend their extensive commercial interests in the Yangzi valley, partly because large gunboats could not move up-river until the spring.

To the consternation of the other treaty powers, the British gave way after mobs, incited by the *Guomindang*, took over their Yangzi valley concessions. In the spring of 1927, as Jiang's armies swept into Nanjing, they took possession of foreign property and killed several foreigners. By the following year, Jiang Jieshi had taken Beijing. Then he established a centralized national government in Nanjing. Shortly afterwards, he served notice that the new China intended unilaterally to abrogate all the 'unequal treaties' imposed on China since the Opium War.

Until 1927, *Guomindang* radicalism had served Soviet interests admirably. It had weakened the British position in China, and driven a wedge between Britain and America. Establishing diplomatic relations with China in 1924 had also helped Russia break out of its international isolation. Then in 1925 the Bolsheviks sought to resume the old tsarist pattern of collusion with Japan. As ever, they did so with an eye as much on Europe as on East Asia.

The 1925 Russo–Japanese Treaty: Rapallo East

The 1925 Treaty which established diplomatic relations between Japan and Russia restored the tsarist pattern of collusion at China's expense, with the United States and the Open Door as the main target. The treaty guaranteed Russia's neutrality in case of Japan's conflict with a third power, which could mean only America. Thus the treaty was tantamount to an 'eastern Rapallo' whose main purpose was to undermine the Washington system.

The 1925 treaty contained secret provisions aimed at China, some of which appear to have renewed the understandings enshrined in the old tsarist treaties. The new treaty tacitly acknowledged Soviet control of the Chinese Eastern railway – which the Soviets had re-established by virtue of their 1924 treaty with China – in return for Japan's control over the South Manchurian railway. The treaty was thus pointed at the Open Door. In China itself, Russian officials and Comintern agitators actively worked to undermine the Washington system.[23] And, demonstrating how the Soviets never forgot the main game in Europe, secret annexes to the treaty also helped Moscow block Rumania's attempts to have the League of Nations endorse Rumania's incorporation of Bessarabia after the First World War. Before the war, the territory had belonged to the Russian empire.[24]

The balance of power in Europe: Locarno

For the Bolsheviks, the United States was now emerging as the main adversary. This was partly because British global power was in irreversible decline. It was also because America was beginning to show an interest in European stability that was most unwelcome in Moscow.

The Bolsheviks had hoped that the 1923 crisis, when France invaded the Ruhr to enforce German reparations repayments, would foster the German revolution. But it failed again. Worse, from the Soviet point of view, the United States began to promote Franco–German rapprochement. America's means of doing so was the Dawes Plan, by which American bankers would lend money to Germany so that it could meet its reparations obligations under the Versailles treaty.

In conjunction with the Dawes Plan, Britain and others sought to bring stability to western Europe by means of the Locarno Treaty system of 1925. The Locarno system sought to foster Franco–German rapprochement by guaranteeing Germany's western frontiers. Germany, increasingly reconciled with the Western powers, entered the League of Nations in 1926.

Stability in Europe was the last thing the Soviets wanted. By 1925, Stalin had become general secretary of the communist party, intent on picking up the mantle of Lenin who had died in 1923. Stalin sought to use Lenin's handiwork, the Rapallo Treaty, as a means of keeping Europe divided. That would foster the intercapitalist war out of which the German revolution would finally emerge. In Europe, Stalin's answer to the Dawes Plan and Locarno was the 1926 Treaty of Berlin, which perpetuated the Rapallo approach to Germany and sought to undermine the 'spirit of Locarno'.

Haushofer's continental bloc

Three years after the Rapallo Treaty had been signed in 1922, the dreams of Haushofer and the *geopolitikers* seemed to be coming true. There was now a global network of treaties which connected with the Soviet Union, Germany (1922 and 1926), China (1924) and Japan (1925). Moreover, these four countries were linked by their shared resentment of the Anglo-Saxon powers.

In 1924, Haushofer set up his *Zeitschrift für Geopolitik* in Munich. During the previous year he had been in contact with Adolf Hitler. Hitler, along with key supporters such as Rudolf Hess, was then in comfortable custody in the Landsberg fortress as a consequence of his part in a failed putsch in Munich. Many of Haushofer's geopolitical ideas were reflected in Hitler's book *Mein Kampf* ('My Struggle'), written at this time. But Haushofer, whose wife was half-Jewish, shared neither Hitler's racist paranoia nor his inclination to look to Britain as an ally. To the contrary, Haushofer and his supporters such as the redoubtable Niedermayer continued to advocate alignment with Russia as the means by which the continental powers could band together to carve up a British empire greatly weakened by the First World War.

But Haushofer's bloc could succeed only if the irredentist powers directed their ambitions towards the British Empire, and avoided clashing with one another. That was never likely to be easy, because irredentism was also festering within the bloc. China had lost Korea and Taiwan to Japan, as well as the vast tracts of territory east of Lake Baikal that it claimed had been lost to Russia. As a consequence of the First World War, Germany had lost to Japan its former colonies in the Pacific, as well as the Shandong peninsula. And Russia had lost south Manchuria and south Sakhalin to Japan as a consequence of the 1904–1905 war.

Then the fostering of Chinese nationalism by the Bolsheviks misfired, with immense strategic consequences. In fomenting Chinese nationalism, the Bolsheviks had sought to undermine the Washington system. But in doing so they released pent-up forces which they were unable to contain. The rise of Chinese nationalism soon undermined the moderates in Japan, unleashing militarist forces there that threatened Russian and American interests alike. Once again, a major realignment was occurring in the East Asian quadrilateral.

The 1929 Sino–Russian war in Manchuria

Five years after the signing of the 1924 Sino–Russian treaty, the two countries were at war. In 1927, Jiang Jieshi turned on the left wing of the *Guomindang*, killing many communists and expelling his Soviet advisers. He then sought to overturn all the 'unequal treaties' that had been imposed on China. The Anglo-Saxon powers and Japan agreed, but Moscow proved resistant. So in 1929 forces of the *Guomindang* and its Manchurian allies took over sections of the Chinese Eastern railway. Widespread fighting then occurred with the troops of General Bliukher's newly created Special Far Eastern Red Army. Because Russia and China had just signed the 1928 Kellogg–Briand Pact, which was supposed to outlaw war, US Secretary of State Kellogg attempted to mediate. But he met no success.

For its part, Japan remained neutral in the Sino–Russian conflict, despite China's efforts to point Japan at Russia. Japan had reason for ambivalence. Jiang Jieshi's assertion of his railway rights, and his unilateral abrogation of previous agreements, threatened Japan's interests as much as they did Russia's. Yet Japan could not relish the sight of the Soviet military power on display in Manchuria. In the face of superior Soviet forces, the *Guomindang* and its Manchurian allies had to back down. For all Jiang's bravado, his forces collapsed at the first sign of serious military pressure. Moreover, by inviting Japan to throw out the Russians, he set a dangerous precedent. Once the Japanese had moved into northern Manchuria, would the 'international community' be able to persuade them to withdraw?

Unlike Jiang, Stalin had shown a deft touch, waiting until Chinese provocations had become obvious to all who had an interest in the maintenance of the treaty arrangements in China. But Stalin always gave close attention to force balances, and was aware of the risks of overextension. So he stopped short of a full-scale invasion of Manchuria and withdrew promptly – as tsarist Russia had failed to do during the Boxer Rebellion. Thus Stalin sought to avoid a collision with Japan.

But he had not counted on Japan's *Guandong* army in Manchuria.[25] In Japan, dangerous forces were being unleashed which soon spiralled out of control. Japan in the 1920s had accepted the constraints of the Washington system because moderate leaders could see the advantages to Japan's economic and security interests, in China and elsewhere. This was also the era of 'Taisho democracy' in Japan under the Taisho emperor. But when China unilaterally sought to abrogate the 'unequal' treaties that underpinned the entire Japanese position in China, Japan received little support from the Western powers.[26] This undermined the moderates in Japan, who in any case had little sympathy for Chinese nationalism. China, torn by warlordism, seemed far from a modern state. And the Japanese were acutely aware of how much the Comintern had been stirring up Chinese nationalism.

Moreover, an agreement that Jiang Jieshi signed with Russia in June 1931 directly threatened Japan's economic interests in Manchuria.[27] Japan had invested greatly in heavy industry there, and depended on its resources, including soy beans. The South Manchurian railway also returned healthy profits. For Japan, Manchuria was now considered a vital interest. Jiang Jieshi did not seem to appreciate the dangers of provoking Japan when none of the Western powers was able or willing to keep the militarists there on a leash. Once again, out of characteristic hubris and miscalculation, China was partly the architect of its own misfortune.

Japan starts to go off the rails

In Japan the economy had turned sour, with large bank crashes in 1927, some of them due to the boycotts of Japanese goods in China. Agricultural distress, even before the onset of the Great Depression, helped to radicalize the armed forces, whose recruits were mostly from rural backgrounds. Many were seeing their parents go hungry and their sisters sold into brothels. In turn, rural distress led to growing insubordination in the army, and the peculiarly Japanese phenomenon of *gekokujo* – the domination by juniors of their seniors. Then the collapse in world trade brought about by the Depression made things much worse.

Japan was also afflicted by its appalling decision-making processes. When the country had faced a palpable threat from the sea in the mid-nineteenth century, the Satsumas and Choshus had been able to sink their differences for long enough to overthrow the Shogunate, reform Japan and meet the Russian threat in Manchuria. But it was downhill all the way after that. Japan's fundamental problem was factionalism. The Choshus, who dominated the army, couldn't make up their minds whether they wanted to fight Russia again, or continue to collude with Russia at China's expense. But colluding with Russia was likely to put Japan on a collision course with the rising power of the United States, a country with far greater resources than Japan. The navy, dominated by the Satsumas, was also divided. Some wanted to fight America, but others thought it was madness to risk war with a much more powerful country. And how could Japan hope to bring a war home to the United States? Moreover, the army and the navy reported separately to the emperor, who had no real power anyway. So there was no-one at the top capable of ordering strategic priorities. That left the field open for those who were organized and determined enough to get their way. Like China, Japan was largely the creator of its own troubles.

In June 1928, elements of Japan's *Guandong* army in Manchuria, which was pretty much a law unto itself, assassinated the Manchurian warlord Zhang Zuolin (Chang Tso-lin). Manchuria then became the theatre for the *Guandong* army's brand of *gekokujo*. In killing the 'Old Marshal', the *Guandong* army radicals blundered. Although he had not always been Japan's pliant instrument, he was far more tractable than his son, Zhang Xueliang (Chang Hsueh-liang) proved to be. The 'Young Marshal' continued his father's policies of encouraging the building of railways and ports which would compete with the Japanese-owned South Manchurian railway. Moreover, he lost little time in throwing in his lot with the *Guomindang*. In October 1928, Zhang Xueliang raised its flag in Mukden, thus reuniting Manchuria with the rest of China. And he soon joined the *Guomindang* in the 1929 war against Russia. With both the *Guomindang* and Russia now contesting Japan's grip on Manchuria, further trouble was not far away. Moreover, in the war with Russia, China had shown dangerous weakness when it proved unable to defend its interests in the Chinese Eastern railway.

Japan grabs all of Manchuria

Trouble soon came, in the form of the 'Mukden Incident' of 18 September 1931 in which dissident Japanese forces dynamited a section of track of the South Manchurian railway. Blaming the Chinese, they then threw Chinese troops out of their barracks in Mukden. The government in Tokyo did not approve, but the *Guandong* army had now slipped its leash. Widespread fighting followed the Mukden Incident, which led to a Japanese takeover of all of Manchuria. It was then renamed 'Manchukuo' ('Manchu Land'). The last Manchu emperor, Pu Yi, who had abdicated in 1911, was installed as Manchukuo's puppet ruler. The United States refused to recognize Japan's incorporation of Manchuria, which was a clear violation of the Open Door.

Thus there was a new collision of interest between Japan and America.

In 1932, the League of Nations sent the Lytton Commission to Japan, China and Manchuria to investigate the 'Mukden Incident'. Its verdict, while damaging to Japan's case, was not hostile to Japan. The report also pointed out that Chinese miscalculation had exacerbated the crisis. Lord Lytton noted that it was not possible for any nation to cultivate hatred and hostility towards other countries and then expect the League of Nations to step in and save it from the consequences of its actions.[28] Once more, the Chinese were architects of their own misfortune. But so were the Japanese. Japan did much to isolate itself when it left the League in March 1933, the walkout being led by the American-educated Matsuoka Yosuke, a prominent member of the Choshu Manchurian clique. With both China and Japan displaying so little skill, they were putty in the hands of a ruthless Machiavellian like Stalin.

Stalin plays divide and rule, as recommended by Lenin

Unlike the Chinese and Japanese, who both put 'face' above interest, Stalin understood the utility of effecting a strategic retrenchment if necessary. He was caught by surprise by the Japanese occupation of all of Manchuria, and unable to do much about it at the time. Because Russia was militarily weak in the Far East, it could not defend its interests in the Chinese Eastern railway against determined Japanese pressure. So Stalin sold the CER to *Manchukuo* in 1935, brushing aside Chinese protests. The sale of the railway having removed an ulcer in his relations with Japan, Stalin then held out to the Japanese the prospect of further collusion pointed at the United States and China. He offered Japan a non-aggression pact, to build on the 1925 Russo–Japanese treaty. But the Japanese were already in the driver's seat and saw no reason to parley with Stalin.

So Stalin worked to gain leverage over Japan by normalizing Moscow's relations with both China and the United States. First he patched up relations with China, ruptured during the 1929 war. Then he sought an opening to the United States, hitherto excoriated by the Bolsheviks as the home of all capitalist evils. Late in 1932, Stalin sent Maxim Litvinov, now Soviet foreign minister, to Washington where the New Deal administration of Franklin Roosevelt was about to assume office. Litvinov was an excellent choice. A fluent English speaker, a Jew married to an Englishwoman, he could ooze charm. So, of course, could Roosevelt.

But Cordell Hull, the dour US Secretary of State, was not easily charmed. Soviet propaganda had long claimed that America had intervened in Siberia in 1918 in order to wrest territory from Russia. This was a deliberate lie, since Trotsky had pleaded, in secret, for American intervention. Thus Hull insisted that Litvinov sign a document setting the record straight. Litvinov thereby acknowledged that US forces had entered Siberia in order to prevent Japanese hegemony there, and he waived claims arising from the Siberian expedition.[29]

The United States also insisted that Moscow promise not to engage in subversive activities in the United States, albeit without much expectation that the promise would be kept. Diplomatic relations were then established. As his first ambassador to Moscow, Roosevelt sent his friend William Bullitt, who was known to be sympathetic to Soviet interests.

Now Stalin could hint to the Japanese that they had better restrain themselves because he had a powerful new friend. Moreover, the development of air power was altering the force balances in the Far East. Japan's wood and paper cities were already within range of heavy bombers based in Vladivostok, just across the Japan Sea. Moreover, the United States might develop bases on the Aleutian island chain, and thus also bring Japan within range of land-based air power. And what if the Soviets were to offer their new friend access to bases in Siberia?

Having played the American card against Japan, why should not Stalin then play the Japan card against America? Why not embroil the two most powerful members of the East Asian quadrilateral in a war of attrition? That might not prove too difficult. It was hardly a secret, for example, that the Japanese Navy had been wargaming conflict with the United States since 1907. Moreover, there was plenty of visceral dislike on both sides, stirred up by racism and immigration issues.

Neither was it a secret that Japanese expansionists were eyeing the resources of Southeast Asia. Japan's build-up of long-range maritime capabilities suggested ambitions much wider than Manchuria. In Southeast Asia, the empires of the European powers lived on, but weakened beyond recall by the First World War. True, the United States evinced a genuine distaste for British colonialism, and had no obligation to defend the empire of Britain or anyone else. But any Japanese advance into Southeast Asia would almost certainly embroil the United States in war with Japan because of American obligations to the defence of the Philippines.[30] It was hardly likely that any Japanese commander would accept the risk of leaving the Philippines behind his line of advance, especially as the development of air power threatened to bring Taiwan and southern Japan within range of US air power based in the Philippines. If Stalin could encourage Japan and America into war, the benefits to Russia would be enormous – once the protagonists had exhausted themselves in a fight to the death, made more vicious by racial antagonism on both sides, Russia could hope to pick up the spoils.

Few senior Americans had sufficient grounding in *realpolitik* to comprehend Stalin's designs. In the State Department as elsewhere, most senior officials were inclined to blame Japan for all of East Asia's problems. That was not surprising, given Japan's appalling behaviour in China, including the bombing of undefended cities. Few in New Deal America were prepared to credit Japan's claims that all of its troubles in Manchuria were due to the machinations of the Comintern. Still, there were some senior Americans who, without wishing to make apology for Japan, saw the hidden hand of

Stalin in helping to manipulate these events. The 'old China hand', John MacMurray, noted in a long memorandum of 1935 that, if the United States was to defeat Japan in a war, no balance of power would result in East Asia. Rather, the USSR would be the beneficiary. He also noted that Russia was as least as dangerous and unscrupulous as Japan.[31]

In July 1935, ambassador William Bullitt, quickly disillusioned with the Soviets, as were most who found themselves posted to Moscow, warned Roosevelt that 'it is the heartiest hope of the Soviet Government that the United States will become involved in war with Japan'.[32] Bullitt predicted that Stalin would seek to stay out of such a war until Japan had been defeated. Then he would take the opportunity to seize Manchuria, and Sovietize all of China. It was an accurate enough prediction of Stalin's intentions, even though in the end the wily Soviet dictator's reach was to exceed his grasp.

3 The road to war 1935–1941

The Second World War was Round Two of the great strategic contests between Germany and Russia for control of Eurasia. This time the struggle had a truly global dimension, with its East Asian component being much more significant than during the First World War. Moreover, the scale of conflict in the western Pacific dwarfed even that of war in the vast spaces of Russia.

War between the United States and Japan was a highly unusual conflict between two maritime powers, the first such clash since the Anglo–Dutch wars of the seventeenth century. Moreover, the war in the Pacific was a strategic consequence of war in Europe. The United States stood in Japan's path when Japan sought domination of China, but saw no interest there that justified the risk of war with Japan. But then Hitler, having been given a free hand by Stalin, overran Western Europe in the summer of 1940. Thus he created glittering prizes for Japan by uncovering the defences of the Southeast Asian colonies of the European powers. That raised the risk that Japan might take Singapore, and thus control the vital node between the Indian Ocean and the China Seas. Although the United States had seen no vital interest at stake in China, it began to see one in the defence of the Gibraltar of the East and all that went with it.

The rise of Hitler

One of the reasons that Hitler overran Western Europe so easily was that Stalin gave him a free hand. Hitler was always the ally that Stalin most wanted.[1] In January 1933, Stalin welcomed Hitler's coming to power, seeing him as a fellow revolutionary who hated the Versailles treaty as much he did. In fact, Stalin had done much to help Hitler, by forbidding the German communists to combine with the socialists in order to oppose the Nazis. Stalin's calculus was that Hitler would provoke a war with the Western powers. Then the resulting chaos would foster the revolution in Germany that Moscow still hoped for. Even after Hitler came to power, Stalin sought to preserve the special relationship with Germany. He turned a blind eye to Hitler's destruction of the German communist party, the largest in the

Comintern. In June 1934, Hitler's murder of now-embarrassing former supporters and possible opponents (the 'Night of the Long Knives') impressed Stalin. It may have been the model for his own even bloodier purges, which began in the summer of 1936.

But by 1934 Stalin must have realized he had miscalculated. Hitler indeed hated the Versailles treaty and the Western powers. But he loathed Slav 'subhumans' even more. Nor had Hitler made any secret of his ambition to carve out living-space (*lebensraum*) at Russia's expense. Alfred Rosenberg, a Russian-hating Balt, was Hitler's chief propagandist, spewing out anti-Slav and anti-Jewish propaganda. That was much to the distress of the *geopolitiker* General Professor Karl Haushofer. Haushofer was all for *lebensraum*. But he wanted Hitler to pursue it in the British Empire, not in Russia.

Hitler's January 1934 non-aggression pact with Poland was especially menacing for Russia. Hitherto, Germany and Russia had kept in close touch on their dealings with the hated Poland that had been reborn at Versailles. Now an irredentist Germany allied with Poland and Rumania represented a menace to the breadbasket of the Ukraine.

The global dimension of Stalin's miscalculations became manifest when Japan joined Germany in the Anti-Comintern Pact of November 1936. The pact was mostly the work of the former champagne salesman, Joachim von Ribbentrop – who competed with Rosenberg for the ear of the Führer – and the Japanese military attaché in Berlin, General Oshima Hiroshi. Even though Poland did not join the Anti-Comintern Pact, by 1936 Germany, Poland, Rumania and Japan had been brought into strategic alignment. That presented the Soviet Union with the palpable threat of two-front war.

'United fronts' and 'collective security' in Europe…

Stalin's response was a shift in the Comintern line towards united fronts, and a change in Soviet diplomatic posture towards 'collective security' and alignment with the Western powers. Now communists everywhere were ordered to cooperate with socialists and others in order to resist the Nazis. The new Soviet diplomatic doctrine of 'collective security' was unfurled by the Soviet foreign minister, Maxim Litvinov. It was symbolized by Russia's joining the League of Nations in 1934, and the signing of mutual security pacts with France and Czechoslovakia in 1935.

Litvinov, as a Jew, had reason to hate and fear Hitler. But it is doubtful that he genuinely believed in the 'spirit of Geneva', as Western governments and publics did. Like all of Stalin's terrified minions, Litvinov slavishly followed the twists and turns of the dictator's policies. Indeed, so adept was he that Litvinov was one of the few Old Bolsheviks who managed to die in his bed. For Stalin, collective security was just another instrument of *realpolitik*, as recommended by Lenin. It was a tool to foster a new division of Europe – this time between Germany and Poland on one side, and France and Britain on the other.

There were few limits to Stalin's cynicism. It was important for his design that France and Britain be able to put up a good fight once war with Germany started. That was because only a war of attrition would create the conditions from which the European revolution could be fostered. So Stalin encouraged the British and French to rearm against Hitler, and ordered the powerful French communist party to support a military build-up.[2] Stalin's motives were understood well enough in diplomatic circles in Moscow. In his dispatch to Roosevelt on 19 July 1935, William Bullitt noted that 'to keep the flames of Franco–German hatred burning brightly is regarded as a vital interest of the Soviet Union'.[3]

But Stalin, seeking as ever to keep his options open, did not shut the door on rapprochement with Germany, even after the 'Black *Reichswehr*' left its secret bases in the Ukraine. (Niedermayer, Haushofer's protégé, left in 1932.) Litvinov's modest status indicated that Stalin did not wish to close off the option of rapprochement with Hitler. The Soviet foreign minister was not even a candidate member of the Politburo, and so could be dumped at any time. For his part, Hitler was also keeping the door ajar. When the Anti-Comintern Pact was formed, the German government told Japan that it did not regard the provisions of the treaty of Rapallo as being contrary to the new pact.[4] That was a signal to Stalin that Hitler might reciprocate his interest in a deal, should circumstances warrant.

…and in East Asia

In East Asia, Stalin needed to keep the *Guandong* army off his back. Having effected a rapprochement with China in 1932, he now sought to promote a new united front there, consistent with the shift in the Comintern line. In 1934, with Stalin's encouragement, the Chinese communists left their base in Kiangsi and began their 6,000 mile Long March to Yenan in the far north-west. There they would be close to the Soviet Union, and subject to greater influence from Moscow. The next step in Stalin's design was to persuade Jiang Jieshi (Chiang Kai-shek) to agree to a new united front. That came about as a consequence of the Xian (Sian) Incident of December 1936, in which Jiang Jieshi was captured – or permitted himself to be captured – by the Manchurian warlord Zhang Xueliang, son of the 'Old Marshal' who had been assassinated by elements of the *Guandong* army in 1928.

Jiang Jieshi was released only after he agreed to a united front with the communists against Japan. It is still unclear what role Stalin played in these murky events, where Zhou Enlai (Chou En-lai) was the key player on the communist side. But the timing, only a month after the Anti-Comintern Pact had presented Moscow with a threat of two-front war, strongly suggests that Stalin had a hand in it. Indeed, Jiang Jieshi's only son Jiang Jingguo (Chiang Ching-kuo) was probably kept in Russia as a hostage until his father agreed to the united front.[5]

Stalin also sought to use 'collective security' as an instrument of *realpolitik* in Asia, as in Europe. He may have been encouraged by the Australian government, which was promoting the idea of a Pacific pact to oppose Japanese aggression.[6] In June 1937, the Soviet ambassador to China suggested that China propose a convention to draw up a collective security treaty in the Pacific Ocean area.[7] Should such a pact prove impossible, he said, Russia would provide China with a strongly worded mutual security pact, a draft of which was duly supplied.

Stalin encourages Japan into the China war

This offer was obviously made to encourage China to resist Japanese probes into north China, thus provoking the *Guandong* army into widening the China war.[8] On 7 July 1937 an incident took place on the 'Marco Polo' bridge, near Beijing. While it is still unclear exactly what happened, Japanese troops were soon pouring into north China. But when Chiang asked the Soviets to make good on their offer of a mutual security pact, they said it was too late. All that was on offer now was a non-aggression pact, which was duly signed in August.[9] Stalin, having encouraged China to resist Japan, and thus provoke the wider war that he so ardently sought, had no intention of becoming embroiled himself.

By the end of 1937, Japan had sent sixteen of its then twenty-four divisions to China. But it soon sank into a swamp of its own making by overrunning a militarily weak China. Japanese forces drove the capital back to Chongqing (Chungking), far up the Yangzi gorges, but they found China too big to conquer. And the more Japan became mired in China, the more it served Stalin's interests. The hubris of the *Guandong* army was as valuable to Stalin as his intelligence assets, which included the Sorge spy ring in Tokyo.[10]

Protecting Stalin's back against Japan

Encouraging Japan into the China war had served Stalin's interests, but he needed to do more to deter Japan from invading the Soviet Far East. Nor could he ignore the threat of two-front war latent in the Anti-Comintern pact. And while Stalin kept open the possibility of rapprochement with Germany, he by no means trusted Hitler. So Stalin relocated much Soviet industry east of the Urals, beyond Hitler's reach – but not so far east that it might come within Japan's grasp. The Soviets had not forgotten the 1918–1922 period, when Japan had occupied the entire Soviet Far East, including Vladivostok. Moreover, Stalin must have been worried that the militarists in Japan might soon get the upper hand. In Tokyo, abortive coups took place in May 1932 (which saw the assassination of prime minister Inukai Tsuyoshi) and in February 1936.

Stalin also tightened his grip on Outer Mongolia by means of a mutual security treaty in 1936. And in order to meet the threat of two-front war, he set up separate unified military commands at both ends of Eurasia, capable of fighting by themselves if Japan cut the Trans-Siberian railway. Russia did not have the option available to Germany in the First World War of rapidly switching forces, via its efficient railways, from one front to another. But its vast spaces were the greatest strategic asset of the Soviet Union.

In order to deter Japan, which enjoyed the advantage of proximity, the Soviets fortified the Amur and Ussuri river valleys along the entire 2,500 mile frontier. Double-tracking of the Trans-Siberian Railway was also begun. By 1937 it had reached Khabarovsk, only four hundred miles from Vladivostok. Vladivostok itself was protected by twenty-one-inch guns – much larger than the British naval guns at Singapore.[11] Heavy bombers were also stationed there. Because the Japanese were operating on shorter, interior lines of communications, the defensively-deployed Soviet forces ground calculated that they needed a three-to-one ratio in order to deter attack.

As a consequence of Stalin's force build-up, the Red Army more than held its own against the probes of the *Guandong* army. The Japanese had been encouraged by the beginnings of the Red Army purges in 1937 to think that Stalin had disastrously weakened Soviet forces. In mid-1938, however, the Red Banner Army rebuffed Japanese probes at Changkufeng in the Manchuria–Korea–China border region, near the coast just south of Vladivostok. Japan's armies had enjoyed easy victories over mostly ill-equipped and poorly trained Chinese troops. They had raped and murdered civilians in huge numbers, including the notorious massacre in Nanjing in late 1937. But the Japanese met their match in the Red Banner Army.

These clashes did not attract much attention in Europe, partly because Europe was now engulfed in the Czech crisis. The crisis was provoked when Hitler sought to detach from Czechoslovakia the German-speaking areas of the Sudetenland. Because the Czech fortifications were within the borders of the Sudetenland, that meant that the Czech state would in effect be disarmed.

Munich and Soviet myth-making

Soviet propaganda claimed that Stalin made his 1939 pact with Hitler purely for defensive reasons. The story went as follows. By capitulating to Hitler at the Munich conference, Britain and France made it impossible for Russia to help the Czechs. The Western allies were also half-hearted in their post-Munich overtures to Moscow. That was because they were seeking to embroil Russia in war with Germany. In desperation, Stalin turned to Hitler. Or so the story went. Of course, after Hitler attacked Russia in 1941, Soviet propaganda had every reason to expunge all memory of Stalin's alliance with the Fuehrer. (In 1948, as the Cold War began, the United States published many relevant documents, to Moscow's fury.[12])

The Soviet Union was certainly excluded from the Munich conference. That was because it was widely distrusted. Nor is there is any evidence of genuine Soviet interest in aiding the Czechs. During the crisis, Count Friedrich von der Schulenburg, Germany's ambassador to Russia, noted that 'whereas the Soviet Union is attempting to force France and Great Britain to take the initiative against Germany, she herself will hold back'.[13] No doubt Jiang Jieshi, contemplating these events from his mountain bastion up the Yangzi gorges, would have recognized the pattern.

By early 1939, the Western democracies were truly between a rock and a hard place, caught between ruthless dictators in Germany and Russia. Britain and France were not seeking to embroil Russia in war with Germany, as the Soviets alleged, not least because their governments were incapable of *realpolitik*.[14] But the Western democracies had every reason to be wary of Stalin. So did the smaller states trapped between Germany and Russia. In the Czech crisis, Poland and Rumania were loath to let the Red Army cross their territories because they feared Moscow would foment coups and install communist governments. In early 1939, Stalin demanded that, in return for joining an alliance against Hitler, he be given a free hand in Eastern Europe. Britain and France knew that, if they agreed to this, they would be endorsing a Soviet takeover of all the buffer states between Germany and Russia.

Facing invidious choices, the Western powers dithered. But in March, Hitler's march into the rump of Czechoslovakia engendered a sea change in British politics. The Fuehrer had previously insisted that he wanted only the re-incorporation of all Germans into the *Reich*. 'I want no Czechs,' he had repeatedly said. Now he was exposed as a liar. Thus, in April, Britain gave an unconditional security guarantee to Poland (and Rumania), and France followed suit.

'Poland must disappear': the Nazi–Soviet pact

The Anglo–French guarantee to Poland caused as much anger in Moscow as it did in Berlin. Now Stalin saw the chance to reconquer those parts of the tsarist empire that Lenin had been forced to give up. As Hitler planned his attack on the Poles, he needed to protect his back by means of rapprochement with Russia. Stalin was quick to send Hitler a sign that a deal was possible. In May, Vyacheslav Molotov replaced Litvinov as Soviet commissar for foreign affairs. Molotov was also in effect prime minister, a much higher status than Litvinov had enjoyed. Hitler did not miss his cue.[15] On 20 August he took the risk of sending a personal letter to Stalin, requesting that he receive Ribbentrop in Moscow almost immediately.

Now Stalin had the upper hand. He knew Hitler was in a hurry, wanting to defeat Poland before the autumn rains. Stalin was also toying with a British and French military mission in Moscow, and that gave him more leverage on Hitler. But Stalin had unfinished business in the Far East, where he was at war with Hitler's supposed ally, Japan.

Division-level fighting had begun at Nomonhan on the Manchurian–Mongolian frontier in May 1939, as a consequence of further probing by the *Guandong* army. Thus Stalin did not agree to receive Ribbentrop in Moscow until he was sure that General Zhukov's offensive at Nomonhan, launched on 20 August, would succeed. Having protected his back in the Far East, Stalin was now free to effect his risky rapprochement with Hitler. So he agreed to receive Ribbentrop on the 23rd. When Ribbentrop arrived, Stalin boasted that Zhukov had just killed 20,000 Japanese at Nomonhan. Of course, Ribbentrop did not care much, even though Japan was supposed to be Germany's ally. In this *realpolitik* world of the great dictators, able to turn on a penny, Japan was outclassed.

The jackals' pact: the partition of Poland

Stalin, exploiting Hitler's urgent need for a deal, exacted maximum concessions. A secret protocol divided Poland into German and Russian 'spheres of interest'. Bessarabia and Finland were declared to be within the Soviet sphere of interest. The Baltic states were trickier, because Hitler wanted Lithuania and most of Latvia, while Stalin craved Latvia's ice-free ports. But Hitler, after a glance at a map, gave Stalin the Latvian ports.

Once the pact was signed, the Soviet propaganda mill reversed overnight. Now the 'fascist hyenas' became 'the German authorities'. Popular fronts were no longer encouraged, except in China where the united front still served Stalin's interests. The new propaganda line of the Comintern was that Russia had turned to Germany only after hopes of alliance with Britain and France had been dashed. The truth can be read in a cable from the Soviet foreign ministry of 1 July 1940, intercepted by the Japanese, which said that 'the conclusion of our agreement with Germany was dictated by the *need* for a war in Europe' (emphasis added).[16]

For those who cared to look, the new Comintern line also revealed much about Stalin's ambition to embroil Japan in a war with the United States. The New York *Daily Worker*, mouthpiece of the American communist party, said that the Nazi–Soviet pact gave 'greater opportunities for the people and government of the United States effectively to check Japanese aggression in the Far East'.[17] One wonders what the readers of the *Daily Worker* might have made of this cryptic comment. Presumably it meant that American communists were being enjoined to drop their campaign against Nazi Germany, and focus on Japan. Indeed, Japan's atrocities in the China war gave the Comintern much ammunition. Few in America knew or cared about the purges and mass executions in Soviet-controlled Mongolia.

Now, with Stalin's problem with Japan resolved, Stalin and Hitler needed to head off any last minute mediation in the Polish crisis by the Western democracies. So Molotov cynically encouraged the Poles to fight.[18] He offered to supply them with war materiel, and the Soviet press urged resistance to German demands. On 1 September, Hitler invaded Poland, triggering British and French declarations of war.

Yet Stalin moved slowly to claim his share of the loot in Poland, despite Hitler's urging. It was not until Stalin had settled on a peace deal with the Japanese at Nomonhan on 15 September that the Red Army moved into eastern Poland on the 17th. As ever, Stalin kept a careful eye on both ends of Eurasia. On 27 September 1939, Ribbentrop returned to Moscow for the further division of the spoils. In return for a slice of Poland previously awarded to Russia, Hitler agreed to hand over Lithuania. That represented a further advance in Stalin's drive to control the exits to the Baltic.

Japan: nasty surprises

All this came as a shock to the Japanese. Hitler had kept them in the dark about his negotiations with Stalin. Ambassador Oshima had not been told until late on 21 August, the very eve of Ribbentrop's departure for Moscow. Soon after the pact was announced, the government of Baron Hiranuma fell, humiliated by Hitler's betrayal. Salt was rubbed in because Stalin had been thrashing the *Guandong* army at Nomonhan at the time the pact was being signed. These reversals of fortune for Oshima and the ultranationalists might have boosted the moderate and court factions had not the European balance abruptly shifted again, as a consequence of Hitler's *blitzkrieg* in the west. For Japan, that created alluring prizes in the Far East. So the moderates found themselves again on the back foot.

Given a free hand by Stalin, the German attack in May 1940 proceeded through neutral Holland to Belgium and France without drawing breath. Hitler also seized Norway. He conquered France with 136 divisions, leaving only seven in the east – showing yet again how valuable Stalin's neutrality was to Hitler. And Stalin was much more than an interested bystander. Under his orders, the French communist party did much to undermine resistance to Germany. In the far north, Stalin helped Hitler by giving him access for a U-boat base near Murmansk. That was especially valuable in enabling Hitler to evade the British blockade, before he was able to gain control of the French and Norwegian coastlines. The Soviet Union scrupulously honoured huge supply commitments from its own production that enabled Germany to circumvent the blockade that had crippled it in the First World War. Moreover, the Soviet intercontinental railway system allowed Germany to import rubber and other vital raw materials from East Asia, via Vladivostok. Now Haushofer seemed on the verge of achieving his Continental Bloc which could circumvent and eventually defeat the maritime powers.

But Hitler's victories were too rapid and overwhelming for Stalin's liking, especially because they contrasted so sharply with the abysmal performance of the Red Army in the 'winter war' against tiny Finland. A further problem for Stalin was that Hitler's *blitzkrieg* created the threat of a new rapprochement between Germany and Japan. This was because Hitler had rendered vulnerable the resource-rich colonies of the European powers in Southeast Asia. An unfinished base without a fleet, the supposed British bastion of Singapore was now not a deterrent, but a tempting target. The Royal Navy was hard pressed in the Atlantic and the Mediterranean, not least because Hitler soon controlled the Atlantic coastlines of Norway and France. Germany had never achieved that in the four years of war after 1914. Now there was no prospect of 'Main Fleet to Singapore', as had been envisaged when the British decided in 1923 to build the base in Singapore after the United States had insisted on the abrogation of the Anglo–Japanese alliance.

Hitler had indeed created temptations for Japan in the 'southern resources area'. In Tokyo, the militants now wanted an alliance with Germany in order to convince the United States that it should not stand in Japan's way. The German–Japanese alignment, which Stalin had demolished in August 1939 by means of his pact with Hitler, was now being rebuilt. And that undermined the moderate prime minister, Admiral Yonai Mitsumasa, a disciple of Kato Tomasaburo, who (as we have seen) had led the Japanese delegation at the 1922 Washington conference.

The Tripartite Pact of September 1940

A new alignment with Germany was high on the agenda of the new government which came to power in Tokyo on 16 July 1940, just after the fall of France, when Prince Konoe Fumimara became prime minister for the second time. His foreign minister was Matsuoka Yosuke, the former president of the South Manchurian railway who had led Japan's walkout from the League in 1933. Matsuoka, apparently having been subjected to racial discrimination during his education in the United States, was viscerally anti-American. The new war minister was General Tojo Hideki, another member of the 'Manchurian clique' – and, like Matsuoka, a member of the Choshu clan which had been pro-German since the Meiji Restoration.

Matsuoka's grand strategy was much encouraged by Ribbentrop. Both were influenced by Haushofer, whose son had worked for Ribbentrop for a time. Matsuoka's goal was to reach a military alliance with Germany as a first step. Then he would use that alliance as leverage on Russia, persuading Stalin to join in a four-power entente composed of Germany, Russia, Italy and Japan. This grand alliance, Matsuoka hoped, would so intimidate the United States that it would be deterred from entering the European war. Once Germany had dealt Britain a fatal blow, Japan could safely seize Singapore, the key to the 'southern resource area'. Thus Japan would avoid entanglement in the European war, while being able to dominate East Asia at low cost. As part of its 'southern strategy', the Japanese Navy had already seized Hainan island in February 1939, and in the following month it occupied the Spratly Islands in the South China Sea.

Lest their ambitions collide, the members of the enlarged jackals' club envisaged by Matsuoka were supposed to direct their *lebensraum* aspirations southwards, towards the spoils of the British empire. But Matsuoka did not know that Hitler had never fully endorsed Ribbentrop's grand strategy. In the summer of 1940, Hitler still hoped to bludgeon Britain into a separate peace. As part of this strategy, he wanted to hold out the prospect to the British that they would be allowed to keep their empire. So Japan's territorial ambitions in Southeast Asia had to be kept on hold, at least for now. Besides, Hitler recalled that the Japanese had helped themselves to Germany's Far Eastern colonies during the First World War. He also despised them for racist reasons. As tsar Nicholas II had done, Hitler referred to the Japanese as 'monkeys'. Neither was he impressed by their constant vacillation, or by their military performance against the Red Army at Nomonhan.

Hitler's strategy in relation to Britain misfired because Winston Churchill, now Britain's prime minister, remained defiant.[19] During the Battle of Britain in the summer of 1940, Hitler failed to establish air supremacy over the British Isles. Thus the English Channel performed its historic role of protecting Britain from the latest Continental tyrant. On 17 September Hitler called off his invasion plans. Seeing that hope of American help was fuelling British resistance, Hitler then changed tack. He now became more amenable to Ribbentrop's advocacy of alliance with Japan as a way of bringing pressure on the United States, in order to deter it from intervening in Europe.

Thus, on 27 September 1940, the Tripartite Alliance was signed in Berlin, bringing Japan into strategic alignment with Germany and Italy. That was an outcome that the moderates in Japan had long sought to prevent. Rumania and Hungary soon joined the alliance. Japan, in joining the Axis, sought to convince the United States that it must now give Japan a free hand in East Asia, because Japan now had a powerful ally. Japan was already moving into French Indochina, with two objectives. One was to cut off Jiang Jieshi's remaining supply lines via Haiphong. The second was to position Japan for a strike on Singapore via its back door in Malaya. Now, except for the Philippines, where the US military presence was exceedingly weak, Japan had virtually enclosed the South China Sea. All of East Asia's marginal seas were now controlled by Japan, thus representing a palpable threat to US maritime interests.

But Japan's new strategy was already misfiring. In joining the Axis, it tied itself more closely to Hitler's chariot wheels. Moreover, Matsuoka was mistaken when he thought that the United States would be deterred by Japan's joining the Axis. On the contrary, the pact widened the scope of America's collision of interest with Japan, hitherto focused on the Open Door in China and the security of the Philippines. Now Japan was seen as part of a threatening global alliance.

Recognizing that Hitler represented by far the greater threat, the United

States stood on the defensive in the Pacific. But in order to deter Japan, President Roosevelt moved the Pacific Fleet to Hawaii, where it would lie on the flank of any Japanese advance southwards.[20] And as Japan moved into French Indochina, the United States planted its foot on Japan's resource jugular, and began slowly to apply the pressure. Japan depended on the United States for 80 per cent of its oil products, 90 per cent of its gasoline, and more than 70 per cent of its scrap iron.[21] In August 1940, Washington imposed a total embargo on trade with Japan, including a ban on all oil shipments. Amazingly, Japan had not anticipated this action. Emboldened by the stiffening of American resolve, Britain re-opened the Burma Road which supplied Chongqing via Rangoon.[22] It had closed the Road in July in response to Japanese pressure.

Desultory talks in Washington continued, but with few prospects of success. Japan had no intention of meeting America's key requirement, which was withdrawal from China. For Japan, this quagmire had become a 'holy war'. By implication, the United States would have allowed Japan to remain in Manchuria. Unlike Stalin in 1935, when he had opted for strategic retreat by selling the Chinese Eastern railway, the Japanese were not capable of strategic retreat in order to better concentrate resources and energy elsewhere. Typical of the hierarchical cultures of East Asia, Japan put 'face' before national interest. Some influential Japanese, such as General Ishiwara Kanji, knew that Japan was playing into Stalin's hands, but they were side-lined.[23] From Munich, Haushofer also enjoined Japan to pull its feet out of the China bog. A Japan mired in China was unlikely to be of much use to Germany. But Haushofer too was ignored.

Stalin must have watched with satisfaction as American policy hardened towards Japan. He had been given two days' warning of the Tripartite Pact, and Ribbentrop assured him that it was not directed at Russia. Given Stalin's highly suspicious nature, it is most unlikely that he believed this. Still, the Tripartite Pact was not all bad news for Russia. True, it increased the risk of two-front war, and thus gave Japan more leverage over Russia. But it also marked another large step on the way to a US–Japan war because it did much to keep Japan pointing southwards.

The Nazi–Soviet pact starts to fray

Now the European balance shifted again because Russian and German interests were clashing from the Balkans to the Baltic. In June 1940, Soviet troops moved into Bessarabia, as per the agreement with Hitler. But the Red Army also moved into Bukovina, which was not part of the deal. When Hitler objected, Stalin backed off.

Rump Rumania was then at risk of falling apart, as Hungary and Bulgaria pressed their territorial claims there. That represented a threat to Hitler because of his reliance on the oil fields at Ploesti. At Vienna on 30 August, Ribbentrop imposed a settlement, then guaranteed the territorial integrity of rump Rumania. Stalin was furious because the agreement was obviously directed at him. Hitler also sent troops into Rumania, whence they could also threaten the Ukraine. Hitler also seemed determined to resist Stalin's efforts to bolt the door to the Baltic. He had occupied Norway and Denmark without consulting Stalin. And at the end of July 1940, Hitler resumed arms supplies to the Finns. In September, he persuaded them to allow German troops to cross into Norway.

Despite this growing collision of interest, was it still possible for Stalin and Hitler to come to a durable agreement on the division of the spoils? It seems that Hitler had not ruled this out. German military planning did go ahead for an attack on Russia. But planning was being undertaken for all kinds of contingencies, including a European coalition against Britain in which Russia was expected to take part. In the mind of the Fuehrer, it seems, the battle between the ideas of Haushofer and those of Rosenberg had not yet been decided. Would Hitler continue to collude with Russia in order to divide the world, or would he attack Russia to achieve *lebensraum* to the East? And whatever choice he made, what role would he seek for his supposed ally in the Far East?

A division of the world? Molotov in Berlin

Thus, when Molotov came to Berlin in mid-November, Hitler devoted considerable time to talking to the Soviet foreign minister, whom he treated with exquisite courtesy.[24] That suggests that Hitler did not see the meeting as a *pro forma* exercise. It was just as well that Hitler and Stalin never met. Hans von Herwarth, a personal observer of these events, believed that they would have struck a rapport.[25]

Fortunately for Western civilization, Hitler's charm had the perverse effect of making Molotov even more rude and truculent than usual, presumably lest he be thought by Stalin as having been too accommodating to Hitler. Unlike Litvinov, Molotov had no charm. (During the Cold War, he was to be known in the West as 'the abominable no-man'.) Thus he succeeded only in exasperating the Fuehrer, who was not accustomed to being interrupted and interrogated. The only thing Molotov and Hitler were able to agree upon with any real enthusiasm was the need to keep the United States bottled up in its hemisphere.[26]

Ever the optimist, Ribbentrop proposed that the Axis powers and Russia join in the dismemberment of the British Empire, suggesting that they all direct their *lebensraum* expansion 'entirely southwards'. Since Japan, Germany and Italy were already doing that, Ribbentrop said, he wondered whether Russia would not also turn to the south for her natural outlet to the sea. Molotov asked pointedly 'which sea?' Therein lay the rub. Ribbentrop meant the Persian Gulf, the Arabian Sea and the Indian Ocean. Molotov meant the Black Sea and the Turkish straits.

After Molotov's visit, Hitler concluded that no accommodation with

Stalin was possible, and dusted off his plan to attack Russia. The abysmal performance of the Red Army in the war against Finland had convinced Hitler that he could defeat Russia in one campaign season. Once Germany had conquered Russia, Britain would be brought to heel. Then the United States, deprived of its strategic redoubt in the Atlantic, would be confined to its hemisphere and eventually brought to heel.

Did Molotov realize that his visit had been a disaster? Possibly not. According to Soviet sources, Molotov returned to Moscow convinced that Hitler was still bent on the destruction of the British Empire, and that the Soviet Union was safe for the foreseeable future.[27] Of course, Molotov, who had so far survived the purges, had every incentive to tell Stalin what he wanted to hear.[28]

Thus Stalin wrote to Hitler on 25 November, accepting the proposals for a four-power entente, albeit with a number of conditions. These included the immediate withdrawal of German troops from Finland, plus a Russo–Bulgarian treaty. Together with a base on the Bosporus to be granted by Turkey, that treaty would have given Russia control of the Turkish straits. The area south of Batum and Baku, 'in the general direction of the Persian Gulf', was to be within the Soviet sphere of influence, meaning that Stalin wanted the oil of the Middle East. Japan was to give up its oil and coal concessions on north Sakhalin.

Complaining with unintended irony that Stalin was a 'cold-blooded blackmailer', Hitler did not reply. Did Stalin mean this letter as a genuine offer that, if accepted, could have formed the basis of an enduring alliance? Or was it a brave show of resolve, meant to deter Hitler? Moscow's repeated inquiries about the letter suggest that Stalin was indeed setting his price for a durable alliance. He seems not to have drawn the obvious conclusion from Hitler's failure to reply.

For now the die was cast. On 18 December, Hitler gave the directive for *Operation Barbarossa*, the invasion of Russia. Thus Rosenberg's ideas had triumphed over Haushofer's. Despite all his promises that he would not do so, Hitler was about to repeat Napoleon's great strategic error – to attack Russia with an undefeated Britain to his rear, and the Royal Navy still operating from its Mediterranean bases of Gibraltar, Malta and Alexandria.

Matsuoka's grand tour

In Tokyo, Matsuoka Yosuke had no inkling that Ribbentrop's grand design, the basis for his own, now lay in ruins. Thus, in March 1941, Matsuoka set out to visit Berlin, Moscow and Rome. The Japanese foreign minister, as he travelled in his luxurious Russian-supplied carriage on the Trans-Siberian railway, boasted to his staff about how he intended to make puppets of Hitler and Stalin.[29] But Hitler, having decided to attack Russia, had nothing to offer him but exhortations to capture Singapore. Matsuoka had no remit to agree to that. Typical of the grossly inept way that Japan conducted its grand strategy, he had set out on this long journey lacking clear instructions on the main issue that interested his German ally.[30] Nor did Hitler tell Matsuoka about his plan to attack Russia, although he hinted at it.

In Moscow, Matsuoka parroted the Ribbentrop line, promising that Japan would allow Russia an outlet to warm waters via India once the British Empire had been liquidated. The port of Karachi was Stalin's for the asking. That did not impress Stalin, since Matsuoka was hardly in a position to deliver the keys to the Raj. But Stalin knew that the Japanese were anxious to protect their backs if they struck southwards. He also knew that Matsuoka would not wish to return empty handed from a long trip of which much had been expected.

For his part, Stalin now also had greater need for a deal with Japan. On 6 April, Hitler attacked Yugoslavia and Greece with thirty-three divisions, less than a day after Stalin had offered Yugoslavia a non-aggression pact. Hungary and Bulgaria then threw in their lot with Hitler, threatening Stalin's Balkan flank. Now the *Wehrmacht* was racing through the Balkans, in much greater force than was required for that task. Was the Ukraine its next objective? Stalin refused to listen to myriad warnings, including from Churchill, that Hitler was planning to attack him. Stalin's paranoia led him to insist that these warnings were provocations designed to embroil him in war with Germany. Still, he apparently thought it would be prudent to take out an insurance policy to protect his back against Japan.

Stalin points Japan at America

Stalin played his cards skilfully, though Matsuoka was hardly an opponent worth his mettle. As part of his negotiating technique, Stalin agreed to the pact only at the last minute. And he insisted on a neutrality pact, rather than a non-aggression pact. That meant that Russia and Japan did not pledge not to attack each other, but only that each would remain neutral if the other were attacked by a third party. Stalin then drove a hard bargain, insisting that Japan liquidate its oil and coal concessions in north Sakhalin. The only concession he made was in relation to the Japanese puppet state in Manchuria, *Manchukuo*. In return for Japanese recognition of the Soviet sphere of influence in Outer Mongolia, Russia agreed to recognize *Manchukuo*. That concession didn't cost him much, since the *Guandong* army had long been in occupation of all of Manchuria.

Once the pact had been signed on 13 April, Stalin made the unprecedented gesture of sending Matsuoka off at the railway station. There he made a great public display of affection for the Japanese foreign minister, as well as for the German officials present. Stalin had good reason to be pleased with his handiwork. The neutrality pact was suitably ambiguous. It could be read as targeted at either Germany or the United States. Either way, it suited Stalin's purposes. In relation to Germany, the pact checkmated the Tripartite Pact. If Germany attacked Russia, Japan would remain neutral. If the pact were read as targeted against the United States, Stalin had offered Japan a free hand if it went to war with America. In Washington, the pact was regarded with justified suspicion.[31]

Thus Stalin had protected his back against Japan, and done much to encourage the Japanese into war against America. Not that the Soviet dictator put much faith in paper treaties. He would be careful to back up the neutrality pact by an adequate force balance in the Far East to make sure the Japanese were not tempted to attack.

In Japan, court and moderate circles regarded the pact with dismay.[32] By playing Stalin's game, Matsuoka had done much to set Japan on the path to war with America. And by allowing Matsuoka so much rope, the feckless Konoe contributed greatly to that outcome. Former foreign minister Shidehara, when he heard of Matsuoka's exuberant send-off by Stalin, wrote that 'one cannot but be astounded by the clever trick of excitement that allows the Kremlin to fish in troubled waters'.[33] Shidehara and other moderates realized that 'there is finally the possibility of provoking a war between Japan and the United States'.[34] In Washington, American diplomats such as Loy Henderson also comprehended what Stalin had achieved.[35]

Hitler attacks Russia, while Japan dithers

On 22 June, Hitler attacked Russia with an enormous army of 149 divisions.[36] From Berlin, the Japanese ambassador predicted a rapid German victory. In Tokyo, Matsuoka urged that Japan attack Siberia. He also wanted to continue the southern advance, even while Japan was still mired in China. Thus he advocated three-front war. That was too much even for the phlegmatic Konoe, and pointed questions were asked about the foreign minister's sanity. Konoe's cabinet was reshuffled in order to dump Matsuoka.

So the Japanese hesitated, while their usual factionalism reigned supreme. The navy wanted nothing to do with war with Russia, which would give it virtually no role. The extremists in the navy had always wanted to fight America, which the moderates knew would be suicidal. The army was also divided. Some wanted to attack Russia, and so sent unauthorized peace feelers to China in order to prevent two-front war. Others, still bent on winning the 'holy war' in China, could not see how an attack on Russia was going to deliver China to them.

From Berlin, as the Japanese dithered, Ribbentrop now urged an attack on Vladivostok rather than Singapore.[37] To encourage Japan to attack Russia, on 1 July 1941 Germany recognized the Japanese puppet government in Nanking, and promised to declare war on America once a US–Japan war started. But the memory of Nomonhan and the presence of the Soviet bombers at Vladivostok did much to deter the Japanese. Nor did they see themselves as servants of Hitler's interests. After all, he had not hesitated to betray them when he made his pact with Stalin in August 1939.

Thus the Japanese decided to await an outcome of the titanic struggle in the West. By August 9 they had concluded that it was too late for an attack northwards that winter. Kept closely informed by his intelligence assets, Stalin was able to transfer about half his forces from the Far East – some eighteen to twenty divisions – across the Trans-Siberian railway.[38] Those hardy and well-equipped Siberian troops played a critical role in the defence of Moscow on 4 December, after Zhukov had launched a counter-offensive. So once again, the Trans-Siberian railway played a critical role in Russia's strategic history, as it had done in the 1904–1905 war.[39]

Japan attacks America

Meanwhile, time was running out for preventing war between Japan and the United States. Although the United States had long opposed Japanese aggression in China, it had seen no interest at stake there that justified the risk of war with Japan. If it had, the *Panay* incident on the Yangzi in late 1937, when Japanese aircraft deliberately attacked a US warship, would have provided a *casus belli*. The interest for which the United States became willing to risk war with Japan was the defence of Singapore, guardian of the vital straits that link the Indian and Pacific Oceans. In May 1941, as the British position in the Middle East deteriorated, Roosevelt wrote to Churchill that control of the two oceans would decide the outcome of the war.[40]

Given the strength of hostility in the United States to the British Empire, as well as the continuing pull of isolationism, President Roosevelt was hardly in a position to acknowledge openly, or indeed to Churchill in private, that America now regarded Singapore as a vital interest. But America's stake in Singapore stemmed from the maritime basis of its own security. If Japan were to take Singapore and then link up with Germany in the Indian Ocean, that would knock Britain out of the war. As it was, the British were barely hanging on. Then America, deprived of its 'unsinkable aircraft carrier' in the Atlantic, would have no means of bringing the war to Hitler. And without a defiant Britain to his rear, Hitler would have much less trouble defeating Russia. After that, he would soon turn his attention to the Western Hemisphere, where he already had a foothold in Latin America.

The Japanese, never attuned much to the thinking of foreigners, could not see that, as they moved into Indochina, threatening Singapore as well as the back door to China, the United States had become more willing to risk war. In February 1941, the counsellor of the US embassy in Tokyo, Eugene Dooman, tried to spell this out to them. Brought up in Japan, Dooman knew most of the Japanese élite intimately. So he told Ohashi Chuichi, the vice minister of foreign affairs (Japan's most senior foreign affairs official), that if Japan threatened the communications of the British Empire, it 'would have to expect to come into conflict with the United States'. Shocked, Ohashi replied: 'do you mean to say that if Japan were to attack Singapore, there would be war with the United States'? Dooman replied that 'the logic of the situation would inevitably raise that question'.[41]

But the prizes were too alluring, and Japan was too full of hubris to back down now. Moreover, the navy was anxiously watching the dwindling of its oil stocks. Thus, on 6 September, an Imperial Conference in Tokyo opted for war. In October, the appointment of Tojo Hideki as prime minister made conflict even more likely. On 26 November, a task force led by six aircraft carriers left Hitokappu Bay in Etorofu in the Kurils. Maintaining strict radio silence, it succeeded in crossing the vast North Pacific undetected. Pearl Harbor was attacked without warning on 7 December. At the same time, Japanese troops landed on the Kra isthmus in Thailand, and in north-eastern Malaya. Their objective was to move down the western side of the Malayan peninsula, and then take Singapore by the back door – as Japan had taken Port Arthur in the 1904–1905 war.

The day after Pearl Harbor, President Roosevelt declared war. Admiral Yamamoto Isoruku, who had served with Togo at Tsushima in 1905, had planned the attack on Pearl Harbor.[42] Yamamoto was no militant. On the contrary, he was a disciple of the moderate admirals Yonai Mitsumasa and Kato Tomasaburo. In fact, his outspoken criticism of the nationalist extremists in Japan had brought him numerous death threats. As Commander of the Combined Fleet from August 1939, Yamamoto had laboured to keep Japan out of the war.

After the die was cast for war, however, Yamamoto planned the Pearl Harbor attack as the only means by which Japan might hope to deter the United States for long enough for Japan to grab the resources of Southeast Asia and erect a defensive screen. Still, Yamamoto predicted that the attack might be a tactical success but a strategic failure. That was because he had been to America and understood the power of the US economy, as few other Japanese leaders did. Shortly after Pearl Harbor, Yamamoto stated his fear that all Japan had done was to arouse a sleeping giant.

Japan had opted for a pre-emptive strike. The United States, with only three aircraft carriers in the Pacific to Japan's ten, had failed to deter Japan. British naval power in East Asian waters had also been insufficient to help deter the Japanese. In mid-year, in the vast distance between Alexandria and Pearl Harbor, a distance of more than half the globe, the Anglo-Saxon maritime powers had only one small aircraft carrier.[43] In October, Churchill sent to Singapore the modern battleship *Prince of Wales*, accompanied by an older battle cruiser, the *Repulse*. The new aircraft carrier *Indomitable* was unable to join the other ships after it went aground in Jamaica. After the *Ark Royal* was sunk in the Mediterranean, *Indomitable* was not sent to Singapore because the Royal Navy was down to one aircraft carrier. So much for 'Main Fleet to Singapore'.

It was Field Marshal Jan C. Smuts, prime minister of South Africa, who saw things most clearly. He warned Churchill of the glaring weakness of stationing at Singapore and Hawaii fleets that were inferior to a Japanese fleet holding the twin advantages of concentration and central geographical position. Japan's strategic maritime advantage was a consequence of the decisions made at the 1921–1922 Washington conference, the complacency induced in the democracies by naval arms control, and the US Congress's subsequent refusal to fund a naval base at Guam. By the time the United States decided to try to reinforce the Philippines, it was too late. 'If the Japanese are really nippy,' warned Smuts, 'there is here an opening for a first-class disaster.'[44] He was soon proved correct.

Seeking to prevent the Japanese landings in northern Malaya, the *Prince of Wales* and the *Repulse*, which lacked air cover in the absence of *Indomitable*, were sunk by Japanese naval aircraft operating from Indochina. Singapore fell in February. Once in control of that vital node, Japan was able to bolt the gate from the Indian Ocean. Now the Japanese were masters of more than half the globe. In the first few months of 1942, the Japanese aircraft carriers that had attacked Pearl Harbor raided northern Australia. They then made a foray into the Indian Ocean, bombarding Colombo on the way. Thus the Japanese Navy chased the British Navy out of the Indian Ocean for the first time in centuries, all the way back to South Africa. Now there was a real risk that Japan might link up with Germany in the Indian Ocean, and knock Britain out of the war. If Germany and Japan had been real allies, that might have happened.

Failures of grand strategy

But Japan and Germany were co-belligerents rather than true allies, and never tried to coordinate their strategy. Moreover, Japan had attacked a country far more powerful than itself, whose centre of gravity lay an ocean and a continent away. Japan knew it could not bring the war home to the United States in its own hemisphere. Rather, it hoped to deter America from interfering in East Asia, and thus to gain a free hand there. The Japanese hoped to defeat the American battle fleet in a war of attrition in the vicinity of the Japanese mid-Pacific mandates, as the US Navy charged across the Pacific to liberate the Philippines. But the Japanese Navy had no means of ensuring that it could bring the US fleet to battle. And as we have seen, Japan's decision-making processes were truly appalling. Tojo, who was both prime minister and army minister at the outbreak of war, apparently did not even learn of the details of the navy's attack on Pearl Harbor until the end of the war.[45] For the navy, this was mere 'operational detail'.

Moreover, Admiral Nagumo Chuichi made a tactical error at Pearl Harbor. After he realized that the US carriers were elsewhere, his fliers were ordered to go after the battleships rather than the oil depots. Then Nagumo refused his fliers' entreaties for another strike. Had Nagumo attacked the oil depots, the US Navy would have had to retreat to the west coast. Then Japan might have been able to occupy an unprotected Australia. This would have deprived the United States of its 'unsinkable aircraft carrier' in the

Pacific, the equivalent of the role that Britain played in the Atlantic. As it happened, by sinking so much of the US battle line at Pearl Harbor, Japan undermined the influence of the Mahanians in the US Navy. Now the Americans were forced to devise new roles for their aircraft carriers, including the task forces that were to do so much to win the war.[46]

Despite its apparent success at Pearl Harbor, Japan was thinking and behaving much less strategically than when it attacked Russia in 1904. At that time, the Meiji leaders knew that they could not bring the war home to the enemy. They had not wanted that war. But when Russian ambition made war inevitable, the Japanese decided how they wished to fight it, and how they intended to end it. Even before the war started, they had sent feelers out to President Theodore Roosevelt to broker the peace. And in Britain, the Japanese had had a most useful ally which could hold their coat, help secure financing of the war, and protect them against Russia's allies. But in 1941, Japan's leaders were incapable of making such connections between ends and means. Having started the war, they had no idea how to end it.

The maritime highway via Vladivostok

After America entered the war, the neutrality pact that Stalin had signed with Matsuoka proved of enormous benefit to the Soviet Union.[47] With other access routes to the Soviet heartland difficult or blocked, vital US lend-lease supplies came over the Trans-Siberian railway, via Vladivostok, from Alaska in Soviet or Soviet-flagged ships, once Japanese forces had been cleared from the Aleutian islands.[48] The 'Alcan highway' was rapidly built in 1943 in order to provide a secure inland route to Alaska, safe from Japanese submarine attack on the US coastal shipping routes.

The Japanese refused to allow Soviet ships to transit the Tsugaru strait, an international waterway. No doubt the Japanese recalled the break-out of the Russian Vladivostok squadron during the 1904–1905 war, after which it passed through the Tsugaru and caused panic in Japan's coastal cities. But the Japanese could not risk also denying the Soviets transit via the Soya strait. That was a difficult and dangerous passage, because the strait was often was closed by ice in the winter and shrouded by fog in the summer. The Japanese sank an unknown number of Soviet-flagged ships in the Soya strait, allegedly by mistake. Yet Japan did not dare to tear up the neutrality pact, lest the Soviets attack in Manchuria, or bomb Tokyo. Thus the maritime highway to Vladivostok, under the noses of the frustrated Japanese, was vital for keeping Russia in the war against Germany.

Stalin looks for the spoils

For Stalin, the war in East Asia was all gain and little pain. Japan was thrown on the defensive as early as mid-1942, after the battle of Midway. As the US island-hopping campaign began to bring the war towards Japan's home islands, the Japanese hoped for divine intervention, as when the 'sacred winds' had scattered the Mongol invasion fleets off Kyushu. But there were no 'divine winds' in 1944, when American maritime power was brought within range of Japan's home islands. The application of maritime power alone rarely inflicts total military defeat, but it did on Japan.[49]

As the threat from the United States drew ever closer, the Japanese hoped that Stalin would strike a deal, along the lines of the old secret treaties. But in April 1945, Stalin unilaterally abrogated the neutrality pact with Japan. The Japanese still didn't see what was coming, partly because Molotov led them to believe that Russia would not attack until the required one year's notice had expired. Konoe wanted to lead a delegation to Moscow, but Molotov fobbed him off. Stalin's answer to these Japanese delusions was his Manchurian *blitzkrieg*, begun on 8 August 1945. That was two days after the American atomic bombing of Hiroshima.[50]

At the Yalta conference in February 1945, Stalin bluffed Roosevelt into promising him the Kurils as well as south Sakhalin.[51] A paper prepared by Professor Blakeslee, which set out the correct history of the Kurils, had been omitted from the Yalta brief.[52] Thus Stalin convinced Roosevelt that the Kurils had been lost to Russia as a result of Japanese aggression in 1904. The truth, of course, was that all of the Kuril chain had belonged to Japan since 1875. In return for a promise to enter the war as soon as Hitler was defeated – which Stalin was bursting to do in any case – Roosevelt agreed that the Kurils be handed over to Russia. It soon became clear that Stalin meant all of the Kurils, including the four most southerly islands that had never belonged to Russia.

In any case, Roosevelt could hardly be expected to be unduly concerned about a few obscure islands that few Americans had ever heard of. His priority was to enlist Russia's help in order to limit the numbers of American casualties expected in the invasion of Japan's home islands. The casualties incurred in taking Okinawa suggested that the cost was likely to be high indeed. Moreover, Roosevelt was hardly in a position to deny Stalin territory that the Red Army would be able to take by force.

Stalin's ambitions met – and thwarted

At both ends of Eurasia, Stalin by 1945 had met almost all the objectives he might have dreamed of when he made his risky rapprochement with Hitler in August 1939. At no cost to Russia, the United States had utterly defeated Japan. But Stalin's *Manchurian* blitzkrieg had entitled him to a share of the spoils. As a consequence of his success at Yalta, he had regained *de facto* control of the warm-water ports and strategic railways of Manchuria. His communist allies controlled North Korea, the United States and Russia having agreed to divide the peninsula temporarily at the 38th parallel. Ironically, apparently unknown to either party at the time, this was the same division that Field Marshal Yamagata had unsuccessfully offered the tsar in 1894.

In Europe, the great capitals of Berlin, Prague and Vienna lay under Stalin's hand. That was largely a consequence of the way he had bluffed the Americans, who believed that calculations about post-war strategy were alien to the way a democratic republic should fight a war. Contrary advice from Churchill had been spurned by Roosevelt, always more conscious of the perceived evils of the British Empire than the real ones of Stalin's.

Stalin had also held on to the Baltic states, acquired by means of his pact with Hitler, and achieved a subservient Finland.[53] The former East Prussian capital of Koenigsburg, renamed Kaliningrad, became Russian territory, thus giving Stalin another window on the warm waters of the Baltic. These were large steps towards being able to make the Baltic a Russian lake, though Denmark had eluded Stalin's grasp. The courses and mouths of central Europe's great rivers – the Danube, the Vistula and the Oder – were either in his hands, or in those of his satraps. Except for a short distance from its mouth, the entire course of the Elbe was also within his grip. Stalin or his allies controlled the Balkans. Peter the Great must have been smiling from his grave. Indeed, Stalin kept a portrait of the great Peter in his Kremlin study.

But one great tsarist ambition had eluded Stalin – the control of the Turkish straits. So it was not long before Molotov started pressing the Turks for bases on the straits, in effect taking up where he had left off in his fateful meeting with Hitler in November 1940. The communist uprising in Greece also threatened Western interests in the eastern Mediterranean. So when Britain, irrevocably weakened by the Second World War, was unable to continue in its traditional role as guardian of the eastern Mediterranean, the United States had to step in. Therein lay the seeds of the Cold War, which began in Europe and then spread to East Asia.

4 The Cold War: first phase

The Cold War was the third, and last, of the great struggles of the twentieth century for domination of Eurasia. As in the two world wars, Europe was the locus of conflict. But over time, the East Asian dimension of the Cold War became progressively more important, as it became a truly global contest.

The Cold War began in Europe – as a strategic consequence of the way the Second World War had ended, with the Red Army dangerously close to domination of Europe. Then the Cold War was brought to East Asia by the communist victory in China, the 1950 Sino–Soviet alliance, and the Korean War. During the Cold War, Germany represented the keys to the kingdom. That was because the key Soviet objective was a reunified neutral Germany that Moscow could dominate by virtue of proximity.

Even though Germany was the global locus of strategic tension, it was in East Asia that America lost 100,000 servicemen during the Cold War. More open warfare occurred in East Asia than in Europe because the regional balance was less stable and more brittle there. Proxy wars took place in the two peninsulas on Eurasia's eastern edge – Korea and Vietnam. But even there, head-to-head conflict was avoided, because nuclear weapons made it simply too dangerous.

In 1989, just before the Soviet Union collapsed, Britain's then prime minister, Margaret Thatcher, told the last general secretary of the Soviet communist party, Mikhail Gorbachev, that 'both our countries know from bitter experience that conventional weapons do not deter war in Europe, whereas nuclear weapons have done so for over forty years'.[1] The Soviets, with their huge tank armies, had no reason to be afraid of conventional war. But they did fear nuclear war, because it would have destroyed their political system.

America's strategic options

By 1949, the United States had become convinced that it would have to maintain a balance of power in Europe by means of forward deployments and enduring alliances. America intervened in Europe's struggles because of the maritime basis of its own security. It chose to deploy forward, and work with allies, in order to counter threats posed by a continental power with hegemonic ambition.

Nuclear weapons and a powerful navy were a necessary but insufficient guarantee of American security. The threat posed by Soviet power was not one of invasion. Rather, the Soviets sought to tilt the global balance in their favour by building up such overwhelming military power that it would intimidate the states on the periphery of the Soviet bloc. Then those states would pre-emptively capitulate, without Moscow's having to fire a shot in anger. Had the Soviet Union achieved that objective, it would have confined the United States to its own hemisphere, unable to set the global rules or even to influence them greatly.

The strategic geography of the Cold War

By 1991, the United States had led to victory a mixed maritime–continental coalition, held together by the global sinews of maritime power. Maritime links were essential to the forward deployment of US forces, which increased pressure on the Soviet Union. American forward deployments also assured allies on the periphery of the Soviet bloc that Moscow would not be allowed to pick them off one by one.

The strategic geography of the Cold War essentially replicated that of the Second World War. In Europe, superpower confrontation was mostly continental, the locus of potential conflict being the Oder–Neisse Line or the 'inner-German border'. But the Soviet Union was *in* Europe, whereas America was an ocean away. Thus the United States needed to be able to reinforce western Europe in time of war by means of an 'Atlantic bridge' of ships – hence the strategic resonance of the Caribbean and Atlantic islands such as Cuba, Greenland, Iceland and the Azores. Superpower confrontation in Europe was mostly continental, but it depended critically on maritime reinforcement.

In East Asia, superpower confrontation was mostly maritime. The strategic geography of East Asia during the Cold War essentially replicated that of the Second World War in the Pacific. In East Asia, America's essential interest until 1971 was the strategic security of Japan, the only industrialized country in the region. Then the United States forged a strategic alignment with China in order to oppose growing Soviet power that threatened them both. China's enmity posed an enormous strategic complication for the USSR, tying down a quarter of its ground forces, and reminding Moscow that war in the west would also mean war in the east.

During the Cold War, East Asia's strategic tensions focused on North Asia, where the interests of all the great powers intersect. But over time, as the terms of engagement of the superpower contest widened, East Asia's 'strategic hinterland' stretched to encompass the island continent of Australia, the Indian subcontinent, and as far west as the Indian Ocean island of Diego Garcia.

Evil – and inefficient – empire

Strategic geography wasn't the only thing that mattered, of course. Abstractions such as the need to maintain a balance of power at both ends of Eurasia could not have sustained the support of the American people for such a long struggle. The Soviet Union was also a threat because of its totalitarian government. Once again, as with Nazi Germany, a would-be European hegemon was a totalitarian state with an ideology repugnant to most Americans.

In 1981 America elected a president who believed that the Cold War could and should be won. President Reagan feared that America could not forever remain on the defensive, depending for its security on a passive containment policy. He also appreciated how much the Soviet Union was undermining Western confidence in Containment. When Reagan demanded that Gorbachev tear down the Berlin Wall, he reflected optimism about the superiority of the American system. He also understood that the Cold War could not be won until the regime in Moscow was made to collapse.

Moreover, Reagan sensed the weakness behind the imposing edifice. Unlike America's 'consensual empire', the Soviet imperium was held together by fear. Neither could its command economy compete with that of a free society. Thus, by the 1970s, with the Soviets spending about a quarter of their GNP on defence, their technological deficiencies were beginning to show. As the USSR became more dependent on Western credits and technology, the United States gained greater leverage.

Reagan knew that the rise of *Solidarity*, the authentic voice of the dissatisfied Polish working class, represented a palpable threat to the Soviet system. Thus in 1981 the Polish authorities were forced to crack down on dissent in the face of a threat that Moscow would again send in the tanks if they did not. Then Gorbachev tried to institute political reforms. But after he started tinkering with it, the system collapsed. In 1991, the reunification of Germany within NATO represented utter defeat for the USSR. Yet in 1945, it had seemed to be on the brink of victory.

1945: The Cold War begins in Europe

The end of the Second World War in 1945 saw Russia, having struggled with Germany for hegemony over Eurasia in two global wars, at last on the verge of success following the defeat of Germany and Japan. If the United States had not intervened, Stalin would have achieved Hitler's goal of the domination of Europe. As early as 1942, the Yale geostrategist Nicholas Spykman had warned that having Russia in control of Europe from the Urals to the North Sea was no great improvement on having Germany dominating Europe from the North Sea to the Urals.[2]

By 1945, the Red Army was in striking distance of the English Channel. Feeding on economic misery, powerful communist parties in France and Italy were obedient to Moscow's dictates. Moreover, Russia was exerting pressure in such traditional places as Iran, Greece and the Turkish straits. In February 1948, a communist coup in Czechoslovakia convinced even the sceptics that Moscow indeed sought hegemony over all of Europe. Soon the countries of Western Europe were clamouring for American protection.

The United States became convinced that its interests required maintaining security in Western Europe by means of forward deployments and enduring alliances, leading into the formation of NATO in 1949. A massive US aid program, the Marshall Plan, did much to assist Western Europe's recovery. One of the reasons the United States was able to gather so many allies in such a short time was that it was able to offer them nuclear protection in order to offset overwhelming Soviet proximate power. The Berlin airlift provided an early test of wills.

Stalin, checkmated in the west, then turned to the east. Like Lenin, he was ever attentive to the anti-colonial potential of Asian nationalism and the opportunities thus presented to distract the Western powers from the main game in Europe. Moreover, the Soviet Union had come out of the Second World War with substantial gains in the east.

Stalin: gains in the East

In 1945, Stalin was greedy for the spoils promised him at Yalta. As we have seen, on 8 August 1945 the Soviet Union declared war on Japan, and the Red Army drove into Manchuria. As a consequence of the Yalta arrangements, President Harry S. Truman, who had assumed the presidency after Roosevelt's death, agreed that Soviet forces should also occupy all of the Kurils. But Truman rebuffed Stalin's demands that the Red Army be permitted to take the surrender of Japanese forces in northern Hokkaido.[3] That deprived Stalin of the right to a share in the occupation of all of Japan. It also saved the population of Hokkaido the horrors of a Soviet occupation.

In China also, the Soviet dictator's reach exceeded his grasp. He pressured Jiang Jieshi (Chiang Kai-shek) into making the concessions which Stalin had persuaded the Western allies to give him at Yalta. By means of a treaty on 14 August, Stalin secured a thirty-year concession lease on Lushun (Port Arthur) and Dalien (Dalny), as well as control over the Chinese Eastern railway. Those gains were tantamount to control over all of Manchuria. The Soviets also stripped Manchuria's industrial assets before Jiang Jieshi's troops could arrive. In China, they behaved the same way they had done in Germany and the other areas of Europe they overran, with mass rape and looting.

Stalin remained ambivalent about the Chinese communists almost to the end when in late 1949 they took power, and the defeated *Guomintang* fled to Taiwan. Above all, Stalin wanted a subservient China. So an enduring alliance with Jiang Jieshi would probably have suited him best. In Yugoslavia after the Second World War, the advent of the independent-minded Josef Tito pointed to problems for Moscow if communists came to power by dint of their own efforts.[4] Moreover, Stalin was careful not to become embroiled in a Chinese civil war, lest that lead to a clash with American forces. But as Mao's forces occupied China's coastal cities, the United States did not intervene. Dean Acheson, who became Secretary of State in January 1949, oversaw a policy of 'waiting for the dust to settle'. Acheson hoped that the Chinese communists would prove to be as independent-minded as Tito. Moreover, the Truman administration, aware that Western Europe was the strategic prize of the Cold War, was wary of being drawn into a land war in Asia. Truman was also fed up with the corruption and incompetence of the nationalist forces.

The Sino–Soviet alliance brings the Cold War to East Asia

In February 1950 the Sino–Soviet alliance transformed the strategic geography of the Cold War, making it a global strategic contest. The confidence of the communist camp had been boosted in the previous year when the Soviet Union tested an atomic weapon, thus ending America's nuclear monopoly.

Stalin, in negotiating the new treaty with Mao – who came to Moscow in December 1949 ostensibly to celebrate Stalin's 70th birthday – preserved most of the gains he had made in his 1945 treaty with Jiang Jieshi, including *de facto* control of the South Manchurian railway.[5] He also retained access to the port of Dalien. In the case of Lushun, formerly Port Arthur, the Soviets were to withdraw by the end of 1952. But the treaty did not make the pull-out final or absolute. An 'additional agreement' was so humiliating to China that it was kept secret. By this provision, China agreed not to allow citizens of third countries to settle or to carry out any industrial, trade or other related activities in Manchuria and Xinjiang. The so-called joint stock companies, by which Russia exerted *de facto* control over the economies of these regions, were also continued. Moreover, Mongolia remained firmly in the Soviet camp.

Like Stalin's treaty with Jiang Jieshi, the new treaty was pointed at Japan. It said that 'in the event of one of the Contracting Parties being attacked by Japan or any state allied with her and thus being involved in a state of war, the other Contracting Party shall immediately render military and other assistance by all means at its disposal'. The Chinese insisted on the latter phrase because it could mean nuclear weapons.

The dimensions of the new Sino–Soviet bloc replicated those of the Mongol empire, threatening to outflank the United States at both ends of Eurasia. Moreover, the bloc preached a revolutionary ideology with considerable appeal in Asia, where the Western powers had been discredited when Japan overran their colonies. The Sino–Soviet alliance also foreclosed any hopes of American rapprochement with the new rulers in Beijing, or any realistic hope that America could drive a wedge between the communist powers. China's militant behaviour, including the seizure of American property and the detention of consular officials, also aroused anger in the United States. Moreover, when Russia and China recognized Ho Chi Minh's communist regime in North Vietnam, it suggested a concerted attempt to outflank the Western powers by undermining France's ability to contribute to common defence efforts in NATO.

Fomenting revolution in maritime Southeast Asia

Southeast Asia, because of its connection with the global balance, offered Stalin potentially rich pickings. Both Russia and China supported communist rebels in the Philippines, where post-independence arrangements in 1946 allowed continuing US access to the naval base at Subic Bay and the Clark air base. Communist efforts at subversion came close to success in the early 1950s until they were defeated by American support for Philippine anti-communists. Because the Philippines is an archipelago, American maritime power was vital in denying reinforcements to the insurgents. In the Dutch East Indies in 1948, Moscow backed a communist insurrection, hoping to exploit the Indonesian revolution against Dutch colonialism. But this failed too, so Moscow did not gain a foothold on the Malacca straits.

Reflecting weakness, China's methods were different from Russia's. China fomented revolution in Burma, and by 1950 communists there had established links with the Chinese communist party over the border. In maritime Southeast Asia, a key target for China was the Malayan peninsula, where Beijing's instrument was the large Chinese diaspora. China probably did not anticipate that the insurrection of the Malayan communist party (MCP) would bring it to power. But even without attaining power, the MCP afforded China large influence at low cost. In Singapore, China's subversive activities focused on the labour unions and the Chinese middle schools. These efforts were rebuffed by a vigorous British response, made easier by the fact that the Anglo–American powers held command of the sea.

The Korean War: all gain and no pain for Stalin, at first

In 1950, Stalin gave the North Korean communist Kim Il Sung a green light to invade South Korea. For Stalin, the Korean war must have seemed all gain and no pain. At low cost and low risk, he diverted American attention and resources from Europe. He also embroiled Mao in a war with the United States, which served his objective of keeping China subservient. But Stalin was keen to avoid a collision with US forces. While encouraging North Korea into the war, he had no intention of becoming entangled himself – though some Russian pilots covertly participated in the war by flying North Korean MiGs.

North Korea struck on Sunday 25 June with a massive armoured attack. Caught by surprise, America entered the war in order to protect prostrate

Japan, and to reassure its European allies that Stalin would not be allowed to pick them off one by one. Occupation forces were rushed from Japan. On 27 June, Truman sent the Seventh Fleet into the Taiwan Strait. That prevented Mao from taking Taiwan. It also discouraged Jiang Jieshi from seeking to invade China and thus widening the war.

Yet the United States was wary of a collision with Moscow. Truman, by obtaining UN authorization for a 'police action' in Korea, avoided the need for a US declaration of war, which might have triggered the Sino–Soviet alliance. For his part, Stalin kept his diplomats from returning to the Security Council, which they had been boycotting because of its refusal to seat Beijing instead of Taipei. Like Truman, Stalin wanted to avoid a US declaration of war. If the United States did declare war, China would be able to invoke its treaty with Moscow, under whose terms the Soviet Union was supposed to 'immediately render military and other assistance with all means at its disposal'. That might mean nuclear war.

Initially the war went well for the North. South Korean and American forces were chased down the peninsula to a narrow perimeter around Pusan. An American Dunkirk loomed. But in September, General MacArthur demonstrated the flexibility of maritime power by landing at Inchon (the port for Seoul), behind North Korean lines. Other landings were made on the east coast. As US and South Korean forces advanced up the peninsula on two fronts, the North Koreans were routed. By late November, American probes in the east had reached the Yalu. Despite myriad warnings of Chinese preparations to enter the war, MacArthur assured Truman that China would not do so. Like Stalin in 1941, the American generalissimo discounted all evidence of impending danger.

China comes into the war

With American forces approaching the Yalu, China's industrial heartland in Manchuria was under threat. Manchuria was reverting to his historic role as the 'cockpit of Asia'. Lacking direct means of communication, China's foreign minister Zhou Enlai sent warnings to Washington via the Indian ambassador to China. These were discounted, not least because the ambassador was distrusted in Washington.

While no doubt comprehending Stalin's designs, Mao had his own reasons for entering the war. He did not want to see Stalin dominating the Korean peninsula and thus achieving his tsarist ambition for a warm-water port there. Whatever Mao's calculations, concern about Chinese casualties was not among them. To the contrary, his armies were bloated with former *Guomindang* soldiers, who represented disposable cannon fodder. (China's losses in the war were to be at least half a million dead.) So China entered the war with massive force, exploiting the gap between the two widely separated prongs of America's northward advance that MacArthur had allowed to develop. America had sought only a limited war, but for China this was all-out war because vital interests were at stake.

In January 1951, Seoul again fell to the communists. Then American forces stabilized a front not far below the 38th parallel. Chinese forces having outrun their supply lines, the war entered a stalemate. In April, after MacArthur had publicly urged an advance into Manchuria, he was sacked for insubordination. For his part, Stalin was content to let negotiations drag on, including about the prisoner-of-war problem.[6] That deepened the hostility between China and the United States, and tied down US forces in Asia. The number of Americans killed in the Korean War amounted to 37,000, two-thirds of them after the war became stalemated. The United States was able to extricate itself only after President Eisenhower succeeded Truman in January 1953. In order to end the war, Eisenhower made a credible threat to escalate it by using nuclear weapons. Stalin's death helped too, since the shaky new leadership in Moscow had reason to reduce tensions. In July 1953 an armistice was signed at Panmunjon.

The Korean War had seemed one of Stalin's great successes. But there were negatives, some of which had become manifest by the time he died. One was the rebirth of the Japanese economy. Another was the re-arming of West Germany within NATO. By 1954, West Germany had entered NATO, with its high command integrated into NATO. That did much to help reassure its neighbours that German militarism was a thing of the past. Meanwhile, in East Asia, the United States was gathering new allies.

The creation of the US alliance system in East Asia: Japan

The Korean War widened the terms of America's engagement, and hence its need for allies. As in Western Europe, the United States needed to deploy forward in East Asia in order to contain Soviet power. Forward deployments exerted pressure on the vulnerable rear of the Soviet Union, thus presenting Moscow with the credible threat of two-front war. In order to project maritime power across the vast reaches of the Pacific, the United States needed bases and allies on, or just off, the East Asian littoral. Of these, Japan was the most important.

The US–Japan mutual security treaty was signed on 8 September 1951, five hours after the San Francisco peace treaty that ended the Pacific War. For the United States, Japan became a vital link in a global chain of maritime power that depended critically on nuclear weapons in order to counter overwhelming Soviet proximate power in Europe. For its part, Japan, in return for furnishing the United States with bases just off the East Asian littoral, was afforded maritime and nuclear protection in ways that did not disturb its neighbours. That essential congruence of strategic interest was to underpin the US–Japan alliance until the end of the Cold War.

Still, all was not smooth sailing. As a consequence of the Korean War, the United States wanted Japan to rearm. That was because America had demobilized so rapidly after the Second World War that it was deficient in manpower, while Japan possessed East Asia's only large reserve of trained manpower. Soon after the Korean War broke out, the Occupation authorities ordered the establishment of a 75,000-man National Police Reserve, which in 1954 became the nucleus of Japan's Self Defense Forces.

But most Japanese conservatives did not want to re-arm. That would be so divisive at home that it might endanger conservative rule. Moreover, Article Nine of Japan's 1946 constitution, written under Occupation auspices, had renounced Japan's right to make war or to maintain armed forces. The mainstream Japanese conservatives, having had this 'peace' constitution thrust upon them, soon came to see its virtues.

Thus John Foster Dulles, the Republican whom Truman designated to negotiate the peace treaty with Japan, found a tough bargainer in Japan's prime minister Yoshida Shigeru. An experienced diplomat, Yoshida represented the Anglophile faction which had preferred to rely on the British alliance and a maritime orientation. For that reason, he had opposed Japan's embroilment in China after 1937. So Yoshida had no difficulty in comprehending that alliance with the dominant maritime power represented optimal security for Japan. Thus he readily agreed to conclude a security treaty with the United States, as well as a peace treaty. But he did not want to re-arm.

Yoshida understood the limits of his bargaining position; the United States could simply continue the Occupation. So he knew better than to insist on the right of prior consultation about weapons to be brought into Japan (which obviously included nuclear weapons) or on Japan's ability to restrict US operations from Japan. Yoshida also had to agree that Japan should recognize Taiwan as the legitimate government of China – even though he would have preferred, like Britain, to recognize China's new rulers.

But Yoshida also had some cards to play. He knew that, over the longer term, the United States could not operate its bases in Japan in the teeth of a hostile government. Moreover, Yoshida comprehended that any attack on Japan would automatically involve an attack on the US bases there. So he saw no need for Japan to re-arm, or to contribute to wider US regional security goals. Besides, other US allies, notably South Korea, remained fearful of Japan. That bolstered Yoshida's case for a minimalist approach to security, which became enshrined as the 'Yoshida Doctrine'.

The Yoshida Doctrine: *realpolitik* with a low profile

The Yoshida Doctrine was founded on cold calculation of interest. Yoshida, like the other conservatives, had no intention of seeing Japan becoming a permanent American ward. Japan's defeat in 1945 had discredited militarism, but there were other paths to great-power status. Still, before Japan could re-emerge as a great power, it had to develop its economic and technological base. So Japan needed America to keep the sea lanes open, to afford access to its markets and technology, and to foster Japan's entry into global trading and economic groupings.

America's policy of containing both the Soviet Union and its Chinese ally did cause some heartburn in Tokyo. Like many others of his generation, Yoshida was a China scholar, having been a consul in Antung in the 1920s. Thus he harboured the dream of a Japan–China condominium in which the resources and manpower of China would be harnessed by superior Japanese technology and organizational skills. Yoshida foresaw, correctly as it turned out, that China was too nationalistic to remain forever yoked to Moscow. But while China was in the first flush of revolution, Japan could look to America to keep China and Russia on a leash.

True, the loss of markets and resources in China was a setback for Japan. But to compensate for these losses, America facilitated Japan's access to the resources of Southeast Asia. Moreover, the United States was willing to look the other way while, *sotto voce*, Japan resumed limited trade with China. How else but by such trade was Japan to feed its hundred million people on small islands lacking natural resources?

Widening the alliance framework: bringing in the great south land

Although Japan was America's key ally in the western Pacific, alliances with the Philippines (1951) and South Korea (1953) afforded the United States access to additional bases on or near the East Asian littoral. Other allies, such as Australia and New Zealand, were remote from the East Asian littoral, and possessed only limited resources and manpower. Still, even such distant allies maximized the advantages inherent in global maritime power. These included flexibility, the choice of where best to apply power, and global intelligence vision. In 1951, Australia and New Zealand – in return for a modest contribution to the Korean war – reaped the strategic dividend of the ANZUS (Australia, New Zealand, United States) Treaty. Now the Western alliance extended from Norway's border with Russia in the Arctic to Invercargill in New Zealand, which looked out on the frozen Antarctic continent. The Cold War had become a truly global strategic contest.

Missing link: Japan and South Korea

Yet in East Asia there remained a critical missing link – that between South Korea and Japan. In Western Europe, rapprochement between France and West Germany had been fostered by the relationship between two old men, Charles de Gaulle and Konrad Adenauer. And after three great wars, France and Germany had learned that the costs of war outweighed any possible benefit. Besides, now Soviet power overloomed them both, and the perception of common threat did much to encourage cooperation.

But Yoshida Shigeru and South Korea's president Syngman Rhee were two old men who could hardly bear to be in the same room together. Nor did the perception of common threat do much to foster rapprochement between Japan and its former colony. There was too much visceral instinct and history, dating back to Hideyoshi's efforts to invade China via Korea and the murder of Queen Min. Thus, despite intense American pressure, South Korea and Japan did not even establish diplomatic relations until 1965.[7]

The first Indochina War

Naturally, the creation of the US alliance framework in East Asia did not deter communist efforts to outflank it. In Southeast Asia in the 1950s, the communists achieved their greatest success in Vietnam, where strategic geography favoured them much more than in maritime Southeast Asia. Like North Korea, Vietnam shared a border with China. China's logistical help was critical to the success of the communist Vietminh when they defeated French forces in 1954 at Dien Bien Phu, near North Vietnam's border with Laos.

Nevertheless, the Vietminh proved unable to reap all the rewards of victory. Under pressure from Russia and China, Ho Chi Minh was denied his main objective – the forcible unification of Indochina under communist rule. At the Geneva conference in 1954, Vietnam was 'temporarily' divided along the seventeenth parallel, with the southern part remaining non-communist. Ho was denied the full fruits of victory because China did not want a powerful united Vietnam on its southern borders. Moreover, Ho and many of the other Vietnamese revolutionaries had long-standing links with Moscow, evoking China's mistrust. Thus Stalin's preference before 1949 for a subservient, divided China on his eastern borders had its counterpoint in Mao's preference for a subservient and divided Vietnam on his southern frontier.

The South East Asia Treaty Organization

With North Vietnam having fallen under communist control, the United States moved to shore up the rest of Southeast Asia by means of the 1954 Manila Treaty. SEATO (South East Asia Treaty Organization) was the organization that gave effect to security cooperation under the Manila Treaty. Members included the United States, Britain, France, Australia, New Zealand, the Philippines, Thailand and Pakistan. In addition, British Commonwealth forces committed to SEATO were based in Malaya and Singapore.

It has become a commonplace to assert that SEATO failed. If SEATO's purpose was to prevent Hanoi from taking over South Vietnam, as it eventually did in 1975, then indeed SEATO failed. Certainly, SEATO was no

NATO, because the Manila Treaty obligations were much less than those under NATO. One problem was that the Southeast Asian countries, like Australia and New Zealand, had little defence capacity. Thus, drawing them into a defence treaty risked overextension by vastly expanding US commitments, without gaining any worthwhile force increments.

And from the outset, one large source of weakness was the non-membership of Indonesia, *primus inter pares* in Southeast Asia. Nevertheless, at a critical time for Southeast Asia, SEATO succeeded in its well-advertised aim of deterring general Chinese aggression. No doubt the Chinese knew that SEATO planning provided for the use of nuclear weapons – and the Chinese were meant to know, there being no more credible intelligence than a genuine military plan. Thus SEATO helped these fragile states emerging from colonial rule to get on their feet by reassuring them that the communist powers would not be allowed to pick them off one by one.

The first Taiwan Strait crisis

On 3 September 1954, while Dulles was in Manila making final arrangements for SEATO, Chinese batteries opened up on Jinmen (Quemoy), a Nationalist island redoubt practically in the harbour of Xiamen (Amoy). Thus Mao precipitated a crisis, apparently intending to dissuade the United States from including Taiwan in SEATO.[8]

The other *Guomindang* island redoubts were Mazu (Matsu) off Fuzhou (Foochow), and the Dachens and other specks of islands further north just off the Chinese coast. More than 50,000 soldiers were on Jinmen alone, comprising one quarter of Jiang Jieshi's best troops. Lacking much of a grip on reality, Jiang intended to use them as stepping stones for the re-conquest of China.

In January 1955, Communist forces overwhelmed Nationalist soldiers on an island just north of the Dachens. Congress then passed the 'Formosa Resolution', giving Eisenhower a blank cheque. Three US aircraft carrier battle groups were sent to the Taiwan Strait, and the option of using nuclear weapons was openly canvassed. America's European allies grew nervous. It is always hard to deter opponents without frightening one's allies, and never more so when nuclear weapons are part of the equation. But beneath the bluff, Eisenhower and Dulles were not willing to let Jiang Jieshi determine whether or not the United States went to war with China. Thus Jiang was pressured to remove his forces from the Dachens. For its part, China did not want another war with the United States. In April, Zhou Enlai announced at the Bandung non-aligned conference in Indonesia that China did not seek war, and the crisis subsided.

Whatever Mao's motives in provoking this crisis, its consequences hardly served his interests. In December 1954, the United States made a security commitment to Taiwan that it had previously refused to consider. Moreover, the Taiwan Strait crisis ended with Dulles having driven a wedge between China and Russia by dangling the carrot of détente at Moscow, while threatening China with nuclear weapons.

Growing tensions between Russia and China

On the surface, all was well between China and Russia. Nikita Khrushchev, first secretary of the Soviet communist party, visited China in September–October 1954. His main purpose was to secure China's support in the power struggle in the Kremlin after the death of Stalin. During his visit, Khrushchev signed a number of agreements and agreed to return the Soviet military bases at Lushun.

Still, tensions were beginning to rise. Despite Khrushchev's support for China in the Taiwan Strait crisis, he saw no interest at stake there that justified the risk of nuclear war with America. Moreover, Mao affected a cavalier disregard of the risks of nuclear war. China's population was so large, and its birth-rate so high, he said, that it could afford to lose millions in a nuclear exchange. That kind of talk was beginning to worry the Kremlin.

Sputnik and the global 'correlation of forces'

Still, both China and Russia became emboldened when, in October 1957, the Soviets launched the *Sputnik* satellite. It was not the 184-pound payload that was important, but the improvements in launch capacity that had been revealed, and hence America's vulnerability to nuclear attack. The Soviets had harnessed the two most formidable military technologies of the Second World War: the atomic bomb, and the ballistic missile – successor to Hitler's V2 rocket (his V1, the 'buzz bomb', was the original cruise missile).

The Eisenhower administration's response to *Sputnik* included the development of the US strategic triad – the Strategic Air Command's fleet of B-52 bombers; land-based Intercontinental Ballistic Missiles (ICBMs); and the nuclear-powered ballistic missile submarines (SSBNs). This strategic triad made US nuclear forces invulnerable to destruction by a decapitating Soviet first strike. The earliest generation of SSBNs was the *Polaris*, the first of which went to sea in December 1960. Of the US strategic triad, the SSBN component was the most secure because it was the hardest to find.

Japan's nuclear allergies

But by this time, changes in America's global strategic posture were inadvertently playing into Moscow's hands because they had the effect of increasing nuclear fears among US allies. Eisenhower's 'New Look' defence policy called for cuts in conventional weapons to be offset by increased reliance on nuclear weapons. Thus, in July 1955, Washington announced that the US Army would deploy atomic cannon on Okinawa. Okinawa, where US bases were heavily concentrated, was administered by the US Army. Having paid a heavy price in blood for Okinawa in 1945, America had detached the island from Japan under the terms of the peace treaty – although Japan retained 'residual sovereignty'. Under the terms of the mutual security treaty, the US military enjoyed *carte blanche* everywhere in Japan, but nowhere more so than on Okinawa.

Still, the outcry about the introduction of nuclear weapons to the island showed that public opinion in Japan, the only country to have suffered a nuclear attack, could no longer be ignored. In 1954, a Japanese fishing boat had been irradiated in the South Pacific by fallout from a US hydrogen bomb test, and a fisherman died. In response to the uproar, prime minister Hatoyama Ichiro released a statement saying that US ambassador John Allison had agreed with foreign minister Shigemitsu Mamoru that the United States would 'consult' the Japanese government before bringing nuclear weapons into Japan.

By this time, Japan's growing nuclear allergies were providing new opportunities for the Kremlin to foster unarmed neutrality in Japan. Throughout the Cold War, the Soviet Union sought to achieve an unarmed neutral Japan that it could control by virtue of proximity – an eastern counterpoint to Soviet ambitions to achieve a reunited neutral Germany that would be subject to Soviet dictates. Thus Moscow sought to convince the Japanese public that American (but not Soviet) nuclear weapons represented an unacceptable threat. The Soviets argued that their nuclear weapons had been deployed in response to those of the United States, and would be removed if American ones were taken away. The logical consequences of that, of course, were never spelled out. If both superpowers had removed their nuclear weapons, Japan (like Germany) would be vulnerable to Soviet assertions of hegemony based on proximity. In 1955, the coming to power of the Japanese Gaullists provided Moscow with new opportunities for undermining the US–Japan security treaty.

Moscow: fostering neutralism in Japan

In October 1954, Yoshida's rival Hatoyama had brought down Yoshida and formed a government with Socialist support. His ambition was to rival Yoshida's achievements by establishing diplomatic relations with the Soviet Union and China, which would give Japan more leverage with the United States. Seizing its opportunity, Moscow proposed a deal encompassing the neutralization of Japan. Soon Molotov, still foreign minister, was touting the virtues of the 'Adenauer formula'.[9]

By this the Soviets meant the normalization of diplomatic relations, while setting aside territorial issues. That is what West Germany and the Soviet Union had done in September 1955. In talks in Moscow, Adenauer had rebuffed the key Soviet demand, which was to recognize the Oder–Neisse border between East Germany and Poland. That would have legitimized the

Red Army's creation of 'facts on the ground' in 1944–1945. But Adenauer wanted to secure the return of West German prisoners of war. He was also somewhat isolated from his allies by the so-called 'spirit of détente' that Stalin's successors had been fostering. That gave Moscow much leverage, and so Adenauer had to agree to establish diplomatic relations, even though that helped to legitimize Moscow's rickety surrogate regime in East Germany.

Then Molotov, with the 'Adenauer formula' in his pocket, used it to pressure Japan. Soviet–Japanese relations could be normalized, he said, if the territorial dispute were set aside. To ratchet up the pressure, the Soviets again voted to keep Japan out of the United Nations, and announced new fishing restrictions in the North Pacific. In Moscow, in July 1956, foreign minister Shigemitsu suddenly caved in to Soviet demands, agreeing to a peace treaty accompanied by the return of only the Habomais and Shikotan (the smaller islands which Japan had always regarded as part of Hokkaido). Apparently Shigemitsu hoped that this deal would meet such acclaim at home that he could secure the prime ministership to succeed the ailing Hatoyama. It was a good example of how political ambitions can have an impact on foreign policy. But Shigemitsu had no remit to broker such a deal. It was all rather reminiscent of how Stalin had manipulated Matsuoka Yosuke in the spring of 1941, as Molotov no doubt remembered. Japanese decision-making processes had not improved much in the interim.

With these opportunistic Japanese politicians in disarray, Dulles had to step in. He told Shigemitsu, in order to bolster his position in negotiations with Moscow, that if Japan gave up its claims to the bigger islands (Etorofu and Kunashiri) the United States might feel obliged to retain Okinawa in perpetuity.[10] No Japanese government could survive that. With Shigemitsu sidelined, Hatoyama himself led a delegation to Moscow. In October 1956, a Joint Declaration terminated the state of war between Japan and the Soviet Union, and restored diplomatic relations. Moscow promised to return Shikotan and the Habomais, but only after a peace treaty had been signed. The Soviets then stopped blocking Japan's admission to the United Nations. Japanese prisoners of war were also returned from their Siberian labour camps, where some 60,000 out of an estimated 600,000 had died in captivity.

Soviet relations with Japan did not improve much. Had Moscow been willing to compromise on the territorial issue, it might have been able to exploit Japan's nuclear allergies in order to drive a wedge between America and Japan. But Stalin's successors were not going to give up the territorial gains he had made. Moreover, any compromise on territorial issues with Japan might open a Pandora's box elsewhere, including in China and Europe.

Still, for alliance managers in Tokyo and Washington, Moscow's efforts to promote unarmed neutrality in Japan pointed to the need to revise the security treaty in order to put it on a more sustainable basis. It was untenable over the longer term for Japan to continue to be party to a treaty that had been imposed on it during the Occupation, when Japan had been in no position to say no. The 1950 treaty had no escape clause or termination date, and it gave the United States *carte blanche* in relation to nuclear weapons.

The 1960 revision of the US–Japan security treaty

Revision of the security treaty was achieved during the administration of Kishi Nobusuke, who became prime minister in 1957. From Japan's perspective, the new treaty represented a considerable improvement on the old. It was to run for ten years, after which it could be abrogated by either party on one year's notice. Thus, after 1970, Japan would be able to 'say no' if it chose to do so.

The United States would no longer enjoy the *carte blanche* it had been given in the original treaty. Although Japan wished to codify the 1955 Shigemitsu–Allison understanding, the United States would not agree to this wording in the text of the treaty. But in an exchange of notes accompanying the treaty (signed by Kishi and US Secretary of State Christian Herter) the parties agreed that major changes to US military equipment in Japan – understood to include the introduction of nuclear weapons – were subject to 'prior consultations'.

In contrast to the 1951 treaty, Japan was explicitly afforded American security protection. Article V of the 1960 treaty says that 'Each Party recognizes that an armed attack against either Party in the territories under the administration of Japan would be dangerous to its own peace and safety and declares that it would act to meet the common danger in accordance with its constitutional provisions and processes.'

For Japan, there were some negatives in the new treaty, notably that Japan was supposed to take action to be able defend itself against external attack. But as has been noted, Japanese governments had comprehended from the onset of the Cold War that that any attack on Japan would involve an attack on US bases there. So Japan was not inclined to respond to US pressure to spend more on defence.

The new treaty also met America's essential security needs. The 'prior consultation' clause in the Kishi–Herter notes could be read as permitting the introduction of nuclear weapons into Japan in an emergency. Article VI of the treaty said that 'for the purposes of contributing to the security of Japan and the maintenance of international peace and security in the Far East, the United States of America is granted the use by its land, air and naval forces of facilities and areas in Japan'. Thus it was understood that Japan would not impede the use of American facilities in Japan for wider Western Pacific security purposes.

Moreover, the treaty documents explicitly acknowledged that the security of the Korean peninsula was critical to the security of Japan. In another set of notes, exchanged on 19 January 1960, the United States and Japan continued the 1951 agreements by which the Japanese government had pledged itself to permit the use of US bases in Japan for the support of the United Nations Command in Korea. In the 1960 notes, this pledge was affirmed and placed within the framework of the new treaty.

Even though the new treaty was much more favourable to Japan than the old, there were widespread demonstrations against it. Riots, which led to the accidental death of a student, prevented President Eisenhower from visiting Japan, and the Kishi cabinet was forced to resign. These protests were aimed partly at the prime minister, for reasons of his background as a member of the pre-war 'Manchurian clique'.[11] Still, even though Kishi had had to fall on his sword, the US–Japan security relationship had been put on a more sustainable basis. And as the economy continued to soar, those in Japan sympathetic to Soviet and Chinese interests found themselves increasingly sidelined.

Following this setback, the Soviets resorted to bluster by declaring null and void the territorial concessions 'promised' in the 1956 Joint Declaration. Moreover, the Soviets added another condition – now even Shikotan and the Habomais would not be returned until all foreign forces had been withdrawn from Japanese soil, and a peace treaty had been concluded between Japan and the Soviet Union.

And in an effort to intimidate Japan, the Soviets tested ICBMs over the Japanese islands, and showered Japan with radioactive fallout from their nuclear tests.[12] Soviet-backed 'peace' groups also sought to ensure that Japan was permanently prevented from acquiring nuclear weapons by tying any 'anti-nuclear' policies to the constitution, which was difficult to alter. But the Kishi government firmly rebuffed this attempt to hobble Japan. Thus, contrary to what many Japanese and foreigners believed, the Japanese constitution did not prevent Japan from acquiring nuclear weapons.

Management of nuclear issues in the US–Japan alliance was also facilitated by the advent of the *Polaris* SSBN. Soon America deployed *Polaris* submarines capable of targeting the Soviet Far East from submerged firing positions in the Sea of Japan. So the United States had no need to station medium-range nuclear missiles in Japan, as it did in Europe in order to reassure its nervous allies in the wake of *Sputnik*. Those SSBNs did not need to enter Japanese ports, though their support vessels often did. Thus the strategic geography of the Japanese islands reduced Moscow's ability to play on nuclear fears in Japan. Moreover, by this time, a further negative for Moscow was that the vast island continent of Australia had been drawn into the central nuclear balance on America's side – as another indirect consequence of *Sputnik* and *Polaris*.

Australia: bringing the island continent into the central balance

Hitherto, the United States had believed that Australia was too far south to be of much relevance to the global balance. But after the *Polaris* programme was accelerated, Australia's long Indian Ocean coastline became a strategic asset for America. *Polaris* submarines carried sixteen nuclear missiles that could reach targets more than 1,000 nautical miles away. Thus these SSBNs were able to target the 'soft underbelly' of the Soviet Union – including the 'secret cities' forming the heart of the military–industrial complex east of the Urals – from submerged firing positions in the northern reaches of the Indian Ocean. *Polaris* could also target Xinjiang, where China had started to build nuclear testing facilities at Lop Nor in 1959.[13] *Polaris* required the establishment of Very Low Frequency (VLF) communications facilities in the Indian Ocean region. Given the broad expanses of that ocean, Australia was a logical choice to host these facilities. In 1962, the Australian government agreed to the establishment of VLF communications facilities at the barren and remote North West Cape in Western Australia.

By the early 1980s, the deployment of longer-range *Trident* SSBNs made North West Cape unnecessary for communication with submarines. But the station had other uses. And by that time, Australia had become even more of a strategic asset for the United States. This was a consequence of the development of satellite technology. In 1969, Nurrungar in central Australia became the only ground station outside the United States for the Defense Support Program (DSP) satellites that detected missile launches.

For the United States and Australia, the establishment of these 'joint facilities' at Nurrungar, and at Pine Gap (also in Central Australia), entailed risks for both parties.[14] The United States became dependent on the fortunes of a foreign government for facilities vital to its strategic security. What if the host pulled the plug, possibly at a critical moment? For Australia, there were also risks, because the Soviet Union could play on nuclear fears in Australia. But for both parties, the advantages of establishing these facilities far outweighed the risks and costs. Australia thus made a large contribution to the command, communications, intelligence and control structure that sustained Western deterrence and broad international security during the Cold War.

And while Australia was being more closely integrated into the US alliance structure, Khrushchev had become ever more aware of the limitations of the Soviet Union's strategic geography, and keen to redress these problems.

The limitations of Soviet strategic geography

Khrushchev, after his 1954 visit to China, had seen for himself the limitations of Vladivostok, and wanted it moved.[15] Khrushchev was interested in maritime power, as shown in 1955 by his appointing admiral Sergei Gorshkov – Russia's answer to Mahan – as Soviet naval commander. As Khrushchev saw, the Soviet empire suffered from the same geographical limitations as its tsarist predecessor.

Even the gains that Stalin had made had not produced the break-out to the open sea that Russia had so long sought. In the Black Sea, Turkey was an American ally guarding both sides of the straits that led into the Mediterranean. In Europe, the Soviet Union still had no warm-water port with open access to the Atlantic. The Baltic remained bottled up by Denmark's membership of NATO. In the far north, Murmansk was icebound in winter. Moreover, to break out into the Atlantic, Soviet warships had to penetrate the NATO barrier in the Greenland–Iceland–United Kingdom (GIUK) gap.

In the Far East, the Soviet Union still faced the same constrictions as it had in the 1904–1905 war. The Japanese archipelago blocked all the exits from Vladivostok, which was in any case icebound for three months each year. Petropavlovsk, the only Soviet base with access to the open sea, was also icebound in winter. Moreover, it could not be supported by land forces because it was on the isolated Kamchatka peninsula, as the Russians had discovered when they were bombarded by Anglo–French forces during the Crimean War. Moreover, these northern waters are often fogbound and treacherous even in summer.

But Russia possessed an asset that Lenin would have envied. Now the Soviets had an alliance with China. If the great Eurasian land powers could combine their resources, they could outflank the United States and its allies. Thus access to China's coastline would overcome the limitations of Soviet strategic geography in the Far East.

Developing the Eurasian bloc: cooperation with China

In order to bolster the Sino–Soviet bloc, Khrushchev boosted technological and military cooperation with China. By means of an agreement signed on 15 October 1957 – just after the *Sputnik* launch – the Soviets agreed to a sharing of nuclear arms and missile technology with China as part of Khrushchev's attempt to integrate China into Soviet global strategy. Vast amounts of technological information were given to China, including a sample medium-range ballistic missile (minus its warhead), a G-class ballistic missile submarine without its missiles, and TU-16 jet bombers.[16] Chinese nuclear scientists were trained in Russia, and Soviet nuclear weapons experts were sent to China. Stalin must have been spinning in his grave.

For his part, Mao had also been emboldened by *Sputnik*. At the fortieth anniversary celebration in Moscow of the Bolshevik revolution, in November 1957, he proclaimed that the East Wind was starting to prevail over the West Wind. But unbeknown to Moscow, Mao had ambitions of his own. In January 1955 China had decided to build its own nuclear weapons.[17]

Still, on the surface, relations remained unruffled. Khrushchev had agreed to return the South Manchurian ports to China, and they were handed over in the following year.[18] So Khrushchev proposed to Mao that they build a 'joint fleet', and that China afford the Soviet Union access to its coasts for his future submarines.[19] The Soviet leader also wanted 'radar facilities' on the Chinese coast for his submarines operating in the Pacific and Indian Oceans. In the light of the extensive help that Russia was giving China, Khrushchev did not expect Mao to refuse.

Rising tensions between Russia and China

But beneath the surface, tensions were rising. China resented the price it had paid to save North Korea, only to see Russia become dominant there. Mao also saw Khrushchev's attacks on Stalin, designed to bolster Khrushchev's position within the Soviet communist party, as attacks on Mao's own position. And while Mao had respected and feared Stalin, for the blustering Khrushchev he had only contempt. Nor had Mao any reason to think that China would be encouraged to command a 'joint fleet' – or to believe that there would be a Chinese finger on the nuclear button of any future 'joint' nuclear forces.

Khrushchev, oblivious to Mao's smouldering resentment, was surprised when the Chinese rejected his initial approach for access to their ports. That rebuff sent the Soviet leader scurrying to Beijing in late July 1958. In his meetings with Mao, he noted that Mao had welcomed suggestions that the Soviet Union and China should coordinate their naval efforts in case of war. He went on to talk about the limitations of Murmansk, the Baltic and the Black Sea. Vladivostok, he said, was better, 'but there as well we are squeezed by Sakhalin and the Kuril Islands – they defend us, but also allow the enemy's submarines to monitor the exit of our submarines'. Yet China, Khrushchev noted, had a long coastline with access to the open seas. It would be much easier for Moscow to conduct the submarine war with America from China's coasts.

Mao provokes another Taiwan crisis

But Mao rejected Khrushchev's proposal. Only three years after the Soviets had left the Manchurian ports, Mao saw this as an intolerable affront to China's sovereignty. Khrushchev had barely left Beijing when Mao provoked another crisis in the Taiwan Strait. This was linked to his disastrous Great Leap Forward, a crash programme of industrialization. The Great Leap symbolized Mao's determination to break free of the Soviet connection, and to defeat his internal opponents. The famine caused by his disastrous policies caused at least thirty million deaths.

Nor was it a coincidence that China started shelling Taiwan's offshore islands on 22 August, one day after Eisenhower had publicly invited the Soviets to negotiate a limited ban on nuclear testing. Mao saw this as an example of superpower collusion. And it was soon obvious that, as in the first Taiwan Strait crisis, Khrushchev saw no interest that justified the risk of nuclear war with America.

The Sino–Soviet split widens

By 1959, Sino–Soviet relations had become acrimonious. The first public signs of a rift appeared that year, when the Chinese press started to criticise 'modern revisionists'. The schism was also visible when Moscow expressed mere 'regret' in relation to the first skirmishes between Indian and Chinese troops that were to lead to the 1962 'border war'.[20] The Chinese were furious at the lack of support from their supposed ally. In 1960, Khrushchev withdrew all Soviet advisers from China.

When the USSR signed a limited nuclear test ban treaty with the Kennedy administration in 1963, China denounced the treaty as a 'dirty fraud' designed to preserve the superpowers' nuclear monopoly. The Sino–Soviet bloc was no more. From there it was downhill all the way to the brink of war in 1969. Soon these great communist land powers, each with far flung and insecure peripheries, were seeking to outflank each other. Over time, the terms of engagement of their struggle widened to encompass Southeast Asia, Central Asia, the Indian subcontinent, the further reaches of the Indian Ocean and even Africa.

The schism might have provided opportunities for the United States to drive a wedge between the communist powers, as Acheson had tried to do before the Korean War. But American policy-makers were unconvinced that the Sino–Soviet split was more than the fraud that Jiang Jieshi said it was. Rapprochement became even less likely after Mao began his Cultural Revolution in 1965 and started to pursue a revolutionary foreign policy pointed equally at Washington and Moscow. Moreover, it was virtually impossible for a Democrat president to make an opening towards China. And soon America became mired in another land war in East Asia, this time in Vietnam. Once again, China was on the other side.

'Limited war' in Vietnam: a US own goal

The drain of the Vietnam War weakened US resolve and bargaining power, encouraging the notion of 'détente' with Moscow. Thus, once again, for the Soviet Union the war was all gain and no pain. Indeed, from the outset, Soviet strategy sought to embroil America in a debilitating conflict. Moscow also hoped that the war would generate sufficient danger on China's southern flank that Beijing would see no choice but to reach painful accommodation with Moscow.[21]

Thus, when North Vietnamese forces broke into the presidential compound in Saigon in April 1975, they did so in Soviet-supplied tanks. During the war, about 80 per cent of Hanoi's military supplies came from Russia, via the ports of Haiphong and Sihanoukville in Cambodia. These supplies were indispensable to Hanoi's eventual victory. Yet the myth persists that the conflict was a 'guerrilla war' derived from local grievances, and that the United States was defeated by a peasant army.

The purpose of America's intervention in Vietnam was to prevent the communist north from taking over the anti-communist south after the two states had been divided at Geneva in 1954. America also aimed to block China's ambitions to the south. Moreover, it sought to keep Southeast Asia out of the communist orbit in order that its resources and markets be kept open for Japan.

The Kennedy administration connived at the assassination of the South Vietnamese president Ngo Dinh Diem, after key US officials thought he had become a political liability.[22] But thereafter America was unable to find a reliable and effective partner in Saigon. In November 1963, Lyndon B. Johnson inherited the war after Kennedy was assassinated. Johnson had two choices. He could have declared victory and gone home, arguing that America should not become embroiled in a land war in Asia when the main game was in Europe. Or he could have chosen to fight the war in Clausewitzian fashion – comprehending that victory is won by the concentration of force in time and space. Among other things, that would have encompassed cutting off the communists' supply lines.

But Johnson fell between two stools. He opted to fight the war, mostly because he did not want to be blamed by the Republicans for 'losing' Vietnam, as Truman was still being blamed for having 'lost' China'. But Johnson also feared the impact of the war on his 'Great Society' plans at home. So he downplayed the conflict, and did not call up the reserves. Thus America opted not only to fight another land war in Asia, but to do so with one arm tied behind its back. The Japanese, recalling their own disastrous 'holy war' in China, tried in vain to warn of the risks of quagmire.

For example, Johnson continually assured Hanoi's communist backers that he would neither widen the war nor threaten the viability of North Vietnam. This was mostly because US policy-makers were haunted by fear of a replay of China's entry into the Korean War. But Johnson's assurances meant that the communist powers had no incentive to restrain Vietnam, and every reason to encourage it.

The Vietnam War also revealed the hollowness of the 'limited war' theories espoused by American liberals such as the Defense Secretary, Robert McNamara. He believed in the 'controlled' use of force designed to elicit 'cooperative' responses from the enemy. The problem with this idea, as with the liberals' approach to arms control, was that the enemy was interested not in cooperating, but in winning. Thus the United States fell into the trap of constantly telling the enemy what it would *not* do – bomb Hanoi or Haiphong, mine the harbours, or mine the dykes and flood the countryside. So the bombing campaign was merely 'tit for tat', responding to communist initiatives in the south. That permitted North Vietnam to use its ancient corvée system to repair dykes and public works, to meet the bombing threat as it increased. Meanwhile, Soviet-supplied anti-aircraft and missile batteries took an increasing toll of US pilots.

Unlike the United States, North Vietnam was a totalitarian state willing to endure endless casualties. In order to limit its own losses, America began to use ugly weapons such as napalm, as well as defoliant chemicals meant to deprive the enemy of jungle cover. Moreover, this was the first conflict shown on television, which brought home to the American public the ugliness of war. And as the casualties mounted, and the strategic interest that was at stake remained fuzzy, opposition intensified. For the United States and its East Asian allies, there were few bright spots during this period. One of them was the rapprochement between South Korea and Japan.

Rapprochement between South Korea and Japan

The improvement in South Korean–Japanese relations was made possible by political changes in both countries, plus the growing sense of common threat after China's nuclear weapons test in 1964. Syngman Rhee was overthrown by riots in 1960, and replaced by a short-lived civilian government. Then, in 1961, the army took over in a coup led by Colonel Park Chung Hee, a graduate of the Japanese military academy in Manchuria. In late 1964, Sato Eisaku, Kishi's younger brother, became Japan's prime minister. His foreign minister, Shiina Etsusaburo, another member of the pre-war Manchurian clique, was given the job of effecting the rapprochement with Seoul. The old *Manchukuo* connections proved useful.

Even though Shiina made a statement of 'regret' about Japan's occupation of Korea, there was still much visceral dislike on both sides. Thus the establishment of diplomatic relations was accompanied by riots in both countries. Moreover, a dispute over the Takeshima/Tokdo Islands in the Tsushima Strait was not resolved. Still, growing economic interdependence helped ameliorate tensions. The infusion into South Korea of Japanese aid (disguised reparations), capital and technology helped an economic take-off, much as the Korean War had earlier lifted the Japanese economy. In Japan, South Korea found market niches vacated as the Japanese moved up the product/technology ladder. Moreover, the Korean *chaebols* followed the Japanese cartel model. Soon much of South Korea's trade was flowing through Japanese trading companies. South Korea's economic take-off also did much to reduce the burden on the United States. Thus the US position in North Asia had been shored up – just as maritime Southeast Asia was coming to the boil.

Bringing Indonesia to the boil – just in time

One of the few positive consequences of the Vietnam War was that it bought time for the Great Game to be played out in Indonesia in ways that fed back into the central balance because it underpinned the security of maritime Southeast Asia. American, British and Australian policy in Indonesia was a high-risk but high-return enterprise. In the mid-1960s, China seemed to be winning the competition for influence in Indonesia, using as its instrument the Indonesian communist party, the PKI, proponent of the Jakarta–Peking axis. Had the PKI succeeded in securing the succession to Sukarno, China would have gained a foothold in the Southeast Asian straits.

By this time, China was in the early stages of Mao's Cultural Revolution. China was also emboldened by its test of a nuclear weapon in October 1964. Sukarno, seeking distraction from his economic failures, was not disciplined enough to be a communist. But he drifted ever leftwards. In 1963, the formation of the federation of Malaysia provided new opportunities for China to exploit the opportunities presented by Indonesia's turmoil.

Britain, in fostering the formation of Malaysia, wanted to combine the predominantly Chinese city-state of Singapore with Malaya, and add the British Borneo territories as well. That would complete the decolonization of Singapore, deflecting leftist pressures there, while at the same time avoiding a Chinese ethnic majority in the federation. China, seeking to outflank the Western powers, denounced Malaysia as a neo-colonialist plot. So did Sukarno, noisily backed by the PKI. Indonesia's 'confrontation' of Malaysia aimed to divert the attention of the Indonesian army to the task of fighting Malaysian, British and Australian forces on Borneo. The PKI hoped thereby to gain more leverage over the presidential succession, which would be played out on the main island of Java.[23]

China supplied arms, via the Indonesian air force, intended to equip the PKI's 'fifth force', a new militia meant to protect the party from the Indonesian army, its rival for power. The air force was heavily infiltrated by the PKI at leadership level, including its commander. The army was divided. In December 1964, to applause from Beijing, Indonesia left the UN because Malaysia had been elected to a non-permanent seat on the Security Council. Malaysian diplomats skilfully used their membership of the non-aligned movement to garner support and isolate Indonesia. But these efforts proved insufficient to keep Malaysia and Singapore together once racially-based tensions boiled over. To prevent widespread violence, Singapore was expelled from Malaysia in August 1965.

But Beijing had little time to celebrate. Tensions in Indonesia were at fever pitch because of the PKI's efforts to promote land reform on Java, often at the expense of Muslim landlords, as well as its attempts to establish its armed militia. After six generals were murdered by communists on the night of 30 September–1 October 1965, an attempted PKI coup was thwarted. Then the Indonesian armed forces launched a crackdown. General Suharto, who commanded the troops in the capital, emerged from obscurity. Sukarno was eventually forced to step down, though he was not put on trial. His overthrow was indeed a bloody affair. This was because the stakes were so high – nothing less than China's control of Indonesia's vast resources and strategic position on the Southeast Asian straits. Had the PKI come to power, the carnage would probably have been even greater, as suggested by the genocide in Cambodia when China-backed communists took power there in 1975.

By 1967, Suharto's New Order had cemented itself in power, its non-aligned foreign policy leaning as much to the West as Sukarno's had tilted towards China. Aid and investment from Japan and the West began to pour into Indonesia. This helped foster economic development, as well as significant improvements in income distribution. Suharto, while no democrat, soon legitimized his regime by virtue of its economic performance.

Moreover, in 1967 the political transformation of Indonesia facilitated the creation of ASEAN, the Association of Southeast Asian Nations. Thus maritime Southeast Asia was stabilized because Indonesia had been brought into civilized relations with its neighbours. And in the nick of time. For, by 1968, America was beginning to sound the retreat in Vietnam.

Vietnam: the Nixon Doctrine sounds the retreat

North Vietnam's *Tet* offensive during the holiday season in February 1968 marked the turning point of the war. While the offensive failed to produce the general uprising that the communists had expected in South Vietnam, it yielded a huge political dividend in the United States and other foreign countries. The Vietnamese politburo appreciated that the war had to be fought with a view to influencing US public opinion in ways that would help the communists gain power, not least by equating this objective with 'national independence'. Thus, after *Tet*, the American public began to question whether the war was being won. As a result President Johnson announced that he would not run for re-election.

Thereafter, US policy was driven by the need to get out of Vietnam. In January 1969, Richard Nixon came to office pledging to find a way out, and in May the first withdrawals of US troops began. In July Nixon, on a tour of Southeast Asia, gave a news conference in Guam where he announced what came to be known as the Nixon Doctrine. The United States would continue to hold a nuclear umbrella over its allies, he said, but would expect them to shoulder more of the burden of their own defence. It was a fig leaf for withdrawal from Vietnam. America's enemies hoped it was a harbinger of a wider retreat from East Asia.

North Korea becomes emboldened

Thus the Stalinist regime in North Korea became emboldened. In early January 1968, North Korean commandos penetrated to the Blue House, the residence of the South Korean president, in an unsuccessful attempt to assassinate President Park Chung Hee. Presumably to distract attention from the outcry that ensued, the North Koreans seized the USS *Pueblo*, an unarmed intelligence-gathering ship, in international waters off Wonsan.

For fear of war, the Johnson administration declined South Korean requests for retaliatory strikes against Pyongyang. The aircraft carrier *Enterprise* was sent to the Japan Sea, but that did little to intimidate the North Koreans. In order to get the *Pueblo*'s crewmen back, the United States was forced to sign an apology. Then, in April 1969, North Korean MiG fighters shot down an unarmed US EC-121 reconnaissance aircraft over international waters ninety miles off the North Korean coast, killing all thirty crew members. Another tepid US response, this time by the Nixon administration, showed how much the Vietnam conflict was causing strategic paralysis in Washington. The behaviour of America's European allies told the same story.

US allies wobble: *Ostpolitik*

Partly as a consequence of widespread opposition in Europe to the Vietnam War, the notion of 'moral equivalence' between the superpowers became widely held at this time – even though Soviet tanks had crushed a reformist Communist regime in Prague in 1968, and a worker's revolt in Poland was put down in 1970. In September 1969 the newly-elected West German Social Democratic government of Willy Brandt began to pursue an accommodationist line to Moscow, known as *Ostpolitik* or 'Eastern policy'.

Ostpolitik reflected calculations that German interests might best be served by manoeuvring between the superpowers – a reversion to Bismarck's 'zigzag' politics that Adenauer had so dreaded. Seeking to anchor West Germany in the West, Adenauer had demanded reunification of Germany on the basis of free elections, as a precondition of any German détente with Moscow. But no free election had ever been held in the east. Moreover, in 1961 the Berlin Wall had been built to prevent East Germans from escaping.

Ostpolitik in fact had its roots in the 1961 Berlin crisis, at Brandt's anger at Kennedy's initially supine response to the building of the Wall. (At the time, Brandt had been mayor of West Berlin.) Pursuit of *Ostpolitik* saw Brandt sign two treaties in 1970 – the Moscow Treaty and the Warsaw Treaty. Thus West Germany gave up claims to Polish territory east of the Oder–Neisse line, and to the Sudetenland in Czechoslovakia. In affirming these borders, Brandt thus endorsed the territorial gains made by Stalin at the end of the Second World War. The new links between Bonn and Moscow were soon strengthened by West German deliveries of high-technology goods to the Soviet Union, for credit, and Soviet exports of raw materials at low prices.

Thus the Kremlin achieved a large step towards its goal of detaching Western Europe from America and making it dependent on the Soviet Union. Russian military power resting on a European economic base would give the USSR undisputed global hegemony. It would in effect achieve Hitler's ambition when, having conquered Western Europe, he sought to annex to it the resources and manpower of Russia. Because of West

Germany's importance and centrality, *Ostpolitik* also encouraged other US allies towards pre-emptive capitulation to Moscow.

The Indian Ocean: Britain moves out, Moscow moves in

With Malaysia in the van, ASEAN started to wobble because of the Nixon Doctrine and British withdrawal East of Suez, which began as soon as confrontation was over. The first appearance of Soviet naval vessels in the Indian Ocean also encouraged capitulationist trends. The British had already lost a strategic redoubt in 1956, when Sri Lanka under a left-wing government moved towards non-alignment. So the British Navy had been forced to leave its base at Trincomalee, the finest natural harbour in the Indian Ocean. From 1967 onwards, British withdrawal East of Suez drew the Soviet Navy into the Indian Ocean, not least from Vladivostok.

Moreover, an increasing Soviet naval presence in the Indian Ocean threatened to allow Moscow to plant its foot on the resource jugulars of America's key allies in Western Europe and Japan, and threaten US maritime dominance of the Indian Ocean. By the early 1970s, 30 per cent of America's oil, 80 per cent of Western Europe's, and 90 per cent of Japan's crude oil imports were coming from countries on or near the Persian Gulf.[24]

In 1964, Moscow began to propose the 'neutralization' of the Indian Ocean. Its main target was the British plan to lease the island of Diego Garcia to the United States. Diego Garcia's location made it part of the strategic periphery of both East Asia and Western Europe because it could facilitate American military operations in any direction. In 1965, the British Indian Ocean Territory, whose centrepiece was Diego Garcia, was carved out of soon-to-be-independent Mauritius. Britain paid Mauritius for Diego Garcia, moved out the island's small population, then leased it to the United States.

Thereafter, Diego Garcia became critical for American maritime strategy in the Persian Gulf and the Western Pacific. It thus became a key propaganda target of the Soviet Union and India (after India became a Soviet ally in 1971) as part of their efforts to achieve 'neutralization' of the Indian Ocean.

Managing nuclear problems with Japan

By this time, problems in the US–Japan alliance required renewed attention in Washington. After 1970, the security treaty would be subject to renegotiation, and Japanese nationalists and leftists were demanding the return of Okinawa. In November 1969, a Nixon–Sato summit decided to return the island. By that time, use of the Okinawa bases for Vietnam-related purposes was making the island an ever-more controversial issue in Japanese politics. Even on the main islands of Japan, demonstrations reached new heights during a visit to Sasebo by the US *Enterprise* in January 1968, the first such visit by a nuclear-powered aircraft carrier.

As a result of the Nixon–Sato agreement, Okinawa was returned to Japan under the terms of the existing security treaty. Thus it was returned 'nuclear free'. That meant that the United States lost the right to store nuclear weapons on the island in peacetime. But under the terms of the side notes to the 1960 treaty, the United States retained the right to reintroduce nuclear weapons to Okinawa in an emergency, after 'prior consultation' with the Japanese government.

Thus the return of Okinawa removed an irritant in the US–Japan relationship without impeding US access to bases there, including their use for regional contingencies. 'Automatic' continuation of the security treaty also avoided a confrontation in the Diet such as had occurred in 1960 – as well as the scrutiny that the US Congress might well have given such a lopsided security arrangement by that time.

Japan thus remained a US ally by choice. If Japanese leaders had really believed that nuclear weapons were irrelevant to their security, or represented unacceptable dangers, they could have abrogated the alliance at any time. But the last thing Japan really wanted was to be left to fend for itself in such a dangerous neighbourhood. Moreover, the presence of US *Polaris* submarines in nearby waters facilitated the return of Okinawa 'nuclear free', because the United States had no need to continue to station nuclear weapons on the island. Thus the strategic geography of the Japanese archipelago continued to facilitate the political management of sensitive nuclear issues in the US–Japan alliance.

Regional implications: the 'Korea' and 'Taiwan' clauses

Moreover, these new arrangements extended, *de facto*, the ambit of Article VI of the US–Japan mutual security treaty. If another Korean War were to break out, the United States would need access to bases in Japan in order to reinforce South Korea. But the South Koreans worried that, if Okinawa were returned to Japan, that might make America's use of bases there subject to Japanese approval in a crisis. Anyone with any knowledge of Japan's decision-making processes would quail at that prospect. Thus, in order to reassure Seoul, the Nixon–Sato communiqué contained what came to be known as the 'Korea clause'.

This said that 'the President and the Prime Minister specifically noted the continuing tension over the Korean peninsula. The Prime Minister deeply appreciated the peace-keeping efforts of the United Nations in the area and stated that *the security of the Republic of Korea was essential to Japan's own security*' (emphasis added). This was the first time Japan had acknowledged that its security was linked to that of South Korea.

There was also a 'Taiwan clause' in the 1969 Nixon–Sato communiqué, saying that 'the maintenance of peace and security in the Taiwan Strait was also a most important factor in the security of Japan'. While not as strong as the 'Korea clause', the 'Taiwan clause' was also a milestone because Japan acknowledged a linkage between its own security and that of Taiwan. Moreover, both the 'Korea clause' and the 'Taiwan clause' pointed to the critical importance of Okinawa to US strategy in the Western Pacific.

Not surprisingly, China complained about both clauses. Thus Zhou Enlai made a well publicized visit to Pyongyang, endorsing North Korean aspirations for the 'independent unification of the fatherland'. Zhou may have been playing to the gallery at home, for the power struggle in China was not resolved until the following September. Mao's putative successor Lin Biao (Lin Piao) mounted an unsuccessful coup against Mao, and was killed, supposedly in a plane crash in Mongolia where he was apparently seeking to flee to the Soviet Union. But the last thing China's leaders really wanted was another Korean War. That was even more so because, by 1969, Mao's provocations during the Cultural Revolution had nearly provoked a war with Russia that China could not possibly win.

The 1969 Sino–Soviet border clashes

The Soviet-led Warsaw Pact invasion of Czechoslovakia in 1968 set a disturbing precedent for China – not least because Mao's involvement of mainforce PLA units in the internal power struggles of the Cultural Revolution had weakened China's defences. Meanwhile, the Soviets had been building up their forces along the Sino–Soviet border. Clashes took place in March on the contested island of Damansky/Chenpao in the Ussuri river, when about thirty Russian soldiers were killed. The Russians responded with a massive artillery barrage. Hundreds of border clashes took place in the following months, including along the Xinjiang–Kazakhstan frontier. With Soviet armour in Mongolia visibly threatening Beijing, the Soviets now threatened Mao's grip on power.

Between 1966 and 1968, some forty-five to fifty Soviet divisions were moved to the Far East via the Trans-Siberian Railway.[25] This was a reprise of the way Stalin had built up his forces from 1935 when he had been confronted by the risk of two-front war. The Soviets were anxious that, if border skirmishes grew into a wider conflict, China might interdict the Trans-Siberian, which ran close to the Chinese border for hundreds of miles. The Baikal–Amur Railway, the BAM, took a more inland route, but was far from finished. It had not been forgotten in Moscow that, in 1904, Japan had attacked Russia before the Trans-Siberian Railway was completed.

But what would the Soviets have done next if they had invaded China? The installation of a pro-Moscow government was not in prospect, because Mao was eliminating the pro-Soviet elements in China's communist party and armed forces. By invading China, the USSR would have invited Japan's problems with China from 1937, or Hitler's with Russia. Moreover, by 1969 the US–China rapprochement was under way. If Moscow had attacked China, it would have risked the threat of US nuclear retaliation. Indeed, in October 1969, without making it public, Nixon put the US Strategic Air

Command on nuclear alert. That was almost certainly a response to a newspaper article by the British journalist Victor Lewis, a known KGB mouthpiece. The article threatened that the USSR was prepared to attack China, and was targeting China's nuclear facilities at Lop Nor in Xinjiang.[26] Nixon's response to Moscow's minatory behaviour, modelled on the threatening posture of the Group of Soviet Forces in Germany, showed that the Soviets now risked driving China and the United States together.

US rapprochement with China

Indeed, rising Sino–Soviet tensions, and America's need to extricate itself from the Vietnam morass, provided a growing convergence of strategic interest between the United States and China. Signals were sent to China, for example by the cessation of Seventh Fleet patrols of the Taiwan Strait. China having emerged from its Cultural Revolution, Mao was soon indicating that he was willing to parley. In July 1971, Henry Kissinger, Nixon's National Security Adviser, used the occasion of a visit to Pakistan to make a secret side trip to Beijing.

The beginnings of the Sino–US alignment represented a sea change in the internal order. No comparable shift in the global balance was to occur until the collapse of the Soviet Union in 1991. China and the United States were now willing to sideline their differences in order to rein in the growth of Soviet power that threatened them both. In similar fashion, during the Second World War Britain, the United States and Russia had sunk their differences in order to combine against Germany and Japan.

5   The Cold War: final phase

From 1971 onwards, China and the United States were allies of convenience, with few illusions on either side. China's support for the United States in the event of war with the Soviet Union was never guaranteed. If possible, China would have sat on the mountain top, watching the tigers fight below. With the United States distracted, China might have been tempted to encourage North Korea to invade the south again, hoping to achieve a reunited Korea subservient to China. The turbulence in South Korean politics at the time offered great possibilities.

But the existence of nuclear weapons made this option too dangerous, underlining how the existence of nuclear weapons prevented world war. Thus strategic geography came into its own once more, as China and the United States combined to threaten the Soviet Union with the prospect of two-front war.

An alignment of convenience

While the *de facto* alliance between Washington and Beijing always had its nuances, it served the interests of both parties, not least in relation to Vietnam. Nixon's priority on coming to office was to extricate the United States from the war, which was costing some 15,000 lives a year. It also suited China when America began to pull out of Vietnam. The 1968 *Tet* offensive had brought about an increase in US troop levels, to a peak of 549,500. For China, that raised the worry – whatever the assurances from Washington – that America might seek to invade southern China if war broke out between China and the Soviet Union.

Nixon, having inherited the Vietnam mess from the Democrats, needed China's assurances that it would not come into the Vietnam war, and would *de facto* help America to get out of Vietnam. Nixon's opening to China did much to help isolate North Vietnam, and that forced Hanoi to negotiate seriously. Moreover, rapprochement with China gave the United States greater leverage on Moscow, and that also served to isolate Hanoi.

In addition, by going to Beijing in February 1972, and then to Moscow, Nixon could also cloak himself in the mantle of peacemaker.

That was essential for his hopes for re-election at the end of the year. Nixon also expected to have to escalate the Vietnam War in order to end it. Thus the US incursion into Cambodia in May 1970 was designed to flush out Vietcong sanctuaries along the border, and close the port of Sihanoukville, by which Moscow was supplying the North Vietnamese and their allies in the south. But the Cambodian foray caused outrage at home, not least when four students were killed by the National Guard at Kent State University.

Nixon's opening to China did help secure his re-election in 1972. Moreover, neither China nor Russia moved a muscle when Nixon intensified the bombing of North Vietnam, and extended it to include Haiphong harbour in December 1972 – in order to force Vietnam back to the bargaining table in Paris. Even though some Soviet merchant seamen were killed, the Russians had wider concerns, especially the Anti Ballistic Missile (ABM) Treaty which they hoped would hobble US missile technology. With both Sihanoukville and Haiphong closed, North Vietnam became dependent on a Russian supply lifeline for heavy equipment that had to come over the Chinese railway system. The Chinese quietly constricted this system because they did not want Vietnamese hegemony over Indochina, especially if it were achieved with Soviet backing.

Vietnam's isolation thus helped convince at the Hanoi Paris Peace Agreements of January 1973, which provided a fig leaf for a US withdrawal from Vietnam. The South Vietnamese were promised extensive military aid, but that was subject to support in Congress. In 1975, the cutting-off of American aid to South Vietnam was to pave the way for the North's victory. But in January 1973, all that mattered for Nixon was that he had found a way out of the Vietnam quagmire.

For its part, China had some shared interests with the United States in relation to Vietnam. Once convinced that Nixon was indeed retreating from Vietnam, China withdrew its forces from its southern frontier and concentrated them on its border with the Soviet Union. Still, even here the US – China relationship had its nuances. Kissinger and Nixon had expected China to press Vietnam to negotiate an 'honourable' peace, but they were disappointed. China could not afford to be seen abandoning North Vietnam. That would not look good in Third World forums, and it also risked pushing Hanoi closer to Moscow. So China, seeking to retain influence over Vietnam, did not cut back its aid to Vietnam and maintained some 80,000 logistical troops there. Sino – Vietnamese relations were further complicated by internal tensions in Vietnam between pro-Chinese and pro-Soviet factions – essentially between Hanoi and the Vietcong – National Liberation Front in the south, which was heavily ethnically Chinese.

Setting aside the Taiwan problem

In the interests of opposing the growing Soviet power that threatened them both, the United States and China were willing to set aside the problem that had brought them twice to the brink of war in the 1950s: Taiwan. This took some ingenious diplomacy.

In the 'Shanghai communiqué', signed during Nixon's visit to China, the two sides set out separate positions. The United States said that 'the U.S. acknowledges that all Chinese on either side of the Taiwan Strait maintain there is but one China and that Taiwan is a part of China. The United States does not challenge that position. It reaffirms its interest in a peaceful settlement of the Taiwan question by the Chinese themselves'. The operative verb, of course, was '*acknowledges*'. That formulation served the interests of both parties for the duration of the Cold War.

American détente with Moscow

For its part, the Soviet Union sought détente from a global position much improved since the 1962 Cuban missile crisis. The Soviets had achieved strategic nuclear parity. By means of a massive arms supply to North Vietnam, they had helped keep America mired in Vietnam at disproportionately low costs to themselves. By 1970, Soviet general secretary Leonid Brezhnev was boasting that no question of importance in the world could be solved without Soviet participation. Partly for reasons of background, Henry Kissinger tended towards pessimism. In May 1972, he told Admiral Zumwalt, the US Chief of Naval Operations, that he believed the American people lacked the will to do what was necessary to achieve strategic parity and maintain maritime superiority.[1] Thus Kissinger set out to cut the best deal he could, before the rot set in further.

Still, Moscow had its reasons for wanting a respite in Cold War confrontation. The inefficiencies of the Soviet command economy were becoming manifest, with all the bloc economies falling far behind the West. Moreover, the Soviet Union's vast military spending was increasing its economic difficulties. Among the satellites, unrest among Polish workers in 1970 was ominous, not least because Poland was among the more advanced of the Eastern Bloc economies. So, by means of détente with the United States, the Soviets sought to gain access to Western technology, investment and food imports. These, Moscow hoped, would help remedy the deficiencies of its command economy.[2] Arms control, another child of détente, was central to Soviet tactics for gaining a winning hand.

Arms control: another American 'own goal'

And so it proved. The Strategic Arms Limitation Agreement (SALT) and the Anti Ballistic Missile Treaty (ABM), signed during Nixon's visit to Moscow in May 1972, did much to hobble America. These agreements had their roots in the arcane arms control theories of the Kennedy liberals. The Kennedy administration managed to turn its victory over the Soviet Union during the 1962 Cuban missile crisis into a defeat by developing the theory of Mutually Assured Destruction or MAD.

While MAD had its origins in the theories of economists who had entered the arms control debate in the 1950s, it was mainly the brainchild of Robert McNamara and his 'whiz kids'. Briefly president of the Ford Motor Corporation, McNamara was a Harvard MBA with no background in military history or strategy. Moreover, he was secretly but viscerally opposed to nuclear weapons, as later became manifest by his membership of the 1996 Canberra Commission which recommended the abolition of nuclear weapons.

Arms control liberals saw arms control as an alternative to open-ended arms competition that would risk becoming unrestrained. Would doubling the nuclear inventory double national security? Or would it diminish it by encouraging the adversary to build his forces? The question arose logically from the Eisenhower administration's development of the US strategic triad (long-range bombers, intercontinental ballistic missiles, and submarine-launched ballistic missiles) and the Soviet response in developing its own triad, which was much more heavily weighted in favour of intercontinental ballistic missiles.

The MAD doctrine had some new twists as a consequence of the technology of the missile age. The logic of MAD ran as follows. Anti-missile defences were unlikely to be totally effective against an attacker's full scale first strike. But if an aggressor struck pre-emptively at an opponent's missile force, destroying a large number of his missiles on the ground, then the aggressor could use his ABM defences to handle the victim's 'ragged' retaliatory second strike. So defences would tend primarily to undermine the effectiveness of retaliatory rather than first-strike forces. In other words, missile defences would create incentives to pre-empt, and were thus held to be 'destabilizing'.

The McNamara liberals who were opposed to US force modernization further contended that counter-value (city-busting) weapons stabilized the strategic balance by reinforcing MAD. By this convoluted logic, Western publics were held to be safer as long as their cities remained vulnerable to nuclear attack. But counter-force (silo-busting) weapons, the liberals maintained, increased the risk of war by making a first strike feasible, and thus encouraging it. The theory of MAD was thus based on the belief that adversaries shared an interest in cooperating in order to avoid a war that none could hope to win.

So, in 1972, the arms control counterpart of MAD, the Strategic Arms Limitation Agreement or SALT sought to 'cap the arms race', or even to avert it, by establishing a rational basis for agreement as to how much is enough. As we have seen, that approach to naval arms control worked in the 1920s Washington agreements. That was because at the time all sides

genuinely wanted peace and were able to agree on what constituted sufficiency. But in 1972 there was a collision of strategic interest which could not
be papered over by arms control agreements. American policy was driven by
wishful thinking. No evidence exists that the Soviets believed that their
vulnerability could strengthen strategic stability. Simple artillerymen at
heart, they just believed that more is better. Thus they resisted all US
missionary efforts to educate them as to their supposed true interests in
strategic stability. Like the Germans in 1914, they were committed to
winning, not stabilizing. That was evidenced by the momentum and character of their strategic programmes, including anti-satellite programmes,
exotic weapons, and improvements in INF (Intermediate Range) missiles.

The Soviet Union's power in the international system depended essentially on its ability to intimidate. So between 1962 and 1972, the USSR
developed five new ICBMs, a new SLBM, and four new types of ballistic
missile submarines. By 1971–1972, the Soviets possessed 1,510 ICBMs,
roughly 500 more than the United States.[3] Far from accepting a mutual
stalemate on the McNamara model, the Soviets were pursuing a first-strike
capability against the US ICBM force of much inferior throw-weight. And
by means of the ABM treaty, the Soviets had hobbled US technology, which
had been far ahead in this field. Moreover, the McNamara liberals did not
seem to understand the strategic geography of the Cold War – that nuclear
superiority was essential for America's ability to deploy forward, hard
against the Eurasian landmass, in order to counter overwhelming Soviet
conventional superiority in Europe, and to reassure allies on the Soviet bloc
periphery that Moscow would not be allowed to pick them off one by one.[4]

Although the Soviets' strategic thinking was apparently unsophisticated,
their understanding of the political efficacy of military power was brilliant.
Thus 'arms control' pursued by both the Johnson and Nixon administrations undermined the West's will to resist. Arms control negotiations gave
Moscow endless opportunities to convince Western publics to fear their own
weapons. All this was well understood in Beijing.

China, alarmed by how America was being lulled into complacency by
arms control, began – *sotto voce* – to support US forward deployments in
the Western Pacific. Privately, Chinese leaders also urged solidarity in
NATO, and for the United States to pay close attention to the southern rim
of Eurasia – Turkey, Iran and Pakistan. The security of those states was a
barrier to a Soviet breakthrough in the Indian Ocean.

Rapprochement with China: the Japan factor

With China no longer objecting to the US–Japan alliance, rapprochement
between China and Japan was soon in train. Still, Nixon's opening to China
came as a shock to Japan's prime minister Sato Eisaku, who had been given
only a few minutes' advance warning of Nixon's announcement in mid-July
1971 that he would travel to China. That loss of face added to tensions within

the alliance caused by growing US dissatisfaction with Japan's mercantilist trade policies, and its refusal to undertake any defence burden-sharing.

In his first meeting with Kissinger on 9 July, Zhou Enlai harped on the threat of Japanese expansionism. He said that the Japanese had 'openly decreed that Korea, Taiwan, and Vietnam are linked up with their security'.[5] As Zhou would have known only too well, that was the reverse of the truth. In fact, Sato had agreed to the 'Korea' and 'Taiwan' clauses in the 1969 Nixon–Sato communiqué only under duress, because he wanted Okinawa back. But Kissinger did not demur too much. No doubt Zhou lost no time in playing Kissinger's reactions back to the Japanese, as further evidence that Kissinger and Nixon could not be trusted.

Thus Zhou subtly helped undermine Sato, the most pro-American Japanese prime minister since his brother, Kishi. Moreover, Zhou was for the first time playing the card of access to the potentially vast China market. Since 1970, he had been saying that Japanese companies involved with Taiwan or South Korea were not welcome in China. Japan was already China's leading trading partner, as a consequence of the cut-off of China's trade with the Soviet Union. So the old Pan-Asianist dream revived. Once Japan had obtained full access to China's markets and resources, the Japanese Pan-Asianists believed, it could reduce its reliance on the United States. Moreover, they hoped, a Sino–Japanese condominium would give Japan greater leverage on America.

This was the old Pan-Asianist delusion of Japan in the van and China in the caboose. China was not seen as an economic threat to Japan, since it was such a poor country, and Mao's disastrous economic policies had made it even poorer. So the Japanese remained confident that they could keep so far ahead on the technology/product ladder that China would never catch up. Nor did the Pan-Asianists see China as a security threat, despite its testing of a nuclear weapon in 1964. Rather, they saw China's development of nuclear weapons as merely defensive, meant to ward off the threat of Soviet blackmail.

Japan and China normalize relations

So, in mid-1972, Tanaka Kakuei, who had come up the hard way to make a fortune in the construction business, defeated the patrician Fukuda Takeo in the elections held to decide Sato's successor. Tanaka ran on a platform of not 'missing the China bus'. Thus Zhou Enlai had done much to undermine the Kishi faction and its traditional orientation towards Taiwan. In July 1972, Tanaka went to Beijing to normalize relations with China, even before China and the United States had set up liaison officers in each other's capitals. Tanaka was anxious to get in first so that Japanese companies could get a foothold in the China market ahead of the American competition. The state of war between China and Japan was ended, and the peace treaty that Japan had signed with Taiwan in 1945 was allowed to lapse. In relation to

Taiwan, Japan negotiated a variant of the 'one-China' formula in which Japan *noted* that 'it fully understands and respects' the position of the PRC that 'the government of the Peoples' Republic of China reaffirms that Taiwan is an unalienable part of the territory of the Peoples' Republic of China' (emphasis added).

China agreed to drop its claim for reparations, although both sides understood that Japan's large-scale aid programme to China was to be a disguised form of reparations. That was welcome to the Japanese because much official development aid, in the form of yen loans, was to flow into the coffers of Japan's construction companies, one of the mainstays of the LDP's Tanaka faction. That all fed the growing corruption of the LDP, which had now been in power for nearly twenty years.

Much to the consternation of Japan's Socialist party, which obediently toed the Beijing line, China no longer objected to the US–Japan security treaty. Moreover, Mao also agreed to set aside the territorial dispute between China and Japan over the uninhabited Senkaku/Diaoyutai Islands in the East China Sea.

The Senkaku/Diaoyutai Islands dispute

The islands became a potential focus of contention when it seemed that oil and gas might be found in the vicinity. Japan has claimed the islands since the Sino–Japanese war of 1894–1895, after which China ceded Taiwan (Formosa) to Japan 'together with all the islands appertaining or belonging to the said islands of Formosa'.[6] But Japan has argued that its incorporation of the Senkakus was separate from its incorporation of Taiwan, so the islands were not included in the territories renounced by Japan under the terms of the 1945 San Francisco Treaty. For its part, China claims that the intent of the Allies in the Cairo and Potsdam declarations was to restore to China all the territories taken by Japan as acts of military aggression, and that includes the Senkakus.

The 1945 San Francisco peace treaty gave the United States administrative rights to the Okinawan chain, including the Senkakus. The US Navy subsequently established firing ranges on the islands, and paid an annual rent to the son of the first Japanese settler of the islands. The 1971 Okinawa reversion treaty provided for the return to Japan of 'all and any powers of administration, legislation and jurisdiction of the islands held under the Japan Peace Treaty'. It was also made clear that Okinawa, including the Senkakus, came within the ambit of the 1960 US–Japan security treaty. Article V of that treaty refers to 'the territories under the *administration* of Japan' (emphasis added).

But the Nixon administration took a neutral position about the *sovereignty* of the Senkakus. This was apparently done in order to avoid taking sides between China and Taiwan, which also claimed the islands, and also to avoid offending China at a delicate stage of Sino–US rapprochement.

Moreover, the Senkakus issue was related to the wider issue of the owner-ship of the other islands in the East Asian 'marginal seas' whose sovereignty had been left in legal limbo by the San Francisco peace treaty – including the Paracel and Spratly archipelagos. Thus, in presenting the Okinawa rever-sion treaty to the US Senate, the State Department asserted that the United States took a neutral position with regard to the competing Japanese and Chinese claims to the islands, despite the return of Okinawa to Japanese administration.[7] In November 1971, China for the first time asserted a claim to the Senkakus. But Mao said that it would be best to leave resolution of the dispute to the next generation. Still, while seeking to downplay any potential discord with Japan in the interests of maintaining the coalition against Moscow, China was laying down markers for the future.

Japan's ruling against collective self-defence

The Japanese were not greatly bothered by the Nixon Doctrine, recognizing it as a fig leaf for US withdrawal from Vietnam. But the period of the 'Nixon Shocks' was to have implications for Japan's security policy once the Cold War was over. This was because Japan, in seeking accommodation with China, made an interpretation of its constitution which further hobbled its own military power. In response to Chinese pressure, the Sato government, subsequently endorsed by Tanaka, allowed Japan's Cabinet Legislative Bureau to rule that the 'peace' constitution did not permit Japan to engage in collective self-defence. So, although the United States was legally bound under the security treaty to defend Japan, Japan was under no obligation to assist the United States. Indeed, it was now legally prevented from doing so, if American forces – *even those engaged in the defence of Japan* – were attacked outside Japan's territorial limits.[8]

Thus, under pressure from China and the China-aligned Socialists in the parliament, Sato negated the effect of the 'Korea' and 'Taiwan' clauses of the 1969 Nixon–Sato communiqué. As we have seen, Nixon had made Japan's acceptance of those clauses a *quid pro quo* for the reversion of Okinawa, which Sato desperately wanted in order to crown his long-running prime ministership. The South Koreans were so angry at Japan's back-pedalling on the 'Korea clause' that Park Chung Hee cancelled a visit to Japan that would have been the first such visit by a South Korean president.

But the Tanaka government was not too concerned about South Korean complaints. For now Japan was riding high. While continuing to reap the benefits of American security protection, at low cost and no risk, Japan had secured access to the vast China market as well.[9] So why antagonize China by clinging to the fiction that Japan would lift a finger to help the United States in any conflict outside the Japanese islands?

Japan's three non-nuclear principles

Japan was also able to have its cake and eat it in relation to nuclear issues. It was able to preach disarmament on the international stage, while also sheltering under the US nuclear umbrella. By 1971, the parliament endorsed Japan's three non-nuclear principles, first enunciated by Sato in 1967. The non-nuclear principles said that Japan would not manufacture or possess nuclear weapons, nor permit them to be introduced into Japan. Thus, as we have seen, Okinawa reverted to Japan 'nuclear free'. Japan also signed the Nuclear Nonproliferation Treaty in 1970, although it took six more years to ratify it. Thus the non-nuclear principles were seen by many Japanese as a garlic necklace to ward off the twin vampires of foreign aggression and domestic militarism.

Japanese Gaullists such as Shintaro Ishihara believed that possession of nuclear weapons would confer upon Japan the great-power status to which it was entitled, as well as make Japan invulnerable to nuclear blackmail. Why was totalitarian China 'entitled' to have nuclear weapons, they asked, and not democratic Japan? But the mainstream conservatives did not accept this argument. They understood that Japan's pursuit of strategic independence would inflame regional tensions and put at risk the regional stability on which Japan's prosperity depended. It would also be highly divisive at home. And for those who cared to look a bit harder, the three non-nuclear principles were tied to the four non-nuclear policies, the most important of which was that Japan would continue to rely on US extended deterrence.[10] Moreover, since Kishi's day, the Japanese government had fobbed off attempts by the Socialists to have the non-nuclear principles linked to the constitution.

Thus, while continuing to enjoy the benefits of US strategic protection, Japan could exploit its status as a unique victim of nuclear attack in order to promote disarmament on the global stage. This would allow Japan to promote itself as something more than just an 'economic animal', and would serve as an eventual platform for its claim to be a permanent member of the UN Security Council. And when it came to political management of the 'nuclear allergy', all Japan had to do was to continue look the other way when US nuclear-capable warships came into its ports. It was almost all too good to be true. Thus Japan was more insulated than was China from the shifts in the global balance when the Nixon presidency started to falter.

The rot sets in: Watergate and its consequences

To China's consternation, the 'correlation of forces' shifted further in Moscow's direction when Nixon had to resign in August 1974 to avoid being impeached over the Watergate scandal. Because Spiro Agnew, Nixon's vice-president, had already been forced to resign in a separate scandal, Gerald Ford became America's first unelected president. Ford's honesty and integrity did much to hold the country together, but it was an unenviable job.

Moreover, in April 1975, Saigon fell, shortly after the communist Khmer Rouge had taken power in Phnom Penh. While America was relieved to put the Vietnam imbroglio behind it, the scenes of helicopter evacuations from the embassy roof in Saigon were a lasting humiliation. Not surprisingly, US allies in Southeast Asia and elsewhere wobbled. With Malaysia in the van, few in ASEAN wasted any time in seeking to reach accommodation with victorious Vietnam.

Moreover, the Soviet arms build-up in heavy and increasingly accurate missiles was even more rapid after the signing of SALT I than before it. Moscow's economic problems were not impeding its ability to spend more on military materiel, as the advocates of détente had hopefully assumed. By 1974, ballistic missiles had become accurate enough to target other missiles in their silos, the phenomenon known as counter-force. Moreover, in 1975, the Soviets began to place multiple warheads (Multiple Independently-Targeted Re-entry Vehicles or MIRVs) on their missiles. The SALT freeze had included only launchers and not warheads. The United States had gone along with this because of its lead in MIRV technology, the superior quantity and quality of its manned bombers, and its greater reliance on submarine-launched missiles.

But within five years after 1975, the USSR would field over 750 counter-force missiles armed with more than 5,400 highly accurate warheads. The United States was limited to 1,054 launchers, and only a portion of those would ever be MIRVed.[11] While the US SLBM programme was making steady progress, submarine-launched missiles still lacked counter-force capability, and would do so until the Trident II missile came on-stream in 1989. Ironically, the ABM treaty, because it limited defences to a single missile field, had encouraged the Soviets to develop more offensive capabilities.

As the Soviets reached for a first strike capability, America remained lulled into complacency by the theology of arms control, and stricken by post-Vietnam strategic paralysis. Thus the confidence of American allies at both ends of Eurasia began to wane. But Kissinger continued to seek yet another arms control agreement, SALT II. Arms control, it seemed, had become an end in itself. So in 1976 a group of alarmed Republicans and Democrats formed the Committee on the Present Danger, which became one of the most successful lobbying efforts in American history. And Democrat Senator Henry 'Scoop' Jackson was increasingly effective in Congress in questioning the logic of détente and arms control. But in the interim, Moscow was emboldened to think that the correlation of forces had moved irreversibly in its favour.

In Europe, *Ostpolitik* had encouraged Moscow to pick up its old idea of a conference on European security. The Conference on Security and Cooperation in Europe (CSCE) held its first meeting in Helsinki in 1975, and ratified the current boundaries in Eastern Europe. Thus it endorsed the gains made by the Red Army in 1945. CSCE, as a Europe-wide security organization, did much to serve Soviet interests. It provided Moscow with endless opportunities to divide and rule in NATO – between Greece and Turkey, for example. It was redolent of the way Stalin, using Litvinov as his instrument, had exploited 'collective security' as a tool to keep Europe divided after 1935, as part of his 'united front' strategy pointed at Hitler and Japan. True, the Helsinki arrangements included a human rights 'basket', which encouraged dissidents throughout the vast Soviet empire. But that did not inhibit Moscow from keeping Soviet dissidents in gaol or internal exile.

Increasing Soviet boldness around the globe told its own story. During the 1973 Yom Kippur War in the Middle East, the United States went on nuclear alert in order to deter Soviet threats to intervene to bail out the Egyptian army, trapped before Cairo by an Israeli counteroffensive. In Angola, where the collapse of Portuguese colonial authority created a power vacuum, the Soviets intervened by means of a massive airlift of Cuban troops in order to defeat forces supported by both China and the United States. Thus, bolstered by strategic parity, the Soviets had demonstrated an ability to insert division-sized military power into a conflict far from their frontiers.

In April 1974, a left-wing coup in Portugal threw NATO into disarray. For a time, there was a risk to the Azores, one of the strategically vital islands of the North Atlantic. This was a palpable threat to American maritime security because a foothold in the Azores would have allowed Moscow to present a much greater threat to NATO's ability to reinforce Western Europe in time of war. The Lisbon coup also had strategic resonance thousands of miles away in Southeast Asia. This was because, in December 1975, Indonesia invaded Portuguese East Timor in order to prevent a takeover by left-wing Fretilin guerrillas. Since Saigon had fallen a few months earlier, and in light of events in Mozambique and Angola, President Suharto refused to take the risk of a hostile enclave being established in the outer islands of the Indonesian archipelago. Japan and Australia also had a strategic stake in East Timor, not least because of the importance to both parties of the iron ore trade between Japan and Western Australia.[12]

Further north, the risk also existed that North Korea would become emboldened as a consequence of the forcible reunification of Vietnam under communist control. Thus US Defense Secretary James Schlesinger said in June 1975 that the United States was ready to use nuclear weapons in defence of South Korea. While China could hardly say so publicly, it shared the US interest in preventing war on the Korean peninsula, not least because it now had a reunited Vietnam on its southern frontier. Just after the fall of Saigon, Kim Il Sung visited Beijing after a fourteen-year absence. It's likely that China hosed down any North Korean ambition to try to emulate Hanoi's success. On its southern frontiers, China was already busy trying to limit Vietnamese power. Indeed, in 1974, China had seized the Paracel islands in the South China Sea from a South Vietnamese garrison, lest they fall into the hands of a victorious North Vietnam.[13] In Cambodia, China was also actively encouraged the Pol Pot regime's cross-border attacks into Vietnam, as a check on Hanoi's ambition.

Jimmy Carter – near disaster

Then in January 1977, the consequences of Vietnam and the Watergate scandal propelled Jimmy Carter into the presidency, with near-fatal results for Western security. The confidence of US allies at both ends of Eurasia was rocked by one of the most strategically inept administrations in US history. Evincing a visceral distaste for 'power politics', Carter employed a misplaced moralism by which human rights concerns were placed at the forefront of US policy. The Soviet Union was thus encouraged to think it could go for broke, since Carter seemed concerned about human rights transgressions almost everywhere but in the Eastern bloc.

The Soviets scored a major victory in 1978 when Carter cancelled the neutron bomb project without even seeking, much less securing, reciprocal concessions from Moscow. That shook the Western alliance. Killing by radiation rather than by blast, the neutron bomb or Enhanced Radiation Weapon would have been especially effective against Soviet mass tank formations. But because the neutron bomb represented a palpable threat to Soviet superiority in conventional forces, it led to a successful Moscow-orchestrated campaign against this 'capitalist weapon' that destroyed people but not property. Carter also cancelled the B1 intercontinental bomber, and dithered about a basing system for the new mobile multiple-warhead MX missile. Meanwhile, the development of increasingly accurate heavy Soviet ICBMs was making America ever more vulnerable to a decapitating first strike.

The United States appreciated the need to modernize its *Minuteman* missiles, which had become vulnerable in their fixed silos. But the argument had become bogged down in Watergate and arms control theology. Finding a secure basing mode for the mobile MX missile, the proposed successor to *Minuteman*, proved elusive during the Carter years. Moreover, in 1977 the Soviets deployed the long-range *Backfire* bomber, a supersonic swing-wing bomber similar in many respects to the B1, which Carter had cancelled. Half of the *Backfires* were assigned naval missions, which significantly improved Soviet ability to prevent America from reinforcing Europe in time of war. The *Backfire* also soon appeared in East Asia, where Carter's ineptitude was causing even more wobbles among American allies.

In 1977, Carter threatened to pull US forces out of the Philippines unless President Marcos improved his human rights record. He also caused consternation among his Asia–Pacific allies when he proposed the demilitarization of the Indian Ocean. That played into the hands of the Soviet Union and its Indian ally, not least because much of the Indian Ocean region was now within range of Soviet air power based in Central Asia. In non-aligned forums, India continued to promote 'nuclear free' zones targeting Diego Garcia.

The Korean Peninsula: Carter's follies

During his 1976 election campaign, Carter said that the United States should remove all nuclear weapons deployed in South Korea. He also insisted on withdrawing all American ground forces from the Korean peninsula. That was despite the fact that North Korea's belligerence remained unabated. In 1976, North Korean troops hacked to death two American officers who sought to cut down a tree which was obstructing their line of sight in the Demilitarized Zone. (The North Koreans preserved in a museum the axe used to kill the Americans – much to the disgust of President George W. Bush when he apparently learned of this during his visit to the DMZ in February 2002.) Carter seemed to think that, if the North were no longer 'threatened', it might be induced to negotiate directly with South Korea. It was not until 1979 that the administration backtracked from Carter's *idée fixe* about withdrawing US ground troops and nuclear weapons from South Korea.

Carter's follies had some positive effect in shaking the Japanese out of their complacency. Thus, in 1978, Japan agreed to new guidelines for defence cooperation. These stipulated greater cooperation in military matters, including sharing of information and joint planning of military exercises. Still, that was only a marginal improvement in Japan's willingness to share the US burden in the Western Pacific. Despite its own equities in Taiwan's continued *de facto* independence, Japan was also willing to accommodate China in relation to the Taiwan problem.

Setting Taiwan adrift?

As we have seen, Japan normalized its relations with China in 1972, having had few qualms about breaking its ties with Taiwan. So Beijing kept reminding Washington of the virtues of the 'Japan formula'. But for the United States, things were not so simple because it had a mutual defence treaty with Taiwan.

True, there was little sympathy in the Carter administration for the Nationalist regime on Taiwan, whereas the administration was quite willing to overlook China's gross violation of human rights. But the Republicans in Congress, where the Taiwan lobby had long been active, would not tolerate the abandonment of Taiwan. Moreover, wider issues were at stake. If America tore up its security treaty with Taiwan, and refused to help Taiwan defend itself, China would be tempted to take the island by force. That would hardly inspire confidence among America's other allies.

The nub of the issue was continuing US arms sales to Taiwan. China, which still saw Taiwan as a renegade province, insisted on the right to use force in order to bring it to heel. American arms sales, Beijing insisted, encouraged Taiwan to defy the mainland. Thus the Carter administration was willing to abrogate the Mutual Defence Treaty with Taiwan, and to fudge the issue of continuing arms sales to Taiwan.[14]

Deng Xiaoping, now China's paramount leader after the deaths of Mao and Zhou Enlai, did not much care for this fudge. But he went along with it because China's strategic position was deteriorating. Throughout 1978, tensions with Russia and Vietnam had been rising, as Vietnam expelled large numbers of ethnic Chinese. Now a third war in Indochina was in the offing. The signing of the Soviet–Vietnamese security treaty on 3 November was a harbinger of what was to come. Deng also wanted to implicate the United States in his planned attack on Vietnam if Vietnam invaded Cambodia. That would help offset the risk that the Soviets might intervene.

In January 1979, during Deng's visit to the United States, America normalized its relations with China. It also announced that the defence treaty with Taiwan would be abrogated on the required one year's notice. Thus the Carter administration played a strong hand badly. China, with growing Soviet and Vietnamese pressure on its borders, was desperate to strengthen its relationship with Washington. Yet the Carter administration had been induced to abandon Taiwan. It fell to Warren Christopher, deputy Secretary of State, to explain US policy in person to Jiang Jingguo, the son of Jiang Jeshi (Chiang Kai-shek). At the insistence of Carter's National Security Adviser Zbigniew Brzezinski, Jiang had been given only two hours' notice of America's intention to abrogate the security treaty. The outrage on Taiwan was such that Christopher was lucky to escape unscathed.

But the Carter administration could not evade Congress, because it needed enabling legislation to formalize the downgraded relationship with Taiwan. The Taiwan Enabling Act which Carter sent to Congress emerged as a quite different document, the Taiwan Relations Act (TRA), secured by veto-proof margins. In effect, the TRA was little different from the abrogated mutual defence treaty. It said that it was the policy of the United States that diplomatic relations with the People's Republic of China rested upon the expectation that the future of Taiwan would be determined by peaceful means. The TRA also said that 'any effort to determine the future of Taiwan by other than peaceful means, including by boycotts or embargoes' would be considered 'a threat to the peace and security of the Western Pacific and of grave consequence to the United States'. In diplomatic parlance, of course, 'grave consequences' is code for war. The TRA further required the president to 'provide Taiwan with arms of a defensive character' and in times of crisis to 'make available to Taiwan such defence articles and defence services in such quantity as may be necessary to enable Taiwan to maintain a sufficient self-defence capability'.

Thus the United States managed to normalize its relations with the

Peoples' Republic without selling out Taiwan. But that was not due to any unaccustomed *realpolitik* on the part of the Carter administration. If Congress had not intervened, Taiwan would have been set adrift.

The Soviet build-up in the Far East

Meanwhile, the Soviet Union continued its remorseless military build-up. This included the expansion of nuclear and conventional forces in the Far East. In 1978 Leonid Brezhnev and his defence minister, Dmitry Ustinov, paid a highly visible visit to the Far East to meet the military commanders, signing a blank cheque to meet their assessed needs. Setting up separate theatre military commands enabled the USSR better to fight an all-out war, thus overcoming the traditional Soviet fear of having to fight a war on two fronts. The first of these theatre commands was established at Ulan Ude, just east of Lake Baikal. Soviet armour was forward-deployed in Mongolia in order to threaten Beijing along the vulnerable Baikal–Yellow Sea corridor, thus replicating the minatory posture of the Group of Soviet Forces in Germany. As we have seen, Stalin had also set up widely separated theatre commands in the late 1930s when he had been faced with the threat of two-front war.

The rapid Soviet build-up also menaced Japan. In 1978, the Soviets stationed a division of troops on the Southern Kurils, visibly threatening Hokkaido. This was meant to punish Japan for signing a peace treaty with China in 1978 that included an 'anti-hegemony' clause pointed at Moscow. Japan, by now accustomed to thinking that its security problems could either be ignored or left to America to resolve, initially responded with signs of pre-emptive capitulation.[15] In 1979, the Soviets deployed SS-20 missiles in the Far East, threatening both China and Japan. The SS-20 was a new, mobile, solid-fuel missile with three warheads and far greater accuracy than the intermediate-range missiles it replaced. All of Europe and Asia, and a large part of Africa and the Middle East, were within range. Thus the SS-20 became a make-or-break test for the Western alliance – one that it nearly failed.

The INF showdown in Europe

It was not surprising that the showdown between the USSR and the Western Alliance eventually was over a mobile missile. What was surprising was that high noon came not over strategic (intercontinental) nuclear missiles, but over intermediate nuclear forces, or INFs. The SS-20 threatened to uncouple Western European security from that of the United States. It was just short enough in range not to qualify as an ICBM or 'strategic' missile under SALT limits. Combined with Soviet parity in strategic nuclear weapons, and conventional superiority, the SS-20 seemed an ideal weapon to intimidate Western Europe.[16] It also provided grist to the Soviet propaganda mill, which alleged that the United States sought to fight a nuclear war only in Europe. It was hard to imagine a more potentially alliance-busting weapon.

True, *Polaris* gave the US a secure second-strike capability, and thus protected Western Europe as well. But as has been noted, until the late 1980s SLBMs were counter-value rather than counter-force weapons – that is, they lacked the accuracy to destroy hardened missile silos. Moreover, *Polaris* (and its successor, *Trident*) lacked political visibility, and hence the ability to reassure the West Europeans.

It was Helmut Schmidt, the Socialist chancellor of West Germany, who blew the whistle on the SS-20. Thus, in December 1979, NATO decided to station *Pershing IIA* intermediate-range ballistic missiles in West Germany.[17] Cruise missiles were to be stationed in Britain, West Germany, Italy, Belgium and the Netherlands. Once these deployments began, NATO insisted that they would stop only if the Soviets stopped their preparations for SS-20 deployment. That was the so-called 'double zero' option.

In both Western Europe and Japan, Soviet 'peace' campaigns targeted Western systems as the source of rising tensions, rather than the SS-20s that caused the problem in the first place. Without the resolve shown by Britain's Margaret Thatcher and French president Mitterrand, the Soviets might well have driven a stake through the heart of the Western Alliance. That was especially so because the Soviets were also throwing down the gauntlet to the United States at sea.

Moscow's 'risk fleet'

Geostrategic assymetries meant that the USSR did not need to match the US Navy in order to win the Cold War. Throughout last century's grand strategic contests, the great land powers did not seek hegemony at sea, because that was not a prerequisite for hegemony on land. What they sought was sufficient maritime power to deter the offshore balancer from playing its traditional role – which was to prevent a continental power from achieving hegemony over Europe/Eurasia.

Like Admiral Tirpitz before him, Admiral Gorshkov did not set out to challenge the dominant maritime power all over the globe. He was not seeking command of the seas, or to develop a navy commensurate with that of the United States. It was not until the end of the Cold War, for example, that the Soviet Union laid the keels of two full-scale nuclear-powered attack aircraft carriers. At the time, the United States had fifteen carrier task forces. But that the USSR did not seek to match the US Navy ship for ship did not mean that the Soviet Union was a 'defensive' power, as so many seemed to think.

Rather, the Soviet Union sought to develop sufficient maritime power to prevent the United States from keeping open the sea lanes to Western Europe, as Germany had sought to do in both world wars. The Soviet Union already occupied the central geographical position in Europe. If the United

States could not reinforce Western Europe in time of war, it could no longer play the role of global offshore balancer, and the Soviet Union would win the Cold War. In 1975, as part of the Soviet Navy's OKEAN 75, the largest naval exercise so far conducted by Moscow, the exercises simulated interdiction of NATO's Sea Lines of Communication (SLOCs). This was why the Soviet 'risk fleet' represented a threat that the United States could not afford to ignore.

Vietnam's Soviet-backed invasion of Cambodia

In Southeast Asia, as elsewhere in the late 1970s, the Soviets were on a roll. Moscow was emboldened to back Vietnam when it invaded Cambodia at the end of 1978, in search of hegemony over Indochina. (The removal of the genocidal China-backed Pol Pot regime was a consequence of the invasion, not its cause.) Vietnam attacked with more than 100,000 men and an armoured division. The USSR armed Vietnam, probably provided high-level strategic guidance on how to conduct invasions, and secured Vietnam against the threat of really serious Chinese counter-attack. Soon Vietnam was deploying forces on Thailand's borders which visibly threatened Bangkok. The concentration of Vietnamese forces was modelled on that of the Group of Soviet Forces in Germany and the Soviet forward deployment in Mongolia that threatened Beijing.

Moscow's reward for its support of Vietnam was the strategic gains accruing from forward deployment into the South China Sea. That came as a consequence of being given access to the former French base at Cam Ranh Bay. For the Soviet Union in 1979, these strategic gains in Indochina strengthened its hand against China because it put pressure on China from an unexpected angle. For Moscow, access to Cam Ranh was also a low-cost way of making life harder for the US, similar to the Soviet lodgement in Cuba.[18]

Even though Cam Rahn was isolated, and its facilities could not compare with those of Yokosuka or even Subic, it represented a competitive start-line for surge deployments into the Indian Ocean. Like nuclear weapons, the strategic advantages conferred by Cam Ranh were not limited to its use in anger. The Chinese were not inclined to take this new threat lying down. In February 1979, China invaded Northern Vietnam. Hard fighting against battle-hardened Vietnamese forces revealed the deficiencies of the PLA, and China suffered some 30,000 casualties. Still, China did capture the mountain fortress and key rail junction of Lang Son in March 1979, which laid open the road to Hanoi.

Then China withdrew, as it had done in its 1962 border war with India. China's purpose was not to stay in Vietnam, but to show Vietnam that it could not exercise regional hegemony in defiance of Beijing. The PLA presence obliged Hanoi to deploy its best forces on the northern border and keep them there for the duration of the war, leaving only second-grade forces available for Cambodia, including many conscripts. Moreover, China displayed considerable propaganda skill in calling its initial cross-border offensive the 'first lesson'.

Vietnam's invasion of Cambodia galvanized ASEAN, which had been hitherto willing to accommodate Vietnamese power. The ASEAN states appreciated the threat to the strategic security of all of their members when the capital of one of them, Thailand, was threatened by vastly superior Vietnamese forces on its frontier. (American forces had been withdrawn from Thailand in 1976, at the request of the Thai government.) Even Suharto's Indonesia, ever suspicious of China and wary of the US–China alignment, was forced to back the Thais. Thus, for reasons of strategic security, ASEAN was compelled to overcome its internal differences, and mount an international effort to counter Vietnam's bid for regional supremacy. Feisty Singapore led the campaign to reverse Vietnam's gains in Indochina, often tangling with Indian diplomats in international forums. Singapore, always the hard-head of ASEAN, recalled some lessons of history – that Japan's move into bases in South Vietnam in 1940 had brought Japan within striking distance of Singapore.

The 'Arc of Crisis' in Southwest Asia

To China's chagrin, Carter's Hamlet-like indecision over a growing political crisis in Iran did much to undermine the Shah. The 'Arc of Crisis' already extended to the Horn of Africa, where the Soviets had shifted support from Somalia to the Mengistu regime in Ethiopia. The fall of the Shah saw a pro-Western authoritarian regime replaced by a fundamentalist Islamic regime far more oppressive than that of the Shah, as well as the taking hostage of employees of the US embassy. They were not released until the day Carter left office – the regime in Tehran comprehending that the incoming Reagan administration would not hesitate to use force. And by the time the Shah fell, the Soviets had invaded Afghanistan. The two events were connected, since the Shah had long opposed Soviet and Indian designs on Afghanistan.

As a consequence of the 1955 visit of Khrushchev and Bulganin to Afghanistan, the Soviets began building roads and tunnels which drew that landlocked and poorly developed country towards Soviet Central Asia. In response, the Shah planned an ambitious network of railways known as the Trans-Persian Railway that would have linked Afghanistan with Iran, and with the Indian Ocean via the Pakistani city of Karachi.[19]

By linking Afghanistan with Pakistan, the Shah's railways would also have provided Afghanistan with a transport link to Western China. For, by that time, China's large western province of Xinjiang had been connected to Pakistan across the high Pamirs by means of the Karakoram Highway, the highest major road in the world. China's link with Pakistan was intended to outflank the Soviet Union and India, which had taken the opportunity presented by Pakistan's internal crisis in 1971 to dismember Pakistan.

The Soviet invasion of Afghanistan

Thus the Soviet invasion of Afghanistan was pointed at China as well as at the 'Main Adversary', the United States. This time, Moscow had been emboldened by America's continuing strategic paralysis to intervene in a Third World conflict with large numbers of its own forces, rather than just with the Cuban surrogates it had used in Angola and elsewhere.

But the Soviet invasion proved too much even for Carter, who famously said that he had learned more about communism in the previous twenty-four hours than in his lifetime to date. When his administration began a rapid build-up in the Persian Gulf, the Indian ocean island of Diego Garcia came into its own as the only major staging point between the Western Pacific and the Gulf. The Afghan War also sounded the death knell to the SALT II arms control package, already in trouble in the Senate. And once the Afghan anti-Soviet *mujahideen* guerrillas had been supplied with shoulder-held 'Stinger' missiles, effective against Soviet aircraft and tanks, the tide of battle began to turn. By 1982, Russia was starting to become mired in Afghanistan in the same way that America had been bogged down in Vietnam, and Japan quagmired in China in the late 1930s.[20] By this time, the Afghan War had helped propel Ronald Reagan into the American presidency, with the unenviable task of restoring the balance in the global 'correlation of forces'.

Reagan: America *redux*

Reagan understood that, if the United States continued to try to convince the Soviets to agree to 'stabilizing' strategic competition, as the McNamara liberals recommended, it would sooner or later lose the Cold War. As it was, the United States was being debilitated by a never-ending passive policy of containment. So, in order to win the Cold War, he set in train a rapid and massive military build-up. The 'Reagan Doctrine' also aimed at providing support for regimes around the world which were opposing Soviet or Soviet-backed forces, with front-line states such as Pakistan and Thailand high on the list. The Reagan administration, believing that arms control had deluded the United States into complacency, also turned towards active missile defences and counter-force (silo-busting) missiles.

By this time, it had become clear that the Soviets were not content with a mutual stalemate in the build-up of missiles, as Western arms control liberals had hopefully expected. Rather, the Soviets were pursuing a first-strike capability against the US ICBM force. The Soviets also violated the 1972 ABM treaty, including by building a massive radar at Krasnoyask in Siberia – which Gorbachev later admitted to Reagan.[21]

Meanwhile, Soviet strategic programmes forged ahead. The global balance would have shifted even more in Moscow's favour had the United States not developed the *Trident* ballistic missile submarines. The first *Trident* went to sea in the early 1980s, armed with twenty-four long-range ballistic missiles each with three accurate W-88 warheads. This gave the US Navy a capability that had so far eluded it. Still, as America's intercontinental ballistic missiles became ever more vulnerable, US second-strike capabilities came to rest on its bomber force, as well as on fewer than twenty-five ballistic missile submarines. Moreover, Soviet anti-submarine warfare capabilities were steadily increasing, not least because of capabilities improved by espionage in the United States.[22] And, as we have seen, it was not until the *Trident II* missile appeared on the scene in 1989 that submarine-launched ballistic missiles had a true counter-force capability.[23]

President Reagan also supported research into missile defence via the proposed Strategic Defense Initiative (SDI). From the time he became Soviet secretary general in 1985, Gorbachev campaigned against SDI, complaining that it was 'destabilizing'. That was because he perceived the palpable nature of the threat. SDI spoke to the heart of Russian technological deficiencies, especially in microelectronics and computers, the basis of any anti-ballistic missile (ABM) system. A controlled society which forbade most of its citizens access to photocopiers was not likely to be able to compete with America in the new technologies.

Tensions between the superpowers thus ran high in the early Reagan years. In December 1981, when martial law was imposed on Poland, Reagan warned Brezhnev that Soviet intervention would invite war. Tensions reached a peak in August 1983, when Soviet interceptors shot down a Korean airliner that had strayed into their air space – even though, as communications intercepted by American intelligence showed, the Soviet pilots had known it was a civilian aircraft.

Still, superpower tensions began to wane as the United States was increasingly able to negotiate from a position of strength, with SDI as its ace in hand. Contrary to the predictions of the arms control liberals, the Soviets became more tractable, not less, as the United States built what Acheson would have called 'situations of strength'. The deficiencies of the Soviet command economy were also becoming ever more apparent. That made it harder for Moscow to subsidize North Korea, Cuba and Vietnam. Moreover, Afghanistan had become a bleeding sore as the United States and China cooperated in funnelling military and other vital supplies to the resistance. Thus the Soviets became more amenable to meaningful arms control deals that did help to reduce tensions. In relation to the SS-20s, for example, NATO achieved its 'double zero' option. Thus the INF treaty was signed in Washington in December 1987. It eliminated the SS-20s and precluded future missiles in this range. Unlike SALT, this led to a real reduction in nuclear arms. Still, tensions remained high in East Asia, especially on the Korean peninsula.

North Korea: state-sponsored terrorism continues

With its bloated military, North Korea's economy was even more ineffi-
cient than that of the USSR. Thus Pyongyang had no answer to the rapid
economic development of the south. Moreover, South Korea was
becoming a democracy. Under American pressure, in 1988 Chun Doo
Hwan – who had come to power by a coup, and ruthlessly put down an
uprising in the south-western province of Kwanju in 1980 – was persuaded
to step down. Power was then transferred peacefully to an elected civilian
president. The 1988 Seoul Olympics were also a success, representing a
coming-of-age akin to Tokyo's achievement in hosting the 1964 Olympics.

North Korea's response was an escalation of state-sponsored terrorism.
In 1983, several members of the South Korean cabinet were killed in a
bomb attack intended to kill President Chun during a visit to Burma.
Then, in 1987, North Korean agents blew up KAL flight 858, killing all
the passengers and crew. North Korea also harboured Japanese Red Army
terrorists who had taken part in hijackings and atrocities around the
world.

The Taiwan problem: the fudge holds

North Korea's behaviour angered Beijing because it kept North Asian
tensions on the boil. China wanted a peaceful environment in which to
build up its wealth and power. Thus China and the United States had a
growing convergence of strategic interest in relation to the Korean peninsula. But problems still existed in relation to that other perennial source
of tensions – Taiwan.

Like South Korea, Taiwan was becoming more democratic, which gave
it a much greater purchase on American interests. Moreover, the mainlan-
ders were now reaching out to the Taiwanese majority. In 1984, Lee
Denghui (Lee Teng-hui), a Taiwanese unelected governor, was made Vice-
President. But the question of arms sales to Taiwan vexed Reagan's
administration as much as it had Carter's. In 1981, China expelled the
Dutch ambassador to Beijing, and withdrew its own ambassador from the
Netherlands, after Holland sold Taiwan two modern diesel-electric
submarines. (The only other submarines Taiwan possessed were Second
World War era Guppies.) Moreover, the issue of American arms sales to
Taiwan, especially modern fighter aircraft, arose again just at the time
that the deepening crisis in Poland required US solidarity with its
European allies, and with China. And Reagan, like all his predecessors
since Nixon, wanted to make a visit to China – which took place in 1984.

So the issue of arms sales to Taiwan was fudged again. In August 1982,
Reagan signed off on what was to become regarded as the Third
Communiqué – the other two being the 1972 Shanghai Communiqué and
the 1979 normalization document. According to the 1982 communiqué,
the United States declared that it did not seek to carry out a long-term

policy of arms sales to Taiwan. Its arms sales to Taiwan 'will not exceed, either in qualitative or quantitative terms, the level of those supplied in recent years since the establishment of diplomatic relations between the United States and China, and ... it intends to reduce gradually its sales of arms to Taiwan, leading over a period of time to final resolution'.

But that was not the end of the matter. There were also the Reagan Six Assurances to Taiwan, made public in the form of a statement made subsequent to the issue of the 1982 Communiqué by John Holdridge, then Assistant Secretary for East Asia in the State Department. The Six Assurances declared that the United States would not pressure Taiwan to negotiate; that it would not serve in an intermediary role between Taiwan and the People's Republic; that it would not terminate arms sales to Taiwan; that there would be no prior consultation with the PRC regarding arms sales to Taiwan; that there would be no revision of the Taiwan Relations Act; and that the United States had not changed its position regarding the sovereignty of Taiwan.[24]

Thus the Taiwan issue was fudged again. And as Jiang Jingguo progressively introduced democracy, his state was re-legitimated along with its economic performance. Whatever Kissinger and Carter might have hoped, Taiwan was not simply going to fade away. The US position remained what it had been in 1972, under the terms of the Shanghai Communiqué. The United States merely *acknowledged* that 'all Chinese on both sides of the Taiwan Strait maintain that there is but one China and Taiwan is part of China'. Moreover, America had always insisted that China did not have the right to take Taiwan by force. But Sino–US tensions over Taiwan remained subsumed, as the 'Second Cold War' intensified.

Reagan's Maritime Strategy

By the 1980s, the United States was thinking about protracted non-nuclear conflict on a global basis that would exploit US strategic strengths. Reagan's Maritime Strategy proposed a 600-ship navy that concentrated on conventional deterrence. This strategy assumed that the USSR would be unwilling to use nuclear weapons, and that it lacked the staying power to win a conventional war.

'Horizontal escalation' proposed taking offensive action against the Soviets from the first moment of general war, in order to shape the conflict. Its ground component was NATO's new concept of 'AirLand Battle'. This envisaged an immediate army offensive, with deep air penetration against the second echelon of Soviet troops. For its part, the US Navy proposed an aggressive maritime strategy based on its fifteen attack carrier battle groups. The development of the *Aegis* air defence system provided a new means of defending America's carriers. Aegis's computers were capable of tracking hundreds of air targets simultaneously, including sea skimming cruise missiles, and could deploy missiles against multiple targets at same time.

The Maritime Strategy envisaged attacking the Soviet 'bastions' in the White Sea and the Sea of Okhotsk which protected the Soviet fleets of ballistic missile submarines (SSBNs). This Soviet bastion strategy had its roots in the mentality of the regime in Moscow. Unlike the United States, the Soviet Union was unwilling to trust its SSBN captains at sea. So centralist distrust led to the novel strategic artform of SSBNs anchored in bastions at both ends of Eurasia, protected by geography, attack submarines and surface ships.

Reagan's Maritime Strategy was developed in unconscious imitation of British naval strategy during the Crimean War, when Britain had employed a global strategy, bombarding Russian bases in the White Sea, the Aaland Islands at the entrance to the Baltic, and Petropavlovsk na Kamchatke at the other end of Eurasia. Reagan's strategy was in fact the classic strategy of the dominant maritime power, taking the fight to a landlocked would-be hegemon, thus exploiting the mobility and flexibility that maritime power confers.

If war had broken out, it is debatable whether the United States would really have risked such high-value targets as its aircraft carriers in operations in confined waters against such a formidable enemy. Moreover, America would have had to go after the Soviet SSBNs so that the carriers could advance forward, thus putting pressure on the Soviets to use their SSBNs or lose them. That was indeed a high-risk strategy – it assumed that the Soviets would not, if push came to shove, resort to nuclear war.

Still, force balances matter as much in peacetime as they do in war. The Maritime Strategy did much to help tilt the 'correlation of forces' against Moscow. Moreover, Japan made an important contribution to the strategy.

The Maritime Strategy and Japan

An essential part of the Maritime Strategy was the development of an effective, high-technology air defence and antisubmarine network around the Japanese archipelago. Fully armed Japanese naval aircraft, alternating on a daily basis with US Navy antisubmarine aircraft, patrolled throughout the Sea of Japan. This convinced Soviet naval commanders that, despite the strength of domestic pacifism, Japan was prepared to fight alongside the United States if necessary.[25]

Japan's strategic geography also facilitated the political management of Japan's contribution to the Maritime Strategy, as it had earlier facilitated the management of sensitive nuclear issues. But this was a bumpy road. At a 1981 summit meeting with President Reagan, prime minister Suzuki Zenko, without understanding what his bureaucrats had written for him, promised that Japan would defend the sea lanes out to 1,000 miles. He also called the United States an 'ally' for the first time. Suzuki recanted such 'militaristic' language, and his hapless foreign minister was forced to resign. Then the inept Suzuki was also forced to quit. In a quirk of fate, he was replaced by Nakasone Yasuhiro, Japan's most hawkish prime minister since the war. Although Nakasone had a weak power base in the LDP, he used a close relationship with Reagan in order to boost his stock at home.[26] In his first visit to Washington, Nakasone referred to Japan as an 'unsinkable aircraft carrier'. He was one of the few Japanese leaders able to comprehend Japan's role in the global balance. For example, at the 1983 Williamsburg summit of the G-7, he opposed Soviet proposals to redeploy SS-20s from Europe to Asia.

Japan's defence of the sea lanes out to 1,000 miles sounded modest. Thus it did not arouse undue opposition at home or in the region. The United States also permitted Japan to build under licence four *Aegis*-class destroyers. Thus Japan became the only country outside the United States to possess this battle management system.[27] Japan's Navy, though it lacked long-range power projection capabilities, was by now a formidable fighting force. Moreover, its capabilities were built to complement, not duplicate or supplant, American maritime capabilities.

Critically, Japan could control all the exits from the Sea of Japan. By controlling these maritime choke points, the United States and Japan made it impossible for the Soviets to feel comfortable that they could, in wartime, support their bases in Cam Rahn Bay and Petropavlovsk. This was because all the critical support had to come out of Vladivostok. The two Soviet aircraft carriers stationed at Vladivostok were also much less capable than the (conventionally powered) *USS Midway*, which had been based in Yokusuka in the mid 1970s.[28] The permanent presence of the *Midway* battle group made the American military presence in Japan far more credible as a deterrent, and a symbol to the region of the importance of the US–Japan security treaty.

Japan's aid programme was increasingly directed to strategic purposes, including to key US allies such as Turkey, Egypt, Pakistan and Thailand. Moreover, in 1986, the Nakasone cabinet abandoned the one per cent ceiling for military spending that had been decided upon ten years earlier. Thus Japan made an important step towards becoming America's ally rather than a mere protectorate. Moreover, in 1987 Japan became more activist in the South Pacific. In order to limit the inroads the Soviets and their surrogates were making in the South Pacific, Japan, in conjunction with Australia, stepped up its aid to the region. That was partly because Japan was worried that New Zealand's defection from the ANZUS alliance threatened to set off another grand debate in Japan about nuclear weapons.

Australia and New Zealand

In 1985, New Zealand defected from the ANZUS alliance when its Labour government refused to continue to accept American nuclear-capable ships in its ports. This marked a notable success for Moscow's 'peace' campaigns. Anti-nuclear sentiment in New Zealand had also been stirred up by French nuclear testing in the South Pacific. The French secret service inadvertently helped the Soviets when it blew up the Greenpeace protest ship *Rainbow Warrior* in Auckland harbour, accidentally killing a crew member.

New Zealand, tucked away in the southwest corner of the vast Pacific Ocean, didn't matter much for reasons of strategic geography – Henry Kissinger rightly referred to it as a 'dagger pointing at the heart of Antarctica'. But New Zealand was also a long-standing democracy. If the 'Kiwi disease' had spread to countries which were critical to American global strategy – such as Japan, Denmark and West Germany – the Soviet Union would have been well on the way to winning the Cold War.

Australia was also important to US global strategy because, as we have seen, it hosted US facilities which were critical to the global balance. Even though, like New Zealand, Australia had a Labour government, it did not emulate the democracy across the Tasman Sea. Longstanding and strong ties existed between the two countries, but their strategic geography was different. Unlike New Zealanders, Australians had experienced attacks on their territory from Japanese forces in 1942 which had never been forgotten. Thus any Australian government that seriously threatens the US alliance does so at its electoral peril. So, while the Australian Labour government emphasized defence self-reliance, and threw some bones to the anti-nuclear lobby, it had no intention of endangering the alliance.[29] Moreover, New Zealand's apostasy gave Australia new leverage in the alliance, from which New Zealand was now suspended. But by then the Cold War was nearly over.

Japan at Cold War's end: free rider?

At the end of the Cold War, many Americans believed that Japan, and not America, had won. Japan, they claimed, was a notorious free rider. Japan had shared no risk, they said, so it had not lost a single serviceman in combat, while America had lost 100,000, nearly all of them in East Asia.

As we have noted, it was not true that Japan had shared no risk during the Cold War. Those Japanese PC-3 pilots who flew missions every other day over the Japan Sea, alternating with their American counterparts, would have been first in the firing line had the balloon gone up.

Moreover, the congruence of strategic interest that had underpinned the alliance since the Korean War had remained intact throughout all the subsequent twists and turns of the Cold War. Because of the maritime basis of America's own security, its strategic needs had been best served by forward deployments, and working with allies at both ends of Eurasia. Unlike nearly all of America's European allies during the 1973 Middle East War, Japan had never given the merest hint that it might restrict American military operations from its territory.

And on the economic front, all was not zero-sum, as the American 'revisionists' would have it. By the 1970s, inexpensive but high-quality Japanese imports were helping to keep down America's inflation caused by spending on the Vietnam War, and by Johnson's refusal to raise taxes until 1968. Moreover, by the end of the Cold War, Japan was subsidizing America's yawning budget deficit because Japanese savings had become the world's largest source of capital. This was not of course due to altruism. The Japanese government was the largest buyer of American treasury bonds, investing at international market rate of return while Japanese savers received virtually no interest at home.

But the 'free rider' accusation was not without a kernel of truth. Japan may not have had a completely free ride, but it was certainly a cheap and profitable one.[30] Japan was incapable of acting on the basis of other than the most narrow self interest. While American military spending averaged six per cent of GNP during the Cold War, Japan's military spending averaged less than one per cent. That five per cent made a huge difference. Despite growing frustration with Japan's mercantilism, the United States had had little choice but to put up with it because of the exigencies of the Cold War.

Japan had also created hostages to fortune. In relation to security affairs, Japanese governments and bureaucrats had taken the easy way out, making little effort to educate the Japanese people about Japan's contribution to winning the Cold War. Kishi's political demise in 1960, at the furore over the renegotiation of the security treaty, stood as a warning to those who were too overt about supporting the United States. Thus head-in-the-sand pacifism remained entrenched. Few stopped to ask what might happen if the wonderful security blanket of the US alliance were ever taken away.

China at Cold War's end: shattered illusions

In the late 1970s, China's paramount leader, Deng Xiaoping, embarked upon a huge gamble. To avoid the economic failures which Soviet military overspending and attempts at autarky had produced, Deng set China on a different course. He sought the benefits of the market while avoiding overspending on the military, thus relegating the military to the fourth of his 'four modernizations'. As a Long March veteran, Deng had sufficient cachet with the military to insist upon this. He sought gradually to build up China's wealth and power, without causing others to fear it and thus be motivated to combine against it. This strategy soon began to pay off. Once Chinese peasants were allowed to grow and sell their own produce – even if they were still tied to the land and not permitted to own it – the Chinese economy started to take off, especially in the coastal areas.

But Deng was no democrat. On the contrary, his model was the economically successful but authoritarian Singapore. Deng was determined to maintain party control, even if communist ideology couldn't be expected to survive the turn to 'market socialism'. But he did not seem to comprehend that the Singapore model had been successful in large part because its long-time leader Lee Kuan Yew ran a clean and efficient government. Moreover, a huge country like China could hardly be compared to a tiny city-state. As soon as Chinese peasants started to get rich, problems of corruption and inflation began to surface. So did demands for greater political freedoms.

In May 1989, the funeral of the Chinese leader Hu Yaobang, a sidelined reformist, provided the opportunity for large numbers to come out in the streets of Beijing. Protests then got out of hand, and in the glare of the foreign media, students – many of them sons and daughters of the élite – occupied Tienanmen Square for weeks. They even disrupted a visit by Gorbachev meant to symbolize the patching-up of Sino–Soviet differences. The regime became even more threatened when workers and ordinary citizens joined the protests. Worse, the students were taking American democracy as their model, creating a papier maché copy of the Statue of Liberty and calling it the 'Goddess of Democracy'. That was all too much for the grizzled veterans of the Long March. Attempts at mediation having failed, Deng sent in the tanks. Hundreds, if not thousands, of unarmed civilians were killed. American illusions about the nature of the regime in Beijing also died at Tienanmen Square – or at any rate they should have.

6   The quadrilateral continues

America's winning of the Cold War saw the resurfacing of the East Asian quadrilateral – indeed, it had never really disappeared, even at the height of so-called East–West 'bipolarity'. With equilibrium restored to Europe, unresolved great-power strategic tensions now focused on East Asia. But the configurations of interest within the quadrilateral had altered, as a consequence of the sea change that had overtaken the global strategic order.

While the United States and China were both enjoying much greater strategic latitude, the other two members of the quadrilateral found themselves in straitened strategic circumstances. Russia, no longer able to use military power to threaten the other members, had become a mere shadow of its former self. In East Asia, it was now little more than an interested onlooker. Japan was also weaker because its economy hit a brick wall at the end of the Cold War. So the Japanese were less able to use their economic power to further their strategic interests.

But it seemed unlikely that Russia and Japan, the weakened members of the quadrilateral, would be able to sink their differences in order to combine against a rising China. They had little to offer each other, and mutual dislike continued to characterize their relationship. Moreover, the unresolved dispute over the Southern Kurils prevented the signing of a peace treaty. Even when Russia was at its weakest, Japan was unable to achieve the territorial concessions that it had expected. The Japanese were not likely to do any better, as the Russian economy and self-confidence started to revive with a shrewd and vigorous new president, Vladimir Putin, at the helm.

Meanwhile, the two strengthened members of the quadrilateral, China and the United States, had become strategic competitors. This was mostly because the collapse of Soviet power had dissolved the common threat that underpinned their cooperation during the latter stages of the Cold War. Moreover, the Taiwan issue, which had never been settled, quickly resurfaced. And when China started to demonstrate blue water ambition, it was certain to collide with America's interest as the global 'offshore balancer'.

China acquired a strategic latitude unprecedented in modern times as a consequence of the collapse of Soviet military power. Relieved of Russian pressure on its frontiers, China was soon pointing east and south strategically, pressing on the vital straits that connect the Indian and Pacific Oceans. In 1992, it reasserted vast territorial claims in the East and South China Seas, and insisted on its right to use force in pursuit of those claims. In addition, a growing foothold in friendless Burma allowed China to press on the Malacca Strait from both directions. China, by virtue of its alignment with Pakistan, which was designed to contain India within its subcontinent, had also acquired a strategic foothold on Pakistan's Indian Ocean coastline.

Chinese pressure on both sides of the Malacca Strait is bound to engage the strategic interests of the United States. The security of the straits, to which Singapore still holds the key, has been a vital American interest since 1940. That is not only because of the maritime basis of America's own security, but also because of America's responsibility for the long-range maritime and resource security of Japan – which is a matter of great convenience to both parties.

The US–Japan alliance remains an essential element in broad regional security. But American and Japanese strategic interests, while still highly congruent, are not quite as congruent as they used to be. During the Cold War, the United States had no choice but to deploy forward, and that meant providing Japan with strategic protection, while Japan undertook no risk and disproportionately few costs. But the end of the Cold War gave the United States more options.

For the United States, forward deployments in East Asia are now more a matter of strategic choice than absolute necessity. Thus the Japanese have more to worry about than during the Cold War, when they were required to do little more than turn a blind eye when nuclear-capable US warships entered their ports. It is not unthinkable, for example, that a future administration in Washington might be tempted to balance power in East Asia by playing off China against Japan.

That strategy recommended itself to Nixon and Kissinger in the early 1970s because they were tired of Japan's relentless pursuit of mercantilism and its dogged refusal to share wider security goals. But in the 1970s, the notion of playing off Beijing and Tokyo, however tempting, remained a chimera because of the overriding imperatives of Containment. Today the United States has wider options.

The Japanese can no longer assume that the United States is obliged to look after all of Japan's security problems. And after fifty years of denial, they are now being forced to recognize that they have a problem with China. China's growing strategic pressure is beginning to cause Japan to become more anxious about its security.[1] For its part, China is ambivalent about the US–Japan alliance.

China's ambivalence about the US–Japan alliance

China is ambivalent because the alliance cocoons Japanese power by providing Japan with nuclear and long-range maritime protection. But the alliance also enables the United States to remain forward deployed in East Asia, a region in which China thinks it is entitled to pre-eminence. Moreover, China believes that the alliance emboldens Taiwan. This is one of the reasons China complains about Japan's participation in research into US missile defence plans such as the Navy Theatre Wide upper-tier system, based on *Aegis*-equipped warships. This system, China alleges, would bring Taiwan under the umbrella of the US–Japan alliance, and thus encourage it to defy China.

China's ambivalence was on display in 1996 when the alliance was given a much-needed upgrade after the neglect of the early Clinton years. The summit between Bill Clinton and Hashimoto Ryutaro did much to ameliorate concerns that US–Japan trade friction might rupture the alliance once the 'glue' of the Soviet threat had disappeared. There were also tensions arising from Japan's inept response to the 1990–1991 Gulf War.[2] In September 1995, a new crisis occurred when three US servicemen raped a schoolgirl in Okinawa.

But the Clinton–Hashimoto summit occurred just after the United States, by means of a naval display in the East China Sea, had checked unexpected Chinese belligerence in the Taiwan strait (see p.150). The summit, long in the planning, was not a consequence of those events, but China did not see it that way. Who in China could forget that China had lost Taiwan to Japan as a consequence of the 1894–1895 naval war? Moreover, Hashimoto had caused an outcry in China (and South Korea) when he visited the Yasukuni shrine, where convicted war criminals are enshrined. That was the first such visit by a prime minister since Nakasone's in 1985.

The summit communiqué focused on new logistical roles for Japan and the potential for future joint development of missile defences. These new arrangements also seemed to expand the geographic scope of the alliance from the area immediately surrounding Japan to a much wider but ill-defined 'Asia Pacific', which might include Taiwan. Moreover, President Clinton signed the declaration in Yokusuka harbour aboard the air craft carrier *Independence*, which had recently returned from its deployment near the Taiwan Strait. The *Independence* was saluted by the *Myoko*, one of Japan's four *Aegis*-equipped destroyers of the *Kongo* class. It was a reminder of who had the real navies in the region.

The United States also upgraded its alliance with Australia at the same time, leading China to complain about being contained by 'crab claws'. And in 1997, revised US–Japan defence guidelines, passed by the Japanese parliament in 1999, effected changes proposed in the Clinton–Hashimoto communiqué. The new guidelines also stated that the ambit of the alliance covered situations in the 'areas surrounding Japan'. China was rebuffed when it pressed to have Japan say that the definition of 'areas surrounding Japan' specifically excluded Taiwan.

Thus, in the summer of 1998, China's second defence white paper – a supposed attempt at greater transparency – criticised US bilateral alliances as 'destabilizing'. Moreover, China tried to intimidate Japan during a visit in late 1998 by the general secretary of the communist party, Jiang Zemin. This tactic backfired badly.

China's bullying of Japan backfires

By this time, China had been emboldened by President Clinton's unprecedented nine-day visit to China in the summer of 1998, the first presidential visit since 1985. China, taking advantage of the president's domestic embarrassments following a sex scandal, insisted that he not visit either Japan or South Korea. While on Chinese soil, Clinton complained about what the United States saw as Japan's inadequate response to the 1997 regional financial and economic crisis. He made no mention the importance of the US–Japan alliance for regional security. And he uttered in public the 'three noes' on Taiwan.[3] All of this puffed up the Chinese, who were already emboldened by Jiang Zemin's 1997 state visit to the United States. There Jiang had been permitted to lay a wreath at the *Arizona* memorial at Pearl Harbor, thus recalling the US–China alliance against Japan in the Second World War. As ever, the Chinese were highly attuned to the political uses of history.

But Jiang Zemin's subsequent visit to Japan was a disaster. It contrasted sharply with the visit a few weeks previously of the new South Korean president Kim Dae Jung, who indicated a willingness to set aside the past and move on. (By this time, Japan had made numerous apologies to South Korea about its occupation of the peninsula, even if these apologies fell short of a Diet resolution.) When in Japan, Jiang Zemin wore a Mao jacket at the Imperial banquet, harped about war guilt, and had no words of thanks for some twenty billion dollars in Japanese aid to China since 1972. Thus many Japanese came to think that China's demands for atonement for Japan's wartime atrocities could never be satisfied, despite the apology that had been offered when Emperor Akihito visited China in 1992.[4] Now the war guilt issue – 'remember Nanjing' – had become a means of extortion. And this in an economy that had long gone sour.

China's leaders seemed to realize they had overreached. So China's more moderate prime minister, Zhu Rongji, visited Japan in October 2000 in order to make amends. Behind that turnaround lay a solid calculus of interest. For China could not be sure that it could contain a Japan that was strategically independent of the United States.

Japan's economy still represents 60 per cent of the GDP of East Asia. Moreover, the Japanese are a technologically adept and highly organized people. Japan's defence budget, although less than one per cent of GDP, is the second largest in the world.[5] And it is widely assumed, in China as elsewhere, that Japan has the technological capacity rapidly to develop nuclear weapons and the means of delivery once the decision to do so had been taken.[6] For all these reasons, it suits China that Japan should continue to rely on the United States for its nuclear and long-range maritime protection.

Thus China and the United States have some shared interests in relation to Japan. But how much are they willing to concede to each other in order to sustain these common interests? Or in relation to their common interests on the Korean Peninsula? For China, one of the problems is that it cannot control North Korea, or stop it from acting in ways that injure China's interests, not least in relation to Japan.

Equations of power on the Korean Peninsula

China's essential strategic interest on the Korean Peninsula is to have the dominant say in the process of reunification. For its part, America's essential interest there is the strategic security of Japan, the interest that has driven US policy since 1950. Neither China nor the United States wants to see North Korea try once again to reunify the peninsula by force. Thus Chinese and American interests are congruent. But they are not identical.

After the peninsula is reunified, Beijing will presumably want the United States to leave its bases in Korea, thus allowing China to revert to its historic role as suzerain of the peninsula. Still, China would have to calculate what impact such a withdrawal might have on Japan. If the US were to leave all of its bases in Korea, Japan would be the only North Asian country hosting such bases. That might make the US–Japan alliance politically harder to sustain, leading to pressures for Japan to become strategically independent.

Tensions on the Korean Peninsula are, like the Taiwan problem, an unresolved strategic residue of the Cold War. But they have taken on new and more dangerous twists. Since the end of the Cold War, Stalinist North Korea has become more threatening to its neighbours because it has developed missiles and weapons of mass destruction. Moreover, the regime in Pyongyang can no longer play Russia and China off against each other to its own benefit, as it was able to do during the Cold War. Attracted by South Korea's burgeoning economy, contrasting so strongly with the economic decline of the north, Russia normalized its relations with South Korea in 1990. China followed suit two years later. Thus North Korea was orphaned by the Cold War. So, in order to prop up its regime amid mass starvation and economic collapse, Pyongyang developed missiles and weapons of mass destruction as instruments of blackmail. North Korea's medium-range *Nodong* missile was first tested over the Japan Sea in May 1993.

North Korean missiles aimed towards Japan, and the American bases there, are presumably intended to impede America's ability to reinforce South Korea in time of war. Thus North Korea learned the lessons of the Korean War, when America rushed forces from Japan in response to the North's attack on the South. Indeed, if American bases in Japan and South Korea were attacked by chemical weapons, that would greatly hamper the ability of American aircraft to attack North Korean forces moving southwards. Given the current balance of forces on the Korean peninsula, the North cannot win a war, even with more than a million men forward deployed. But there is no certainty that its leaders understand that. Moreover, Seoul is so close to the border that it could be severely damaged by North Korean rocket and artillery attacks.

So far, the North's policy of extortion and blackmail has succeeded remarkably well. In 1985, North Korea signed the NPT (Nuclear Non-Proliferation Treaty), at Soviet urging, and in the hope of acquiring Soviet nuclear technology. This was not forthcoming, but North Korea pursued a clandestine policy of developing nuclear weapons. From the 1990–1991 Gulf War, North Korea apparently drew the conclusion that the United States would have been deterred from taking military action against Iraq if Washington had known that Iraq's weapons of mass destruction programme was as advanced as later became apparent.

Joining the NPT was also useful because, by threatening to leave it in March 1993, North Korea provoked a long-running crisis that was resolved to its ultimate benefit. The crisis erupted when North Korea refused to accept International Atomic Energy Authority (IAEA) inspections of suspect sites because Pyongyang had discovered that the IAEA, after the Gulf War, was much tougher than it had anticipated. North Korea's threats of war included threats to turn Seoul and Japan into 'a sea of fire'.

The 1994 Korean nuclear crisis

The Korean nuclear crisis revealed a US alliance system in disarray, as Kim Il Sung no doubt intended. (Kim died during the crisis, but supposedly continues as head of state from his coffin, a bizarre state of affairs even by North Korean standards.) In May 1994, North Korea raised the stakes by removing the fuel rods from its nuclear reactor, making it impossible for the IAEA to trace the history of the reactor and thus to estimate how much weapons-grade fissile material North Korea had extracted. The United States apparently believed that North Korea possessed enough material for one or two weapons. In June, it withdrew from the IAEA. The Clinton administration moved *Patriot* missile defence batteries to South Korea, and threatened a blockade and an implicit use of force.

The crisis was defused, but not resolved, when President Clinton agreed that former President Jimmy Carter should visit Pyongyang. For its part, China also put pressure on Pyongyang to end the crisis. Even though China had recognized South Korea, it maintained links and influence with the North, including the supply of missile technology. One of China's many interests in North Korea is that it does not want to see a collapse of the northern regime leading to a huge outflow of refugees to Manchuria.

Thus, for fear of war, and because of the lack of support from its key allies, the United States agreed to a deal suggested by Kim Il Sung, brokered by Carter, which rewarded North Korea for flouting its obligations to the

NPT. The deal went as follows. In return for freezing its known nuclear programme, North Korea was to be provided with two supposedly proliferation-resistant light water nuclear reactors, as well as heavy fuel oil to supply electricity while the reactors were being built. For the purpose of building the new reactors, the Korean Peninsula Energy Development Organization (KEDO) was created, with funding mostly from South Korea, Japan and the European Union. So North Korea, without being forced to reveal its nuclear history, was afforded the international recognition that it craved. It also achieved direct negotiations with the United States, and that threatened to drive a wedge between the United States and South Korea.

There were supposedly some teeth in the North Korean nuclear agreement. The light water reactors were not to be handed over until IAEA inspections had been concluded, and the IAEA had thus been able to certify that it could fully account for North Korea's past nuclear activities. But that would take years. When the time came to place the cores in the light water reactors, would the United States and its allies insist on the fulfilment of these conditions? As the KEDO project gathered pace, would not it gain its own momentum, thus providing incentive to let North Korea off the hook? Moreover, experience with Iraq had shown that it was not so difficult to fool the IAEA. And there was nothing to prevent North Korea from developing its missile programme, and presumably its chemical and biological weapons programmes.

Then, as a consequence of the regional economic crisis in 1997, the former South Korean dissident Kim Dae Jung was elected president in December. Kim then pursued a 'sunshine policy', based on the misplaced hope that unilateral concessions might elicit better behaviour from the North. In mid-2000, Kim Dae Jung travelled to Pyongyang to meet Kim Jong Il, the 'Dear Leader' and successor to his father Kim Il Sung. This rapprochement brought Kim Dae Jung the Nobel Peace Prize, but little else.

As might have been anticipated, the benefits of the 'sunshine policy' have all flowed to the North. The regime there has been kept on life support with food and other aid from South Korea, as well as from the United States and other donors. (The United States is in fact the main donor.) Countries such as EU members and Australia flocked to recognize North Korea, thus giving the regime respectability. Moreover, the prospect of reunification has fuelled nationalism in South Korea, directed at both the United States and Japan. So-called détente on the peninsula has also done much to lull most of the South Korean population into believing that war is now unthinkable.

The Korean dimension in the US–China–Japan triangle

The 1994 Korea nuclear crisis also caused a crisis in the US–Japan alliance because the United States was forced to plan Japan *out* of its military preparations. Under the terms of Japan's Status of Forces Agreement with CINCUNC (Commander in Chief, United Nations Command), Japan gave the green light for the United States to stage forces through major American bases. But the Clinton administration wanted Japan to do more. It wanted Japan to cut off remittances from Koreans in Japan who were sympathetic to the North; to help in the evacuation of non-combatants from South Korea; and to provide rear area logistical support for the hundreds of thousands of US troops expected to stage through Japan.[7]

But Japan said that most of these requests could not be met because of the 1972 Cabinet Legislative Bureau ruling that Japan could not engage in collective self-defence. Under this interpretation of the constitution, Japan could not even use government aircraft to evacuate its own nationals from South Korea, let alone other nationals. Moreover, the Maritime Self-Defence Force commander told his US Navy counterpart that Japan could not provide ships for surveillance and minesweeping, unless there were a UN imprimatur for such action. Because China, North Korea's *de facto* ally, possessed a veto in the Security Council, that was highly unlikely. The US–Japan alliance seemed on the road to rupture until Carter's intervention defused the crisis.

Moreover, Japan miscalculated when it tried to help resolve the North Korean nuclear problem by means of international arms control pressure. During negotiations in 1993 on the indefinite extension of the Nuclear Non-Proliferation Treaty (NPT), the Miyazawa government dragged its feet, apparently in order to maintain pressure on North Korea to stay in the NPT. Japan also forced the other members of the G-7 to water down a June 1993 communiqué endorsing quick adoption of the indefinite extension of the NPT. But Japan came under international criticism for being seen to be dangerously hinting at its own nuclear option.[8]

The 1998 *Taepodong* launch

In August 1998, North Korea galvanized Japan by testing a three-stage long-range solid fuel missile, the *Taepodong*, over the Japanese islands. The North Koreans said the missile had launched a satellite. But, like *Sputnik* in 1957, it was not the payload that mattered, but the improvements in launch capacity that had been revealed, and hence Japan's vulnerability to missile attack. North Korea had demonstrated launch capabilities considerably in advance of those predicted by American intelligence, even if the final stage of the missile did not separate properly. Some Japanese politicians even called for a pre-emptive strike against North Korea – even though Japan did not possess military aircraft capable of getting to Pyongyang and back, and no-one seemed to be recommending a return to the *kamikaze* tactics of the Second World War.

The Clinton administration was alarmed by this manifestation of volatility in Japanese politics, and the sorry state of the security debate there. But the administration made matters worse by taking a relaxed attitude to the *Taepodong* launch, seeing it more in counter-proliferation terms than as the equivalent to America's own experience with *Sputnik*. The Clinton administration also raised hackles in Japan by continuing to expect the Japanese to help fund the KEDO project, even though Japan had announced suspension of its funding. Moreover, the Japanese believed – apparently without foundation – that the United States had not provided them with timely intelligence on the *Taepodong* launch. Indeed, the problem seems to have been largely on Japan's side, because of its inadequate intelligence coordination and assessment machinery. This was a reflection of Japan's continuing problems with rampant factionalism.

Japan's response was both to strengthen its alliance with the United States, and to do some hedging. The *Taepodong* launch consolidated support in Japan for passing the new defence guidelines in the Diet. In October 1998, the Japanese government also announced its participation in research with the United States into theatre missile defences (TMD), in the form of the Navy Theater Wide system based on *Aegis* cruisers and destroyers. Trilateral coordination with the United States and South Korea was also improved, by means of the creation of the Trilateral Coordination and Oversight Group (TCOG) in April 1999.

But Japan also decided to acquire its own intelligence satellites, at considerable expense. This was partly to shore up the Mitsubishi Electric Company's troubled H-2A rocket programme. The move was also intended to break the monopoly of the Japan Defence Agency on the processing of satellite imagery, and to locate these functions more centrally in the Cabinet Intelligence Research Office. But more than techno-nationalism or turf battles was at stake here. Japan's hedging by buying and operating its own satellites was another sign that Japanese and US interests were not quite as congruent as they had been during the Cold War. Moreover, North Korea did not seem to be deterred from provocative behaviour.

North Korean spy boats

In March 1999, the government of Obuchi Keizo authorized Japan's Navy to use live ammunition to halt two North Korean spy ships in Japanese waters after Japan's coastguard had given chase without success. These spy ships apparently engage in espionage in Japan, and run drugs and high technology equipment to North Korea. On this occasion, only warning shots were authorized until almost at the end, and the ships got away. But in December 2001, Japan's coastguard cornered another North Korean spy ship. After the ship engaged the Japanese with rocket-propelled grenades, the coastguard responded with machine gun fire. Then the North Korean ship blew itself up, with the loss of all the crew. By the time it sank, the ship was in waters which China claims as part of its Exclusive Economic Zone.

Despite China's complaints, Japan went ahead with plans to salvage the ship. And to make the point, when Japan made a preliminary investigation in May 2002, one of Japan's *Aegis* warships of the *Kongo* class was hovering, albeit well over the horizon. It was a graphic illustration of how much North Korean provocations were doing not only to increase Sino–Japanese tensions, but of Japan's willingness to stand up to China. In June, salvage efforts confirmed that the North Korean spy ship had indeed carried rocket-propelled grenades. But the North Korean issue was not the only source of rising Sino–Japanese tensions. So was the Taiwan issue.

The Taiwan problem in the US–China–Japan triangle

The Taiwan problem, like that of the Korean Peninsula, was an issue that had not been settled during the Cold War. China had never given up its right to use force against Taiwan. For its part, despite the mantra of 'one China', the United States had never conceded that China had that right.

Taiwan emerged from the Cold War as a market-oriented and prosperous democracy of twenty-three million people. Democracy on Taiwan is thus an affront to the legitimacy of the authoritarians in Beijing, who have been elected by no-one. Their ruthlessness against their own people in 1989 contrasted with the vibrant, if somewhat rambunctious, democracy developing on Taiwan.

Nevertheless, China hoped to regain Taiwan by credible threat of force, in the same way that Hitler had gained the German-speaking areas of Czechoslovakia in 1938 – in the expectation that others would acquiesce through fear of war. China did not want to have to use force against Taiwan, not least because that would disrupt the peaceful environment which China needed in order to build up its own wealth and power. In fact, an attack on Taiwan would almost certainly fail, and that might well bring down the regime in Beijing. In 1982, that is what had happened to Argentina's military regime after it invaded the Falklands Islands and lost the subsequent war with Britain. And if China were to try to invade across the often-stormy hundred-mile width of the Taiwan Strait, it would invite a repetition of Hitler's problems with the English Channel in 1940.

Rather, China sought to take Taiwan by intimidation, after having successfully isolated the recalcitrant island from all those who might otherwise be tempted to support it. As we have noted, the Dutch were punished in 1981 for selling two submarines to Taiwan. The other Europeans then quickly ran up the white flag. And if China were to perceive that the balance of force in the Taiwan Strait was tilting in its favour, it would be tempted to take the island by force. Thus, in 1992, the Bush administration sold F-16s to Taiwan mainly to counter China's purchase of Russian SU-27s. (There were of course votes in Texas in the F-16 deal.)

The 1995 Taiwan Strait crisis

The 1995 Taiwan Straits crisis began in July 1995, when China launched surface-to-surface ballistic missiles ninety miles off the tip of northern

Taiwan. The crisis had its origins in the shabby treatment accorded to President Lee Denghui, when he stopped over in Hawaii in May 1994. This upset many members of the now Republican-dominated US Congress, not least because Lee was a democratically-elected leader. In the following year, when Lee sought to give an address at Cornell University, his alma mater, he was initially refused a visa. Congress was outraged at this snub, made more notable because the Irish Shin Fein leader Gerry Adams, considered a terrorist by Britain, had just been given a visa despite protests from London.

Congress duly voted 395 to 1 to give Lee his visa. Secretary of State Warren Christopher had assured Beijing this would not happen, but now he had to backtrack. China was already up in arms because in March 1994 Lee Denghui had given an interview to a Japanese writer where Lee – a Presbyterian – compared himself with Moses leading his people to the promised land. Lee, who had also studied at Kyoto University, intimated that he preferred Japanese to Chinese culture – a calculated insult which few in Beijing could ignore. And in June, Lee made his trip to Cornell, where he gave a political address to his class reunion.

In July, China conducted military exercises which included the launching of nuclear-capable missiles in the East China Sea, north of Taiwan. China was no doubt pleased to see that Taiwan's stock market dropped, and capital flight took place. In December, another round of Chinese military exercises was timed to coincide with Taiwan's parliamentary elections. The Clinton administration contented itself with sending a task force led by the aircraft carrier *Nimitz* through the Taiwan Strait, the first such passage by US warships through these international waters since 1979. But the message was blunted when Washington said that the task force's passage was due to bad weather – the weather had actually been fine. That timidity served only to embolden China.

The 1996 Taiwan Strait crisis

In March 1996, China fired ballistic missiles which bracketed Taiwan's ports, in an attempt to intimidate Taiwan during its first presidential election. These tactics backfired, because Lee Denghui won in a landslide victory. China's missile firings included the firing of nuclear-capable M-11s within ten miles of Taiwan's major ports, Keelung and Kaohsiung.

Despite the existence of the Taiwan Relations Act, which specifically refers to blockade, China apparently did not expect the United States to respond. As it happened, Admiral Liu Huaqui was visiting Washington at the time. Liu, a Long March veteran and China's answer to Mahan, reported directly to premier Li Peng. US Defense Secretary William Perry told Liu that he, as a former artilleryman, understood the significance of China's bracketing of Taiwan's ports. Perry warned Liu of 'grave conse-quences' – diplomatic code for war – should China attack Taiwan. No such language had been used to China for a quarter of a century. Moreover,

Perry's words were backed by action when the United States sent two aircraft carriers to the vicinity of the Taiwan Strait.

One of the repercussions of this incident was that China made a nuclear threat to the United States. A senior Chinese general, believed to be Xiong Guangkai (deputy chief of staff and chief of military intelligence), told Charles W. Freeman, Jr, a retired senior state department and defence official, 'You will not sacrifice Los Angeles to protect Taiwan'.[9] So much for China's No First Use pledge – its propaganda pledge not to be the first to use nuclear weapons. Moreover, Taiwan was not the only source of growing Sino–American strategic tension. Problems in the South China and East China Seas were also beginning to loom.

The South China Sea and the US–China–Japan triangle

Tensions in the South China and East China Seas are mostly a consequence of China's greater strategic latitude since the collapse of Soviet power. This enhanced latitude fired China's sense of historical grievance and strategic ambition. It is not that China suddenly became powerful with the end of the Cold War. Rather, it was no longer pinned down by the Soviet Union and its allies. The collapse of the Soviet Union, and the removal of its forces from Mongolia, lifted the strategic pressure on China from the north-western quarter. Since the late 1970s, heavily-armoured Soviet forces there had visibly threatened Beijing along the vulnerable Baikal–Yellow Sea corridor. Indeed, the retrenchment of Soviet troops from Mongolia was East Asia's strategic equivalent of the withdrawal of the Group of Soviet Forces from Eastern Germany, whence they had long threatened Western Europe.

Soviet forces were also greatly drawn down in Central Asia, across the border from China's vast and strategically sensitive province of Xinjiang. In the immense space between the Caspian Sea and the Chinese border, the Soviet collapse left in its wake a motley collection of weak states which represent little threat to China. To the south, China's strategic latitude was also enhanced. Deprived of its Soviet ally, Vietnam was forced to withdraw from Cambodia, and was brought to heel. (It subsequently sought dubious refuge in ASEAN.) To China's south-west, India was also deprived of its Soviet ally.[10] China sought to contain India by providing rival Pakistan with missiles and nuclear technology, some of which also came from North Korea.

Thus, with the end of the Cold War, China was relieved of strategic pressure on all of its land frontiers. It was soon pointing east and south, pressing on its maritime frontiers in the East China and South China Seas.[11] Even before the end of the Cold War, in 1986 the PLA Navy had begun to practise 'surge deployments' out into the Pacific, landing on uninhabited and virtually unknown islands where Japanese and American forces had fought nearly a half century before.

China's purchases of sophisticated Russian weapons began in 1992, when it bought twenty-four Su-27 advanced all-weather fighters. By buying these fighters, China greatly extended its power projection capabilities over its contiguous waters, and represented a heightened threat to Taiwan. In 1993, China acquired from Russia advanced surface-to-air missile systems, towed-array anti-submarine sonar, multiple-target torpedo control systems, nuclear submarine propulsion systems, and technology improving the range of its undersea-launched cruise missiles.[12]

In 1999, China signed a further contract for forty Su-30 ground-attack aircraft. A contract for approximately forty more Su-30s was signed in 2001. China also showed an interest in acquiring aircraft carriers.[13] And in 1994, China ordered four Russian *Kilo*-class attack submarines. Eight more were ordered in May 2002. These ultra-quiet submarines were developed by the Soviet Union specifically to target US aircraft carriers. China has also bought two *Sovremmeny*-class destroyers, with two more on order. The *Sovremmeny*, with their SS-N-22 (*Mosquit* or *Sunburn*) missiles, were developed to combat the *Aegis*-class US cruisers that protect aircraft carriers. Apart from being designed to deter US aircraft carriers in any future Taiwan Strait crisis, these acquisitions give China a reach sufficient to create a strategic buffer at sea much wider than it previously possessed.[14] Currently, Chinese arms purchases from Russia amount to some one billion dollars annually.

China pushes in the South China Seas

Not long after the Cold War ended, China's new strategic latitude, bolstered by its arms purchases from Russia, began to have unwelcome manifestations in the South China Sea. China was already well positioned in relation to the weak states to its south. In the latter stages of the Cold War, Beijing's alliance of convenience with America had given China a legitimate role in Southeast Asian security for the first time – with common opposition to Vietnam's Soviet-backed occupation of Cambodia serving as China's instrument. As we have noted, China had already demonstrated its ambition in the South China Sea when it forcibly occupied the Paracel archipelago in 1974, just before the communist victory in Saigon in 1975.

Driven by the search for power and resources, China's extensive territorial claims in the South China Sea represent the greatest threat to strategic security there.[15] Soon after the end of the Cold War, miscalculation by the Philippines, a founding member of ASEAN, did much to let China into the South China Sea. By insisting that the United States leave its bases in the Philippines in 1991, the Filipinos removed the chief means by which the United States could protect them. And by hobbling American maritime mobility, they emboldened China.

In February 1992, China's rubber-stamp parliament approved a law on territorial waters and contiguous areas which reaffirmed China's extensive territorial claims in the South China and East China Seas. China also asserted the right to evict the warships of other maritime powers from its territorial waters. Moreover, China required all foreign warships to give notice of intent to pass through China's claimed territorial waters, and to receive permission before doing so. The area that China claimed was vastly increased, and included the Paracel and Spratly archipelagos, as well as the Senkakus.

Apparently at the behest of the PLA, China asserted the right to use force in pursuit of these claims – in effect, asserting the right to use force against two US allies, Japan and the Philippines. China was emboldened, and Japan dismayed, by the near-silence from Washington. In the absence of a strategic approach in Washington, legal approaches became dominant. Thus the Clinton administration made only feeble protest at China's 1992 declaration, *even though China had asserted the right to use force against two US allies.*

South China Sea issues are strategic issues with legal faces. True, the United States has no vital interest in the question of who owns the scattered reefs and atolls of the South China Sea. But it does have a vital interest in freedom of the seas, and in Japan's resource security. Evidence then came to light early in 1995 that China had seized Mischief Reef in the Spratlys, which the Philippines also claims. Had the US Navy still been in Subic Bay, that seizure would have been unlikely. Mischief Reef is well within the Philippine 200-nautical-mile Exclusive Economic Zone. China subsequently built a four-storey concrete structure on the tiny outcrop, which is barely above high tide, complete with helipad and gun emplacements – while claiming that this was a mere fisherman's shack.

Again, America's response was tepid. Moreover, China's seizure of Mischief Reef did much to demonstrate the impotence of ASEAN. When China seized the reef, the other members did little to support the Philippines, partly because they thought the Filipinos had contributed to their own misfortunes.[16]

China also played divide-and-rule within the newly-constituted ASEAN Regional Forum (ARF). The ARF is East Asia's only security forum, even though it consists of little more than an annual meeting of foreign ministers. Since many of the ASEAN states have conflicting territorial claims in the South China Sea, they have been unable to combine in defence of their interests.

Over time, ASEAN's disarray and timidity will allow China to pick off the other claimants one by one. For the moment, China lacks the long-range military capacity to enforce its claims over the South China Sea. So it bides its time, while insisting that it will negotiate with these weak states only on a bilateral basis. Meanwhile, the ARF is useful to the Chinese, since they use it to undermine the US alliance system in East Asia. The Cold War is long over, China says, so why does the region still need these alliances? In seeking to intimidate the ASEANs, China holds all the high cards. As the 'Middle Kingdom', it enjoys the advantages of size and geographical centrality. China is also the only great-power, nuclear-weapons state, and member of the United Nations Security Council, with territorial claims in the South China Sea. (As a permanent member of the Council, China could veto any military action against it under the terms of the UN Charter.)

The *chutzpah* terms under which China 'ratified' the UN Convention on the Law of the Sea (UNCLOS) in May 1996 were testimony to China's blue water ambitions, as well as to its penchant for manipulating international law. In ratifying UNCLOS, China made archipelagic claims to the Paracels, by drawing baselines around the whole group – despite the fact that China is a continental rather than an archipelagic state under the terms of UNCLOS. This had no doubt been China's intention from the time it seized the Paracels in 1974. In the South China Sea, China is playing a long game.

The Chinese see time as a strategic asset, in much the same way that the Soviet Union saw space (distance, not the cosmos) as a strategic asset. Believing that time is on its side, China can afford to be patient. With America's scuttle from Vietnam much in mind, the Chinese say to the ASEANs *sotto voce*, 'remember Saigon: the Americans are unreliable. Sooner or later they will leave, so you had better accommodate us now, lest the price of future accommodation be made higher'. Some regional countries, while unwilling openly to defy China, hedge their bets. Singapore, for example, has built a berth at Changi Naval Base which can accommodate visiting US aircraft carriers. And for a while at least, there were some in Southeast Asia inclined to resist China.

Indonesia and Australia: growing resistance to Chinese pressure

Indonesia, for reasons of distance, size and visceral instinct, remained willing to resist China until after Suharto's fall in 1998. Moreover, it was prepared to combine with others in order to do so. Indonesia, whose suspicions of China dated back to the Mongol invasion in the thirteenth century, did not even normalize its diplomatic relations with China until the Cold War was over. Nor had its leaders forgotten China's efforts to take power in Indonesia in the mid-1960s. Thus, in December 1995, Indonesia entered into an unprecedented strategic alignment with Australia, a US ally.

The Agreement to Maintain Security (AMS) was a classic balance-of-threat response to Chinese strategic pressure in the South China Sea, especially Jakarta's belated realization that China's territorial claims might extend as far south as the Natuna Islands. The Natunas are the site of a huge gas field – the world's largest – and guard the eastern entrance to the Malacca Strait. Indonesia's suspicions were aroused when China gave assurances that it did not claim the Natunas themselves, but gave no such assurances about the gas fields. Moreover, China's claims appears on its maps as a dotted line, arousing more suspicion in Jakarta.

Indonesia and Australia, in acknowledging their shared security concerns, were willing to set aside the East Timor issue, which had been an ulcer between them since Indonesia's 1975 invasion of former Portuguese East

Timor. It was the first time that non-aligned Indonesia had entered into such an alignment with a foreign state. Indonesia also registered its displeasure with China's 'ratification' of the Law of the Sea convention in 1996, by holding unprecedentedly large exercises in defence of the Natunas. In addition, Indonesia made it clear to China that it considered that the baselines that it had drawn in the Paracels were illegal, and should not be repeated in the Spratlys.

But the Indonesia–Australia strategic alignment did not prove robust enough to survive the departure from the scene of its principals. In 1998, Suharto's fall was accompanied by East Timor's voting for independence. This was accompanied by widespread violence from anti-independence militias, backed by the Indonesian army. This aroused public opinion in Australia, long critical of Indonesian brutalities in East Timor, and led to Australia's UN-authorized intervention in the territory in September 1999. The demise of the Indonesia–Australia strategic alignment thus ended, it seems, the prospects for concerted resistance to China coming from any quarter in Southeast Asia. But while it was now 'jelly to the south', China's probes into the East China Sea met the bedrock of the US–Japan alliance – although there were a few wobbles along the way.

East China Sea tensions: the Senkakus

The Senkakus problem had been set aside, but not resolved, during the Cold War. As we have seen, Mao, in the interests of forging a strategic alignment with America in the early 1970s, was keen to avoid sources of potential trouble with Japan. Thus he was willing to shelve the dispute over the Senkakus. But once the Cold War was over, China began to probe towards the East China Sea. One reason was that China became a net importer of oil in 1993, and its vast demands for energy were fuelling a drive to find oil and gas in its adjacent waters.

China's probes towards the Senkakus started in late 1995, when it began sending ocean surveillance ships and oil drilling rigs into waters close to the islands. Soon the conflicting claims of Japan and China became embroiled in Law of the Sea issues. On 20 July 1996, Japan ratified the Law of the Sea, declaring a 200-nautical-mile Exclusive Economic Zone (EEZ) that included the Senkakus. This was in conflict with China's claim. Japan argued that the continental shelf should be divided along the median line between China and Japan. For its part, China advocated the natural prolongation of the continental shelf, which would give China most of the disputed territory, including the Senkakus. Moreover, as we have noted, in 1992 China asserted the right to use force in pursuit of its territorial claims. This was bound to cause resentment in Japan.

In July 1996, the right-wing Japan Youth Federation built a makeshift lighthouse on the Senkakus. It then applied to Japan's Maritime Safety Authority (MSA) for approval. While the MSA did not approve, it did say it had no legal grounds for removing the lighthouse from private property. With elections approaching in Japan – the first to be held under a new single member constituency system – the LDP campaigned on the platform that the Senkakus belonged to Japan.

China initially may have seen a handy issue with which to divide Taiwan from Japan, since Taiwan also claims the islands. But if driving a wedge between Taiwan and Japan was China's intention, it soon backfired. One reason was that passions were being aroused in Hong Kong. With Hong Kong due to revert to China in 1997, democracy activists there saw the Senkakus as an issue on which the Beijing government could be painted as having neglected national interests. Thus the arousing of nationalist sentiment in China was dangerous for Beijing, which soon pulled back.

But in September 1996, a freighter carrying Hong Kong activists approached within twelve nautical miles of the Senkakus, and was stopped by Japan's Maritime Safety Authority. Five activists jumped overboard, and one drowned. In early October, more activists landed on the islands, planting the flags of both China and Taiwan. And by that time, the Clinton administration's position on the Senkakus had hit a sensitive nerve in Japan.

As we have seen, at the time of the Okinawa reversion in 1972, the United States said that, although it did not take sides as to the sovereignty of the Senkakus, the islands came under the ambit of the US–Japan security treaty. While not wishing to offend China – in the interests of the rapprochement then under way – the United States had also seen the need to reassure Japan. By 1996, this had all been forgotten in Washington.

Nicholas Burns, the State Department spokesman, was asked at a press briefing what US obligations might be in case of a conflict between China and Japan. Burns replied that the issue was 'hypothetical', saying merely that he was confident that the issue could be resolved without the use of force. As Japanese indignation mounted, it was left to a Pentagon spokesman to mollify the Japanese by restating the official position that the Senkakus came within the ambit of the security treaty. But the Japanese were hard to mollify, suspecting that Washington's mishandling of the Senkakus question was another manifestation of the Clinton administration's inclination to put China's interests before those of Japan.

Japan: the need to think harder about security

The imbroglio over the Senkakus was a sign of changing times, as well as an indication that Japan was losing leverage within the alliance. The Japanese had spent the Cold War artfully dodging what they saw as US attempts to entangle Japan in its security problems. They were able to get away with this because they knew that the United States could not abandon them or their vital interests even if it wanted to. But for Japan, the Senkakus problem raised for the first time the risk of abandonment. And behind that specific concern lay the worry that the United States might in future seek to balance power in East Asia by playing off China against Japan.

Moreover, changes in technology increased the possibility that the United States might rethink the wisdom of forward deployment. There were now voices in the United States arguing that Chinese and North Korean missiles were making fixed bases and high-value targets such as aircraft carriers far too vulnerable – equivalent to the battleships of the 1930s. Far better, they argued, for the United States to withdraw to an offshore position and maintain a balance of power from there.

Thus, for the first time since 1945, the Japanese had to start thinking hard about their security. They had only three choices – to shore up their alliance with the United States by becoming more willing to share risk; to reach painful accommodation with China; or to go it alone. The last two choices had little appeal, even though it was no longer taboo in Japan to talk about nuclear weapons.[17] Strengthening the alliance was in fact the safest choice, even though it carried some risk of entanglement, for example in the Taiwan issue. That was because it is always safest in the long run to add one's weight to one's own side and help make sure that it wins. That was what America's European allies did during the Cold War, although it was a close run thing over INF in the mid-1980s. Moreover, no alliance can be sustained indefinitely when one party assumes most of the costs and all of the risks. That is especially so when the common threat, the 'glue' of the alliance, has evaporated.

But large sections of the Japanese political establishment had become used to ignoring security problems, or expecting the United States to resolve them. Since 1945, Japanese society in general had become extraordinarily averse to risk. Thus it was hard for many Japanese to realize that if you live in a dangerous neighbourhood, and in a self-help world without a common government or enforceable rules, risk-free choices simply do not exist. Moreover, the Japanese political system has been in paralysis for the past decade. The Liberal Democratic Party, in power for far too long, is corrupt and incompetent, while the opposition consists mostly of LDP renegades who are little better. Moreover, Japan suffers from its traditional problems in making decisions – rampant factionalism, and hence difficulty in seeing the big picture and the main game. And as the Clinton years showed, when the United States was unable to think and act strategically it could hardly expect its allies to be able to do so.

In January 2001, Japan's worries about abandonment were ameliorated when the Bush administration came to power, with a demonstrated intent of restoring the US–Japan alliance to the centre of its East Asia strategy. Still, by then the Cold War had been over for more than a decade. It was hard to avoid seeing that Japan's strategic options had been constricted, and its leverage within the alliance reduced. As it happened, the next fluctuation in the East Asian quadrilateral rebounded to Japan's benefit. But no guarantee existed that this would always be so.

The aftermath of the terrorist attacks in the United States: Russia

After September 2001, the equations of power within the quadrilateral shifted again as the result of the impact of the terrorist attacks on the United States. The initial consequences were that Russia and Japan gained some leverage on the other members, while China was a net loser.

President Vladimir Putin, whose KGB background well equips him to comprehend the equations of power, moved swiftly to take advantage of new strategic circumstances after 11 September 2001. He made sure he was the first foreign leader to telephone President Bush. Putin knows that the threat to Russia now comes not from the West, but from the South, and potentially from the East. Moreover, Russia needs both the United States and Europe. It cannot hope to recover economically, and regain international influence, if it is locked in conflict with the United States. Besides, there were other advantages to Russia in aligning itself with the West after the terrorist attacks.

Now the Western democracies would be less critical of Russia's crackdown on the Muslim Chechens in the Caucasus – a campaign that included the use of heavy artillery in urban areas, and the levelling of the Chechen capital, Grozny. All of these were violations of human rights far in excess of Israel's 2002 incursions into Palestinian territory in search of the militants who were orchestrating suicide bombings in Israel. But the 'international community', while censoring Israel, was more or less willing to turn a blind eye to Chechnya.

Putin also seized the chance to improve his position *vis-à-vis* China. In June 2001, Jiang Zemin visited Moscow to sign a new security treaty which China sought to point at the United States. The fact that Jiang went to Moscow to sign the agreement did not disguise the fact that Putin was a reluctant bridegroom at this wedding. In order to gain leverage against the Bush administration, Russia and China asserted that the 1972 Anti Ballistic Missile Treaty was a 'cornerstone of strategic stability'. As we have seen, the treaty had in fact been a means by which the Soviet Union had succeeded in hobbling US missile defences under the dubious doctrine of Mutually Assured Destruction or MAD, which had been so appealing to Western arms control liberals. In 2001, China saw the new treaty with Russia as a means of making it harder for Russia to cut a separate deal with America on the ABM Treaty. Not without cause, the Chinese feared that Putin might come to an understanding that would betray their interests.

Thus Russia and China were useful to each other. But little trust existed between them. Many Russians, including influential sectors of the military, worried that in selling sophisticated military equipment to China they were feeding a hand that would eventually bite them. Who could forget that Mao had once said that China would one day present the bill for the vast tracts of territory that China claimed were taken by Russia from the time of the Treaty of Aigun in 1858? Moreover, Russia was steadily losing people in the

Far East because much of the population in Soviet days had relied on military spending and subsidies that no longer existed. Meanwhile, the burgeoning Chinese population in Manchuria was pressing on the Amur frontier. The Chinese, always far more enterprising than Russians, were also gaining a grip on the Siberian economy.

Thus the new strategic circumstances after September 2001 provided new opportunities for Russia. Putin seems to have understood that America would now be even more committed to missile defences. Even if Russia continued to object, America would unilaterally abrogate the ABM treaty – a bilateral treaty – by giving Russia the required six months' notice. So Putin sensibly decided to accept the inevitable, and salvage what he could elsewhere. As the United States prepared to make war in Afghanistan, in order to hunt down Osama bin Laden and his *Al Queda* networks which had lodged there, Putin also realized that Russia could not prevent America from gaining a strategic foothold in Central Asia. So he played cleverly from a weak hand.

Russia, in order to help oust the *Taliban* in Afghanistan, provided arms and equipment to the Northern Alliance. The Alliance had been a Russian client since the mid-1990s when the *Taliban* took over all of the country except the Panjir valley, which the Tajik-dominated Northern Alliance still held against the mostly Pushtun *Taliban*. Russians were also in command of the tank forces and helicopter gunships that broke down the Taliban front lines. Moreover, Russia provided intelligence to the United States, and agreed to overflights of its air space.

Milestones in the Russo–American rapprochement included Putin's summit with Bush in Moscow in May 2002. That put the seal on an arms control agreement to slash nuclear arsenals on both sides to about a third of their previous levels, from just under 6,000 operationally deployed warheads to around 2,000. Reflecting weakness, Russia had to concede virtually all America's demands, including the right to store rather than destroy warheads. Putin received little in return, except for the fig leaf that the new agreement will be in the form of a treaty. And even that treaty will be subject to abrogation on three months' notice. While wishing to give Putin a face-saver as a hedge against Russian revanchism, the Bush administration does not intend to be hobbled by arms control agreements of the kind the United States entered into in the 1970s.

Russia was also rewarded with membership of a new NATO–Russia Council. The new council, while not conceding Russia a veto over NATO decisions, will give Russia a voice in NATO decision-making in relation to shared concerns such as counter terrorism and counter proliferation. Russia's new status will also make it more palatable for the military and conservatives there to swallow the inevitable further expansion of NATO into the former territory of the USSR by incorporating the Baltic countries. Putin, not wishing any trouble on his eastern frontiers while he rebuilds Russia's wealth and power, was punctilious informing the Chinese about his dealings with the West. Still, the talk about NATO stretching in future from 'Vancouver to Vladivostok' cannot have been music to the ears of the rulers in Beijing.

China: strategic latitude restricted

China, which had been a major beneficiary of the way the Cold War ended, found its strategic latitude constricted as an unexpected consequence of the terrorist attacks in the United States. Seeking advantage, especially over Japan, China quickly announced support for America in the war on terrorism. With a leadership succession in train, and economic and social strains from joining the World Trade Organization ever more apparent, China was anxious to repair tensions with Washington following the April 2001 EP-3 reconnaissance aircraft incident.[18] China did make some gains after the terrorist attacks in the United States. American criticism of China's crackdown in Tibet and Xinjiang was muted. Moreover, President Bush travelled to Shanghai in October 2001 for the Apec summit. He also visited China in February 2002 to commemorate Nixon's visit to China in February 1972, and received vice-president Hu Jintao, Jiang's putative successor, in Washington in April 2002.

But for China, these gains were outweighed by large negatives. If China had anticipated that the United States would be willing to set aside Taiwan's interests in order to secure China's support in the war against terrorism, it miscalculated. To the contrary, during his 2002 visit to China, George W. Bush upheld American commitments to Taiwan.[19] In May 2001, the administration, confirming the president's prior indication that he would sell to Taiwan whatever it needed to defend itself, agreed to sell the island the biggest arms package in a decade, including eight diesel submarines and four *Knox*-class frigates. There was no subsequent backtracking from these commitments.

Indeed, in March 2002, Taiwan's defence minister was permitted to travel to a private conference in Florida, where he met senior US officials on the margins of the gathering. That was the first such visit by a Taiwan defence minister since America abrogated its security treaty with Taiwan in 1979. And when president Bush visited China, he was careful to go to Japan and South Korea first, and to spend more time in those countries than in China.

To China's consternation, when the United States made war in Afghanistan it bypassed the UN Security Council. China had apparently offered the United States a bargain not to block the United States in the Security Council, in exchange for reduced US arms sales to Taiwan. But if so, China badly misjudged US intentions. It was soon clear that the United States had no intention of rounding up a posse and then giving it a Security Council imprimatur. Moreover, America refused to label the Uighurs in Xinjiang as 'terrorists'. And China's hopes that the United States would become bogged down in Afghanistan soon proved illusory. On the contrary, the Afghan War showed that America's ability to project power from a distance had improved leaps and bounds since the 1990 Gulf War. (The importance of the island of Diego Garcia for the US bombing campaign was also underlined.[20]) Those improvements in US capabilities did not bode well for China in contemplating a future clash over Taiwan.

America's growing foothold in Central Asia also undermined China's efforts to use the Shanghai Coordination Organization (SCO) as its instrument. Designed mainly to combat Islamic extremism, the group included China, Russia and the four central Asian states of Kazakhstan, Uzbekistan, Kyrgysztan and Tajikistan. The SCO was also a means by which Russia and China could jointly contain US influence in landlocked Central Asia, which has significant reserves of minerals, oil and gas. Moreover, China saw the SCO as a tool which would help China to stabilize its landward frontiers, thus leaving it free to concentrate on Taiwan and the South China Sea. The SCO was also intended to be another platform, apart from the ASEAN Regional Forum, from which China could undermine the US alliance network in East Asia.

But, by mid-2002, China's strategy in relation to the SCO was in tatters. Thus Chinese leaders were reduced to using the occasion of the June 2002 SCO meeting in St Petersburg to complain about the US foothold in Central Asia, especially in Uzbekistan. To make things even worse, Putin also implied that the United States would be welcome to join the SCO.

For China, with Central Asia suddenly looking much less promising, the outlook on its southwestern frontiers was not much better. True, there were some gains. China was happy to see the demise of the *Taliban* rulers of Afghanistan, because it believed, or professed to believe, that the *Taliban* had permitted Uighur training camps in Afghanistan. But the outcome of the war was not much to China's liking. The interim Afghan government was led by the moderate Pushtun, Hamid Kazai, which suited China well enough. But although charming and articulate, Kazai wielded little authority. That was mostly in the hands of the Tajik-dominated Northern Alliance, oriented towards Russia and India, which held the key portfolios of interior, foreign affairs and defence. All three ministers had lost no time in paying their respects in New Delhi. Thus Afghanistan seemed once again to have fallen between a Russo–Indian nutcracker. Moreover, growing – if limited – US–India defence cooperation represented a setback to China's strategy of keeping India contained in its subcontinent.

Pakistan, while still a good friend of China, was drawing closer to the United States, including by allowing America to set up listening posts in northern Pakistan, bordering Xinjiang and Tibet. China is also uncomfortable with the growing US presence at Pansni in Beluchistan. That is close to the port China is building at Gwadar, which is to be linked with Karachi via the Makram coastal highway.[21]

And while China was confronted with these unwelcome new complications on its landward frontiers, on its seaward periphery the outlook was little better because Japanese warships were operating in the Indian Ocean for the first time since 1942. But China could not openly complain about it. Japan was throwing off some of its constitutional restrictions because the government of Koizumi Junichiro was determined not to repeat the fiasco of the 1990 Gulf War. Thus, after a shaky start, Japan moved with unaccustomed speed to provide non-combat naval support for the United States, including by refuelling US warships in the Indian Ocean.[22] Moreover, Koizumi had already indicated that he believed that Japan should abandon the ruling, adopted in 1972 in order to appease China, that it was prohibited by its constitution from engaging in collective self defence.

On China's southern maritime periphery, the United States was also increasing its military presence. The year 2002 saw the return of the US military to the Philippines, where US forces acted as advisors to Filipino troops battling Abu Sayyaf Muslim extremists and kidnappers in Mindanao. While the US Navy will not be returning to Subic Bay, it is likely to make port calls and demonstrate an increasing presence which is welcomed by the Arroyo government. Since the Chinese lodged on Mischief Reef, the Philippines has seen good reason to shore up its alliance with the United States. The annual *Cobra Gold* military exercises with Thailand were also broadened to include other Southeast Asian countries, as well as Australia. This was a means by which regional countries could welcome an increased US military presence, and hedge against growing Chinese power, without drawing too much attention to themselves.

Moreover, at the end of September 2001, the US Quadrennial Defense Review talked about strengthening the 'Asian littoral' in order to maintain a balance of power in East Asia. President Bush's State of the Union address in January 2002 also seemed to implicate China when he referred to Iran, Iraq and North Korea as an 'axis of evil'. All three are beneficiaries of the Chinese proliferation of missiles and other military technology. And in March 2002, leaked accounts of the new US Nuclear Posture Review indicated that China was one of seven countries targeted by US nuclear weapons.[23] While the Bush administration had welcomed China's support in the war against terrorism, it had also demonstrated that Beijing no longer had a monopoly on *realpolitik*.

Thus, as a consequence of the US response to the terrorist attacks, the equations of power in the East Asian quadrilateral have fluctuated once more. Russia, while still weak, now has a skilled operator in the driver's seat. Japan moved quickly to strengthen its alliance with the United States, while China has lost out on most counts. With the war in Afghanistan drawing to an end, now all the players in the East Asian quadrilateral had to start to think about how they would respond if the United States attacked Iraq as the next step in its war against terrorism.

For all US friends and allies, this was shaping up as a major test of political skill. Those who moved nimbly were likely to reap rich rewards, while the United States was likely to take a dim view of fence-sitting allies. Japan, for example, had to start thinking about what might happen in relation to the Iraq problem if Russia turned out to be a more useful partner for the United States than Japan did. After all, Russia had been allied with America in two world wars. It could become a security partner again, should circumstances warrant. As shown by the despatch of an *Aegis* destroyer to the Gulf in late 2002, Japan seems to have taken the point that it must demonstrate its worth as an ally - even if its role in an Iraq war were confined to rear area support the end of the Cold War, there is no collision of strategic interest between Russia and America – though there is a problem with Russian arms sales to China, which threaten to upset the balance in the Taiwan Strait. If that rather large problem can be resolved, the next fluctuation of the East Asian quadrilateral might see Russia and the United States moving closer together in order to check a rising China.

That would please neither China nor Japan. But it is a reminder of the fact that America's essential interest in East Asia lies in the striking and maintenance of equilibrium, rather than in any particular configuration of the East Asian quadrilateral.

Conclusion:
war without end?

Since the first East Asian war of the modern era, the region has seen ten great-power wars, counting the Cold War. At one time or another, each member of the East Asian quadrilateral has fought each of the others. Russia and Japan fought four times – 1904–1905; 1918–1922; 1938–1939; and 1945. Russia and China went to war in 1929, and came to the brink in 1969. China and America fought in Korea between 1950 and 1953, and came to the brink over the Taiwan Strait in 1954 and 1958. Japan and the United States were at war between 1941 and 1945. China and Japan fought in 1894–1895, and between 1937 and 1945. Then Russia and the United States squared off in the Cold War. Although they avoided a head-on clash, mostly because the existence of nuclear weapons made it too risky, they fought proxy wars in Korea and Vietnam, as well as in Afghanistan – a part, albeit a distant one, of East Asia's 'strategic hinterland'.

Like Afghanistan, Manchuria the 'cockpit of Asia' was afflicted with unfortunate strategic geography because it was where the expanding Russian Empire was checked by those determined to stand in its way. Manchuria was the locus of conflict for five of East Asia's wars – between China and Japan in 1894; between Japan and Russia in 1904; between China and Russia in 1929; between Russia and Japan in 1938 and 1939; and between China and the United States from 1950 to 1953. Moreover, the roots of the 1941–1945 Pacific War lay in Manchuria, in Japan's growing collision of interest with the United States after 1905 when Japan sought to shut the Open Door in America's face.

The fluctuations within the quadrilateral have been equally remarkable. When Japan and China clashed in 1894, Russia sided with China, hoping to pick up the spoils – which were not on offer because Japan won. Then when Japan and Russia went to war in 1904, the United States cheered Japan. China also sided with Japan, seeing it as the lesser of two evils. That proved to be a miscalculation, because after 1905 Russia and Japan lost no time in colluding at China's expense. Their collusion then engaged American interests in defending the Open Door in China. During the First World War,

Japan, Russia and the United States were allies of a kind. When China and Russia went to war in 1929, Japan and the United States sat on the sidelines.

Then, as Japan increasingly encroached upon China in the 1930s, the United States sought to stand in the way. But suspicion between Bolshevik Russia and capitalist America was such that they were unable to sink their differences in order to combine against Japan. So, to reduce the risks of two-front war, as Japan and Germany moved into strategic alignment in the late 1930s, Russia encouraged Japan into war, first with China, and then with the United States. When Japan and the United States did go to war in 1941, Russia stood on the sidelines, although it became an American ally in the war in Europe after being its itself attacked by Nazi Germany, its recent partner in carving up Europe. Meanwhile, China was an American ally of sorts, while husbanding resources supplied by the United States in order to square off later against internal foes. Then Russia attacked Japan in 1945, just in time to pick up its share of the booty. After 1949, Russia and China allied against the United States and Japan. Then China switched sides in 1971, thus helping the United States defeat Russia.

Given these gyrations over the last century, fluctuations among the quadrilateral can be expected to continue. Currently, the greatest source of tension is between the United States and China. That is because China seems bent on hegemony over East Asia and its contiguous seas – an ambition which the United States cannot afford to ignore in the interests of its own maritime security. Moreover, with Russia having turned towards democracy, however imperfectly, China is now the only member of the quadrilateral which still has an authoritarian government. Is conflict therefore inevitable between China and the United States? Before trying to answer that question, let us first dispense with various panaceas for managing strategic tension in East Asia.

The economic interdependence fallacy

The most popular of these panaceas is the notion that economic interdependence prevents wars. Just before the outbreak of the First World War, Norman Angell wrote in *The Great Illusion* that 'globalization' made it illusory to think that countries could increase their wealth or territory by military means. War in Europe was now unthinkable, he wrote, because the European powers would not be so deluded as to undermine their essential economic interests. The European economies were intertwined, and their royal families were intermarried. As in Europe in 1914, it is a dangerous fallacy in East Asia today to think that economic interdependence of itself makes great-power war less likely.

Since the September 2001 terrorist attacks in the United States, Americans are less likely to think that 'it's all economics now'. Indeed, the idea that economic forces drive history is too simple. What is striking is the interaction of economic development, technological progress, plus strategic geography and the driving force of interest in shaping international relations. Economics, politics and strategy interact in complex ways. But economic interdependence of itself cannot guarantee security.

It would be especially dangerous, for example, for Japan to think that it could use its economic power to ensure its strategic security. On the contrary, Japan's wealth could make it an inviting target. Moreover, China's minatory behaviour in relation to Taiwan points to the fallacy of the argument that it's 'all economics now'. Some eighty or so billion US dollars of Taiwanese investment in China, and thirty billion dollars of cross-Strait trade annually, do little to inhibit Beijing from threatening the recalcitrant island. As the trade and investment links grow, so does the number of nuclear-capable missiles opposite Taiwan. By mid-2002, the number had reached approximately 400. 'Marry me or I'll kill you' is indeed a novelty in international politics.

Democracy as panacea

Another popular misconception is that the increase in the number of democracies in East Asia could be a panacea for unresolved strategic problems. It may be true that stable democracies do not threaten one another. But Japan is the only such democracy in East Asia. Moreover, there is more to democracy than the existence of parliaments and representative governments. While South Korea and Taiwan have made remarkable progress, both have some way to go. In South Korea, for example, the advent of democracy has made the fostering of anti-Japanese nationalism an ever-present temptation for its politicians. President Kim Dae Jung has done his best to dampen down such sentiments, but his successor might think differently. Meanwhile, north of the 38th parallel on the Korean Peninsula, the world's most repressive and militarist regime is kept on life support because of its ability to intimidate others.

Even when countries abandon authoritarian rule, stability can be hard to come by. In 1998, Indonesia turned towards democracy after the overthrow of Suharto. But democracy proved to be no panacea. Indeed, Suharto's demise left a power vacuum that even competent leaders would be hard pressed to fill, and these do not seem to be in prospect.

The multilateralist myth

A third fallacy is that East Asia's great-power tensions can be resolved by arms control, diplomatic process and multilateral institutions. At the end of the Cold War, optimists hoped that a multilateral security organization could be formed in Asia, along the lines of the Conference on Security and Cooperation in Europe (CSCE). Those aspirations informed the creation of the ASEAN Regional Forum (ARF). But the ARF is trying to build upon sand.[1] Misplaced hopes in the Forum are a consequence of the view that international tensions rise from confusion and misunderstanding, rather than from collisions of strategic interest.

On the historical record, multilateral security cooperation has worked in only three circumstances. The first was in combining to meet a common danger, such as the alliances which formed against Napoleon and Hitler, or the Western Alliance which was created to meet the Soviet threat after 1945. Setting aside differences in order to meet a common threat can make strange bedfellows – for example, despite visceral enmity going back centuries, Turkey and Greece cooperated in NATO because Soviet power threatened them both.

The second success of multilateral security has been in cleaning up the mess after victory has been won. That has essentially been the role of the CSCE (now the Organization of Security and Cooperation in Europe, OSCE) after the Cold War. Helping the loser to save face has been an important consideration in helping to reduce the risk of Russian revanchism. But until the Cold War had been won, the CSCE was a tool of Soviet *realpolitik*, in the Leninist tradition.

The third success of multilateral security was the 1922 Washington Settlement in East Asia. This prevented a naval arms race between the United States, Britain and Japan. Two of the parties, Japan and Britain, knew they lacked the resources for such an arms race with America. In the United States, which could afford an arms race, saner elements were able to stop the US Navy from continuing to build against Britain, a country with which America had no collision of strategic interest. The Washington Settlement thus suggests that arms control can indeed work when it suits the interests of the participants – as long as they genuinely want peace and can agree on what constitutes sufficiency – that is, on 'how much is enough?' But the Washington Settlement was no proof against changing times, especially the rise of militarism in Japan.

Despite these successes of multilateral security, the limitation of destabilizing arms and military technology transfers by means of multilateral cooperation has yet to prove successful if a clash of interests already exists. For example, the so-called 'international community' is uninterested in sanctions against China for its illicit or dubious weapons technology transfers. The arms control fraternity, whose impetus came originally from the appalling casualties of the First World War, keeps forgetting that weapons do not cause wars. Thus efforts to abolish weapons cannot prevent wars. Weapons are not in themselves the cause of great-power tension, though the character and production of weapons can heighten tension and uncertainty when a collision of interest is already present.

Arms control is not a palliative that can reconcile those who are already on a collision course. That is why it is a delusion to think that, in current circumstances, approaches based on arms control and diplomatic process –

however deeply attractive to diplomats and academics – can ameliorate rising tensions between China and the United States.

The neo-isolationist delusion

The neo-isolationist approach is flawed for different reasons. American neo-isolationists think that the United States should 'come home', and shelter behind its vast oceans. They say that, if the United States were to withdraw from East Asia, China and Japan would be compelled to resolve their differences and Japan would no longer be able to free-ride on America.[2] But if the United States were to give up forward deployment at both ends of Eurasia, it would be risking its own security.

Eurasia was the essential interest that made it imperative for the United States to 'contain' the Soviet Union during the Cold War. The maritime basis of American security means that its strategic needs, even after the end of the Cold War, are best served by continued forward deployment and enduring alliances at both ends of Eurasia. Isolationism is in fact the most dangerous choice for a maritime power. That is because it concedes all the initiative to the enemy, including the choice of when and where to apply force. Winston Churchill understood this in the dark days of 1940, when a different prime minister might have advocated pre-emptive capitulation to Nazi Germany. Thus Churchill pursued an aggressive naval campaign in the Mediterranean. That was the only way to take the fight to Hitler, and thus to show America that Britain would not throw in the towel. Paradoxically, what seemed to be the most dangerous option was in fact the course that carried the least risk, as well as the best hope for eventual victory and the retention of national independence.

The lesson of history is that, for the United States as the dominant maritime power, it is far less costly in the long run to remain forward deployed, and thus help shape regional balances at both ends of Eurasia. Currently, without the United States 'keeping the ring' in East Asia, underlying visceral enmities could easily get out of hand. Tensions are rising between China and Japan, while South Korea remains unreconciled to Japan. If the United States did leave the region, it would probably be forced to come back on some future occasion under less advantageous circumstances. That was the longer term cost of US isolationism after the First World War, when in 1940 the United States found itself scrambling to meet palpable threats which had appeared at the opposite shores of both its great oceans.

Currently, to acknowledge that America's best option is to balance power at both ends of Eurasia by means of forward deployment and enduring alliances is not to say that the US–Japan alliance can be sustained on its current lopsided basis, with America shouldering all the risk. On the contrary, the alliance is highly vulnerable to external shocks of the kind presented by the 1990–1991 Gulf War and the 1994 North Korean nuclear crisis. So the United States needs to maintain pressure on Japan, despite its continuing political paralysis. The first thing the Japanese must do is to change the constitutional ruling, adopted in 1972 in order to appease China, that Japan cannot engage in collective self defence.

Reaching strategic accommodation with China?

Some observers who reject neo-isolationist approaches believe that the United States must reach strategic accommodation with China. Because China is a continental power, and the United States is a maritime power, they say, East Asia is now 'bipolar'. Thus tensions will not get out of hand because bipolarity is likely to produce stability. Twenty-first century bipolarity, Robert Ross argues, 'should be relatively stable and peaceful, in part because geography reinforces bipolar tendencies towards stable balancing and great-power management of regional order.'[3] This analysis reflects the belated rediscovery of strategic geography by the political scientists.[4] Ross's policy prescription is that the United States must accommodate China's interests. Zbigniew Brzezinski arrives at the same policy point via a somewhat different route. He argues that America cannot have a geostrategy for mainland Asia unless it reaches accommodation with China.[5]

Does the 'offshore balancer' really need China's acquiescence in order to maintain a balance of power in East Asia? Do geostrategic asymmetries necessarily mitigate conflict? History suggests that the answer to both questions is 'No'. During the Cold War, the United States was a maritime power and the Soviet Union was a continental power. But these geostrategic asymmetries did not produce peace. On the contrary, the clash of interest arose because the Soviet Union emerged from the Second World War as a near-hegemon in Eurasia. The United States then concluded that, because of the maritime basis of its own security, it could not tolerate Soviet domination of Eurasia. Spykman had warned of the risk of Soviet hegemony as early as 1942.

Yet response must always be commensurate with threat. Thus it serves no purpose to exaggerate the nature of the challenge posed by China.[6] Currently, China does not represent a threat to the United States remotely resembling that formerly represented by the USSR, when it possessed huge military power and stretched across Eurasia, threatening US allies at both ends. Thus containment of China is not yet required, and may not be in the future. But if China does indeed seek hegemony over East Asia, that will represent a challenge that the United States will not be able to ignore. In the interim, America needs to keep its alliances in good repair, while encouraging China further into the global economy, where market forces may indeed act as 'solvents of tyranny'.

The tangle of interests

The key to East Asian security is the tangle of interests among China, Japan and the Korean Peninsula. Because of the maritime basis of American security, this tangle is bound to catch US interests.

The most dangerous Sino–US tensions exist in relation to Taiwan, because the Taiwan issue touches on central issues of power in China. No contender to high office in Beijing can afford to appear soft on Taiwan. Moreover, the central government can rely on Chinese nationalism in enlisting public support on the Taiwan issue. Thus the United States must not risk pushing Beijing into a corner on a core issue of sovereignty in which China may not think 'rationally', in terms of US definitions of rationality. In 1941, the United States sought to deter Japan, but the Japanese were not making 'rational' calculations according to American ways of thinking. Rather, they were provoked into making 'use it or lose it' (mis)calculations.

America's essential interest in the Taiwan issue is that China should not get away with the use of force. It is not the question of who rules in Taipei. Neither will any government in Washington allow any government in Taiwan to determine whether or not the United States goes to war with China. At the heart of the Taiwan issue is Beijing's insistence that it has the right to use force to bring the renegade island to heel, and the inadmissibility of this precedent for many countries. The United States is the only country capable of standing in China's way if it seeks to use force to reintegrate Taiwan. While others will cheer from the sidelines, they will do so silently. Thus, for American policy, the difficulty is likely to arise because there is a potential conflict in trying to balance the risk of pushing China into a corner against the imperative of stopping it from 'recovering' Taiwan by force or threat.

Apart from Taiwan, the greatest risk of war in East Asia is on the Korean Peninsula. There, America's essential strategic interest is what it has been since 1950 – the strategic security of Japan. Thus the starting point of American policy on the Korean Peninsula must be how it plays in Tokyo, not in Pyongyang. That is why it was a mistake for the Clinton administration to seek to come to a deal with North Korea just before it left office. Pyongyang had considerable leverage because its leaders knew that Clinton was keen to secure the Nobel Peace Prize which had eluded him in the Middle East. The proposed agreement would apparently have traded the freezing of Pyongyang's long-range *Taepodong* programme for the end of production and deployment of the *Nodongs*. But the existing *Nodongs* would have been left in place, and thus able to threaten Japan.

Given the nature of the regime in Pyongyang, it is hard to see any way forward other than containment.[7] Given the lack of reciprocity from North Korea, Kim Dae Jung's 'sunshine policy' in now in tatters, not least because of the clashes in the Yellow Sea in late June 2002 that left five South Korean sailors dead.[8] But US policy is vulnerable because America's continuing military presence on the peninsula depends on Seoul's agreement. Partly as a consequence of the 'sunshine policy', anti-American and anti-Japanese nationalism is rising in South Korea. In December 2002, South Koreans elected Roh Moo-hyung. He said during the campaign that if North Korea and the United States went to war, South Korea should remain neutral. Moreover, the very economic success of South Korea has complicated matters because of the opening it has given to China. Thus a real problem exists in basing US policy on an economically successful South Korea which, encouraged by China, is likely to overplay or misplay its hand.

In broader terms, security in East Asia requires that the United States and Japan pay close attention to the importance of maritime force balances, and to the health of their alliance. This is because the balance of power in East Asia is the paradigm that demonstrates the salience of maritime power to broad international security.

There are other illustrative examples, most prominently the need to guarantee the security of the industrial world's oil supplies from the Persian Gulf. This, of course, has become tied up with America's war on terrorism, and the threat posed by Iraq's pursuit of weapons of mass destruction. But with the Pacific nexus increasingly driving world economic growth, the need to establish a stable power equilibrium in East Asia is an imperative of international security that the United States cannot afford to ignore.

Notes

Introduction

1 Ironically, far more Europeans were killed in Europe after the Cold War than during it, as a consequence of the turmoil in the former Yugoslavia. But the 'wars of the Yugoslav succession' did risk conflict among the great powers. Even during NATO's 1999 bombing campaign in Kosovo, undertaken to prevent 'ethnic cleansing' of Kosovar Muslims by Serbs, no risk existed that Russia, historically the protector of the Serbs, would fight on their behalf.

2 Cf. John J. Mearsheimer, *The Tragedy of Great Power Politics*, New York, Norton, 2001.

3 For the view that China is headed for economic and political turmoil, see Gordon G. Chang, *The Coming Collapse of China*, New York, Random House, 2001.

4 For an introduction to strategic geography, see Colin S. Gray and Geoffrey Sloan, eds, *Geopolitics, Geography and Strategy*, London, Frank Cass, 1999.

5 A 'core area' emerges at a centre of hydrographic convergence; for example, in the case of Britain, in the Thames Valley, which faces the English Channel. Power and authority radiate along the river networks and/or sea-lanes, forming a distinctive centre of political power and authority. See John P. LeDonne, *The Russian Empire and the World 1700–1917: The Geopolitics of Expansion and Containment*, New York, Oxford University Press, 1997, pp. 1–20.

6 For a recent introduction to China's traditional approaches to security, see Michael D. Swaine and Ashley J. Tellis, *Interpreting China's Grand Strategy: Past, Present and Future*, Santa Monica, Ca, RAND, 2000, chapter 3.

7 Le Donne, *The Russian Empire*, p. 18.

8 John W. Garver, *Protracted Contest; Sino–Indian Rivalry in the Twentieth Century*, Seattle and London, University of Washington Press, 2001, p. 280.

9 *Ibid.*, p. 244.

10 *Ibid.*, p. 281. In 1961, when China was looking for leverage against India as tensions grew in the Himalayas, it returned the relic to Ceylon.

11 Ronald P. Toby, *State and Diplomacy in Early Modern Japan: Asia in the Development of the Tokugawa Bakufu*, Stanford, Ca, Stanford University Press, 1991, p. 172.

12 It was a *samurai* practice to cut off the heads of slain enemies, to prove how many they had killed. Because heads were too large to transport easily from Korea, Hideyoshi opted for noses and ears.

13 Except for the Burma–India–China theatre, the Second World War in the Pacific was fought entirely in or over islands, if the Malayan campaign of 1941–1942 is counted as an island campaign because its object was the capture of Singapore.

14 The analogy is not exact because there is more than one exit through the Southeast Asian straits.

1. East Asia to 1905

1 In the age of capitalism, the effect was to contain costs. The unit cost of moving vehicles against the resistance of water was (and remains) cheaper than flanged wheel on steel rail, which is itself cheaper than rubber tyre on asphalt. The same is true of moving aluminum through the air, the great cost here being the initial lift. These cost considerations explain the short era of canal transport, which was important to early industrialization. I am indebted to A. D. McLennan for these observations.

2 Hence the double-headed eagle became the symbol of the Russian state when Ivan the Great married the niece of the last Byzantine emperor Constantine XI. Thus in 1547 Ivan IV ('Ivan the Terrible') was crowned as tsar, when Moscow took over as the inheritor of the Byzantine empire. One head of the eagle looked east towards the Turkish menace, the other to the west, the only source of aid.

3 Walter A. McDougall, *Let the Sea Make a Noise: Four Hundred Years of Cataclysm, Conquest, War and Folly in the North Pacific*, New York, Avon, 1993, p. 48.

4 John P. LeDonne, *The Russian Empire and the World 1700–1917: The Geopolitics of Expansion and Containment*, New York, Oxford University Press, 1997, p. 169.

5 *Ibid.*, p. 182.

6 In August 1862, a party of four English riders crossed the path of the Satsuma *daimyo* near Yokohama. When they failed to dismount to show respect, the *daimyo's* retinue attacked the foreigners, killing one. The attack was hardly surprising, because *samurai* had long been authorized to cut down Japanese commoners if they failed to show respect, or even if they behaved in an 'unexpected manner'.

7 Le Donne, *The Russian Empire*, p. 332.

8 Denis and Peggy Warner, *The Tide at Sunrise: A History of the Russo–Japanese War, 1904–1905*, New York, Charterhouse, 1974, p. 90.

9 The Koreans' defiance also helped spark the 1877 Satsuma rebellion, when the Satsuma leader Saigo Takamori was turned down by the other *genro* when he proposed invading Korea to teach the Koreans a lesson.

10 Warner and Warner, *The Tide at Sunrise*, p. 55.

11 Hisahiko Okazaki, *A Grand Strategy for Japanese Defense*, New York and London, Abt, 1986, p. 21.

12 Warner and Warner, *The Tide at Sunrise*, p. 121.

13 Lake Baikal, four hundred miles long, lay directly across the route, so it could not be bypassed. It was also surrounded by high mountains. Thus this section of the railway, which skirted the southern shore, had not been finished by 1904. The Russians were using ferries in summer, but in winter the troops had to walk. Supplies were carried by horse-drawn sleds, which sometimes fell through the ice.

14 For a recent account, see Constantine Pleshakov, *The Tsar's Last Armada: The Epic Voyage to the Battle of Tsushima*, New York, Basic Books, 2002.

15 Warner and Warner, *The Tide at Sunrise*, p. 304.

16 *Ibid.*, p. 147.

2. Unstable balance 1905–1935

1   Denis and Peggy Warner, *The Tide at Sunrise: A History of the Russo–Japanese War, 1904–1905,* New York, Charterhouse, 1974, p. 574.

2   Most railway construction in the US and Canada was market-driven. But there were consciously strategic motives in relation to the Pacific Railroad, which linked California to the rest of the country, as well as in relation to the Gadsden Purchase by which the United States gained extra territory along the New Mexico–Arizona border with Mexico. That helped make the border easier to defend. In Canada, national and strategic interests intervened in some cases, for example in the decision to build the Canadian Pacific Railway north of Lake Superior. The logical and cheaper route lay to the south, but that would have taken it through US territory. The Canadian Pacific's southern route (its second line) was also meant to tie British Columbia more tightly to Canada.

3   Hisahiko Okazaki, *A Grand Strategy for Japanese Defense,* New York and London, Abt, 1986, p. 62.

4   For Japan's railway empire in South Manchuria, see Ramon H. Myers, 'Japanese Imperialism in Manchuria: The South Manchurian Railway Company, 1906–1933', in Peter Duus, Ramon H. Myers and Mark R. Peattie, *The Japanese Informal Empire in China, 1895–1937,* Princeton, N.J, Princeton University Press, 1989, pp. 101–132.

5   For a history of the secret treaties, see Bruce A. Elleman, 'The 1907–1916 Russo–Japanese secret treaties: A reconsideration', *Journal of Cultural Studies,* 25, March 1999, pp. 29–44.

6   Walter A. McDougall, *Let the Sea Make a Noise: Four Hundred Years of Cataclysm, Conquest, War and Folly in the North Pacific,* New York, Avon, 1993, p. 480.

7   Warner and Warner, *The Tide at Sunrise,* p. 575.

8   For Japan in the First World War, see Frederick R. Dickinson, *War and National Reinvention: Japan in the Great War, 1914–1919,* Cambridge Ma, Harvard University Press, 1999.

9   David C. Evans and Mark R. Peattie, *Kaigun: Strategy, Tactics and Technology in the Imperial Japanese Navy, 1887–1941,* Annapolis, Md, Naval Institute Press, 1997, p. 168.

10 Japan's interest in Fujian was longstanding. In negotiations leading up to the June 1907 Franco–Japanese treaty, Japan had expressed an interest in Fujian. Ernest Batson Price, *The Russo–Japanese Treaties of 1907–1916 Concerning Manchuria and Mongolia,* Baltimore, Johns Hopkins Press, 1933, p. 32.

11 W. G Beasley, *Japanese Imperialism 1894–1945,* Oxford, Oxford University Press, 1987, p. 158.

12 Price, *The Russo–Japanese Treaties,* p. 121.

13 The revolutions occurred in February and October by the Orthodox calendar, and March and November by the (Western) Julian calendar. Hence Russians refer to the 'October revolution'.

14 For Haushofer and Niedermayer, see Milan Hauner, *What is Asia to Us: Russia's Asian Heartland Theory Today and Yesterday,* London, Routledge, 1992, chapter 8.

15 Warner and Warner, *The Tide at Sunrise,* p. 585.

16 Nicholas John Spykman, *America's Strategy in World Politics: The United States and the Balance of Power,* New York, Harcourt Brace, 1942, p. 195.

17 A. Whitney Griswold, *The Far Eastern Policy of the United States,* New Haven and London, Yale University Press, 1938, p. 216.

18 The text of Trotsky's letter can be found in Bruce A. Elleman, *Diplomacy and Deception: The Secret History of Sino–Soviet Diplomatic Relations, 1917–1925,* New York, Sharpe, 1997, p. 31.

19 Marius B. Jansen, *The Making of Modern Japan*, Cambridge, Ma, Belknap Press of Harvard University Press, 2000, p. 519.

20 For the naval aspects of the Washington agreements, see Christopher Hall, *Britain, America and Arms Control, 1921–37*, New York, St Martins, 1987; and Robert Gordon Kaufman, *Arms Control During the Pre-Nuclear Era: The United States and Naval Limitation Between the Two World Wars*, New York, Columbia University Press, 1990.

21 Milan Hauner, *What is Asia to Us?: Russia's Asian Heartland Theory Yesterday and Today*, London, Routledge, 1992, p. 170.

22 Bruce A. Elleman, *Diplomacy and Deception*: The Secret History of Sino–Soviet Diplomatic Relations, 1917–1927, New York, Sharpe, 1997, p. 131. By means of a secret protocol, Moscow retained most of the personnel positions on the railway.

23 Akira Iriye, *After Imperialism: The Search for a New Order in the Far East, 1921–1931*, Cambridge, Harvard University Press, 1965, p. 55.

24 For details, see Bruce A. Elleman, *Diplomacy and Deception*, pp. 252–258.

25 Guandong (Kwantung) means 'east of the barrier'. The barrier refers to the Shanhaikuan pass, which links China proper with Manchuria.

26 For an elaboration of this theme, see Arthur Waldron, ed, *How the Peace was Lost: The 1935 Memorandum: Developments Affecting American Policy in the Far East*, Stanford, Hoover Press, 1992.

27 Under this agreement, China would have been allowed to buy the Chinese Eastern Railway, in return for allowing Soviet goods into Manchuria duty-free. That would have wiped out the Japanese competition. Bruce A. Elleman, *Modern Chinese Warfare, 1795–1989*, London, Routledge, 2001, p. 190.

28 Elleman, *Modern Chinese Warfare*, p. 191.

29 Elleman, *Diplomacy and Deception*, p. 30.

30 The United States was seeking to set the Philippines on the road to independence, or adrift (depending on how you look at it), by means of the 1934 Tydings–McDuffie Act, which provided for independence after ten years.

31 Waldron, *How the Peace was Lost*, p. 5.

32 George W. A. Baer, *A Question of Trust: The Origins of U.S.–Soviet Diplomatic Relations: The Memoirs of Loy W. Henderson*, Stanford, Ca, Hoover Institution Press, 1986, p. 469.

3. The road to war 1935-1941

1 Even after the war, Stalin often said in the hearing of his daughter Svetlana, 'Ech, together with the Germans we would have been invincible.' Milan Hauner, *What is Asia to Us? Russia's Asian Heartland Yesterday and Today*, London, Routledge, 1992, p. 177.

2 Robert C. Tucker, *Stalin in Power: The Revolution from Above, 1928–1941*, New York, Norton, 1990, p. 344.

3 George W. A. Baer, *A Question of Trust: The Origins of U.S.–Soviet Diplomatic Relations: The Memoirs of Loy W. Henderson*, Stanford, Ca, Hoover Institution Press, 1986, p. 469.

4 John P. Fox, *Germany and the Far Eastern Crisis 1931–1938*, Oxford, Clarendon Press, 1982, p. 203.

5 Jiang Jingguo (Chiang Ching-kuo) had been in the Soviet Union since 1924, and had married a Russian. See Jay Taylor, *The Generalissimo's Son: Chiang Ching-kuo and the Revolutionaries in China and Taiwan*, Cambridge, Ma, Harvard University Press, 2000.

6 The Australians had proposed the non-aggression pact at the Imperial Conference in May–June 1937. When the proposal became public, Japan complained loudly. T. B. Millar, *Australia in Peace and War: External Relations Since 1788*, second edition, Botany, Maxwell Macmillan, Australian National University Press, 1991, pp. 57–58. Japan's complaints may have drawn Stalin's attention.

7 John W. Garver, *Soviet–Chinese Relations 1937–1945: The Diplomacy of Chinese Nationalism*, Oxford, Oxford University Press, 1988, p. 19.

8 According to Jonathan Haslam's account, Bogomolov, the Soviet ambassador to China, exceeded his remit in making this offer, in which he was supported by the Soviet military attaché, Major-General Lepin. Both Bogomolov and Lepin soon fell victim to 'the terror'. Jonathan Haslam *The Soviet Union and the Threat from the East*, Pittsburg, University of Pennsylvania, 1992, p 91. Was Bogomolov executed for too-independent action? Or did Stalin, as he so often did, simply liquidate those who knew too much? Given the circumstances of 1937, when the purges were spreading, it seems unlikely that Bogomolov and Lepin would have risked Stalin's wrath by exceeding their brief. And the offering of a pact to China, and then its sudden withdrawal, were highly characteristic of Stalin's tactics of seeking to embroil others in war.

9 The Japanese soon got wind of this pact, including a secret section that detailed closer military and political links between the two parties. Bruce A. Elleman, *Modern Chinese Warfare, 1795–1989*, Routledge, London, 2001, p. 204.

10 On Sorge and his spy ring, see Chalmers Johnson, *An Instance of Treason: Ozaki Hotsumi and the Sorge Spy Ring*, Stanford, Stanford University Press, 1964, and Robert Whymant, *Stalin's Spy: Richard Sorge and the Tokyo Espionage Ring*, London and New York, L.B. Tauris, 1996.

11 The myth persists that the British guns could not fire in a landward direction. On the contrary, when Singapore fell in February 1942 the guns were still firing. But they were firing naval ordnance, which was of little use against land targets.

12 Department of State, *Nazi–Soviet Relations 1939–1941*, Washington D.C, 1948.

13 Carl Schorske, 'Two German Ambassadors: Dirksen and Schulenburg', in Gordon Craig and Felix Gilbert, eds, *The Diplomats 1919–1939*, New York, Columbia University Press, 1980, p. 490.

14 The British prime minister, Neville Chamberlain, was incapable of *realpolitik*. Winston Churchill, who certainly was capable of it, was out of favour, not least because he was the leading British critic of Munich. In any case, Churchill at the time was an advocate of alliance with Russia. That did not mitigate Soviet paranoia about him, because of his prominent role in the Allied interventions of 1918–1919.

15 Stalin had been sending other signals, for those who cared to look. The Polish communist party, which was likely to oppose vehemently any Nazi–Soviet deal (which would obviously be at Poland's expense), was a particular target of Stalin's terror. So were the Old Bolsheviks, who were also likely to oppose a deal with Hitler. By the end of 1938, astute political prisoners, observing the new kinds of inmates coming into the prison camps, were predicting a Nazi–Soviet pact. Robert C. Tucker, *Stalin in Power: The Revolution from Above, 1928–1941*, New York, Norton, 1990, p. 525.

16 Chihiro Hosoya, 'The Japanese–Soviet Neutrality Pact', in James William Morley, ed, *The Fateful Choice: Japan's Advance into Southeast Asia, 1939–1941*, New York, Columbia University Press, 1980, p. 311.

17 Anthony Read and David Fisher, *The Deadly Embrace: Hitler, Stalin and the Nazi–Soviet Pact 1939–1941*, New York, Norton, 1988, p. 298.

18 *Ibid*, p. 292.

19 Knowing that American intervention was the only way Britain could win the war, Churchill struggled to stay in the conflict long enough for Roosevelt to convince the American public that Britain's survival was vital for America's own security. Thus Churchill employed that classic strategy of British maritime power, a Mediterranean strategy. The Royal Navy drove the Italian fleet back into port, and ruthlessly sank the French fleet lest it fall into Hitler's hands.

20 Waldo Heinrichs, *Threshold of War: Franklin D. Roosevelt and American Entry into World War II*, Oxford, Oxford University Press, 1988, p. 10.

21 *Ibid.* p. 7.

22 The Burma Road had been opened in January 1939, as China's response to Japan's seizing of all the ports in southern China in the previous year. Cargoes were unloaded in Rangoon, shipped north by rail or barge to Mandalay and Lashio, and then trucked over difficult mountain roads to southwest China. In mid-1940, Japan had cut the Haiphong route into Indochina when it occupied French Indochina with the approval of the new Nazi collaborationist government in Hanoi run by the Vichy French.

23 As a colonel in the *Guandong* army, Ishiwara Kanji had been one of the architects of the 1931 Manchurian Incident. But thereafter he realized how much Japan was playing Stalin's game by miring itself in China. Far better, he thought, for Japan to ally itself with China against Russia – with Japan in the lead, of course. No friend of the United States, he had also spent considerable time in Germany, and was apparently influenced by Haushofer's geopolitical thinking. In April 1937, Ishiwara, now a Major-General, was appointed Chief of the Operations Division of the General Staff. After fighting broke out on the Marco Polo bridge, Ishiwara realized that Japan would fall into the same kind of trap that Napoleon had fallen into in Spain. Mark R. Peattie, *Ishiwara Kanji and Japan's Confrontation with the West*, Princeton, Princeton University Press, 1975, p. 302. When Ishiwara returned to China as Vice Chief of Staff of the Kwantung army in the autumn of 1937, he continued to oppose the China war. Not surprisingly, Ishiwara soon found himself sidelined.

24 It says something for the self-imposed isolation of the Bolsheviks that this was the first time Molotov had set foot on foreign soil.

25 Hans von Heywarth, *Against Two Evils*, New York, Rawson, Wade, 1981, p. 186. 'Johnnie' Heywarth had been present at Ribbentrop's meeting in Moscow in August 1939, and had (at considerable risk) tipped off the Americans about what had taken place. He was later linked with the plot to assassinate Hitler, but managed to escape detection. After the war, he became West Germany's first ambassador to Britain.

26 Paul Schmidt, *Hitler's Interpreter*, London, Heinemann, 1951, p. 215.

27 Haslam, *The Soviet Union and the Threat from the East*, p. 147.

28 Molotov was such a toady that he continued to serve Stalin after his own wife was arrested.

29 Hosoya, 'The Japanese–Soviet Neutrality Pact', p. 71.

30 John Huizenga, 'Yosuke Matsuoka and the Japanese–German Alliance', in Gordon Craig and Felix Gilbert, eds, *The Diplomats: 1919–1939*, Princeton: Princeton University Press, 1953, p. 638.

31 Heinrichs, *Threshold of War*, p. 52.

32 For the contentious view that the Emperor was primarily responsible for leading Japan into war, see Herbert P. Bix, *Hirohito and the Making of Modern Japan*, New York, Harper-Collins, 2000. See also Peter Wetzler, *Hirohito and War: Imperial Tradition and Military Decision Making in Prewar Japan*, Honolulu, University of Hawaii Press, 1998.

33 Hosoya, 'The Japanese–Soviet Neutrality Pact', p. 83.

34 *Ibid.*
35 Heinrichs, *Threshold of War*, p. 232, n. 7.
36 There is no credible evidence that Stalin was preparing to attack Germany at this time.
37 Chester Wilmot, *The Struggle for Europe*, London, Collins, 1952, p. 90
38 Did Stalin believe Sorge, who by now had an excellent track record, but whose reporting Stalin had rejected before 22 June? That is hard to know, since Stalin suspected everyone. Moreover, he relied heavily on signals intelligence. He would also have known that the *Guandong* army could not delay any attack much beyond the autumn since it was not equipped for winter warfare, unlike his own Siberian troops.
39 By 4 December, the Japanese task force sent to attack Pearl Harbor had left its base in the Kurils. Did Stalin know of its presence? If so, he would have known that a task force of six aircraft carriers was pointed at the United States, not at Vladivostok. The Japanese naval forces had been careful to keep strict radio silence. Still, it was a large presence, and Stalin had many listening posts in the region. If Stalin did know that Japan was about to attack the United States, that would have increased his confidence in committing the last of his reserves to the desperate battle to save Moscow.
40 Heinrichs, *Threshold of War*, p. 81.
41 *Ibid.*, p. 35.
42 See Agawa Hiroyuki, *The Reluctant Admiral: Yamamoto and the Imperial Navy*, Tokyo, Kodansha, 1979.
43 H. P. Willmott, *Empires in the Balance: Japanese and Allied Pacific Strategies to April 1942*, Annapolis, Md, Naval Institute Press, 1982, p. 128.
44 *Ibid.*, p. 129.
45 Evans and Peattie, *Kaigun*, p. 460.
46 The carrier task forces combined the strength of many hundreds of aircraft, surface ships in close support, and a revolutionary system of mobile supply bases that overcame the problems presented by the vast distances of the Pacific. Added to the capabilities of the carrier task forces were the amphibious assault capabilities developed by the US Marine Corps. Together they comprised an offensive force capable of isolating and overwhelming any island bastion defended by the Japanese navy. *Ibid.*, p. 491.
47 See George Alexander Lensen, *Strange Neutrality: Soviet–Japanese Relations during the Second World War*, Tallahassee, Florida, Diplomatic Press, 1972.
48 The other routes were the difficult and dangerous convoy routes to Murmansk, and the equally difficult route via Iran and the Persian Gulf.
49 That is not to argue that the dropping of atomic bombs on Hiroshima and Nagasaki was unnecessary. On the contrary, diehards in Japan were reluctant to give up even after the second bombing. Moreover, as President Clinton said in 1995, on the fiftieth anniversary of the end of the war, President Truman had no other choice on the basis of the evidence presented to him – including the vast number of expected American casualties in plans to invade Japan's home islands – but to authorize the first (and so far only) use of nuclear weapons in anger. The democracies had finally found the weapon that made the costs of war too high for the dictatorships.
50 That was a coincidence, though many Japanese still do not think so. Stalin attacked Manchuria as soon as he could after the defeat of Germany. Stalin knew about the bomb from his spies in the Manhattan project, but he did not know when it would be dropped, or what effect it would have. But he did know Japan was on its knees, and so hastened to get his share of the spoils. Stalin also sought a fig leaf of international law by announcing the unilateral abrogation of

the neutrality pact in April 1945. But the pact remained technically still in force by August, because abrogation required one year's notice. So this was a fig leaf of the thinnest kind.

51 On 3 September 1945, after Russia had declared war on Japan to get its share of the spoils, Stalin said quite falsely that 'As you know, in the war with Japan Russia suffered defeat at that time. Japan used Tsarist Russia's defeat to seize South Sakhalin from Russia, to gain a foothold on the Kurile islands and thereby lock in our country in the East from all egress to the open sea'. Haslam, *The Soviet Union and the Threat from the East*, p. 3.

52 For the text of the Blakeslee memorandum of 28 December 1944, see John J. Stephan, *The Kuril Islands: Russo–Japanese Frontier in the Pacific*, Oxford, Clarendon Press, 1974, pp. 240–244.

53 In September 1944, the Finns, who had fought like lions as co-belligerents with Germany in what they called the 'Continuation War' against Russia, agreed on an armistice. The terms involved territorial losses and heavy reparations, but were moderate compared with what later happened to other small states on the borders of the Soviet Union. Under the skilful leadership of Marshal Mannerheim, the Finns were able come to terms with Moscow while their military capabilities still gave them something to bargain with. In order to survive, small countries afflicted with bad strategic geography need to be both tough and smart.

4. The Cold War: first phase

1 Kenneth L. Adelman, *The Great Universal Embrace: Arms Summitry – a Skeptic's Account*, New York, Simon and Schuster, 1989, p. 83.

2 Nicholas Spykman, *America's Strategy in World Politics: The United States and the Balance of Power*, New York, Harcourt Brace, 1942, p. 460.

3 See Bruce A. Elleman, Michael R. Nicols and Matthew J. Ouimet, 'A Historical Reevaluation of America's Role in the Kuril Islands Dispute'. *Pacific Affairs*, vol. 71, no. 4, Winter 1998–99, pp. 492–495.

4 Cuba was not a counter-example, because the Cuban communists captured Fidel Castro after he seized power in 1959. The hostility and proximity of the United States made it more or less inevitable that Castro would seek Soviet support, since Cuba's geography had much to offer Moscow.

5 For details of the negotiation of the treaty, see Sergei N. Goncharov, John W. Lewis, and Xue Litai, *Uncertain Partners: Stalin, Mao, and the Korean War*, Stanford, Ca, Stanford University Press, 1993.

6 Many Chinese and North Korean prisoners did not want to go home. The Western democracies had guilty memories of how they had forcibly repatriated Soviet prisoners of war after 1945, to meet firing squads or lingering deaths in Stalin's camps.

7 For Japan's post-war relations with South Korea, see Victor Cha, *Alignment Despite Antagonism: The United States–Korea–Japan Security Triangle*, Stanford, Ca, Stanford University Press, 1999.

8 Thomas J. Christensen, *Useful Adversaries: Grand Strategy, Domestic Mobilization, and Sino–American Conflict, 1947–1958*, Princeton, N.J, Princeton University Press, 1996, p. 195.

9 For details of these negotiations, see Donald C. Hellmann, *Japanese Foreign Policy and Domestic Politics: The Peace Agreement with the Soviet Union*, Berkeley and Los Angeles, University of California Press, 1969.

10 This was the origin of the so-called 'Dulles threat'. See Ellemann *et al.*, 'A Historical Reevaluation of America's Role in the Kuril Islands Dispute'.

11 Kishi had been part of the pre-war 'Manchurian clique', a member of the Tojo cabinet as Minister for Commerce and Industry, and Vice-Minister for munitions. He served three years in gaol from 1946 as a 'Class A' war criminal.

12 James W. Morley, 'Japan's Image of the Soviet Union 1952–1961', *Pacific Affairs*, vol. 35, no. 1, Spring 1962, p. 57.

13 John Wilson Lewis and Xue Litai, *China Builds the Bomb*, Stanford, Ca, Stanford University Press, 1988, p. 177.

14 Pine Gap was established to serve as the ground control station for a CIA–National Reconnaissance Office satellite programme initially code-named RHYOLITE. These satellites, stationed over Borneo and the Horn of Africa, were designed to intercept the telemetry from Soviet and Chinese missile tests, and secondarily to intercept VHF and UHF communications. Jeffrey T. Richelson, *America's Space Sentinels: DSP Satellites and National Security*, Kansas, University Press of Kansas, 1999, p. 50.

15 Constantine Pleshakov, 'Nikita Khrushchev and Sino–Soviet Relations', in Odd Arne Westad, ed, *Brothers in Arms: The Rise and Fall of the Sino–Soviet Alliance, 1945–1963*, Washington D.C. and Stanford, Ca, Woodrow Wilson Center Press and Stanford University Press, Cold War International History Project Series, 1998, p. 235.

16 *Ibid.*, p. 233.

17 For details, see John Wilson Lewis and Xue Litai, *China Builds the Bomb*.

18 Stalin had gained the South Manchurian ports at Yalta in 1945, and had hung on to them in his 1945 treaty with Jiang Jieshi and his 1950 treaty with Mao.

19 *The Khrushchev–Mao conversations of 31 July–3 August 1958 and 2 October 1959*, Woodrow Wilson Cold War International History Project Series, online at <http://ccihp. si.edu/files/zubok-mao> (accessed 12 July 2002).

20 See David Allen Mayers, *Cracking the Monolith: U.S. Policy Against the Sino–Soviet Alliance, 1949–1955*, Baton Rouge and London, Louisiana State University Press, 1986.

21 Richard C. Thornton, *The Nixon–Kissinger Years: The Reshaping of American Foreign Policy*, New York, Paragon House, 1989, p. 118.

22 See Ellen J. Hammer, *A Death in November: America in Vietnam, 1963*, New York, Dutton, 1987.

23 For these events, see Arnold C. Brackman, *The Communist Collapse in Indonesia*, New York, Norton, 1969.

24 Elmo R. Zumwalt Jr, *On Watch: A Memoir*, New York, Quadrangle, 1976, p. 360.

25 Richard C. Thornton, *The Nixon–Kissinger Years*, p. 33.

26 *Ibid.*, p. 21

5. The Cold War: final phase

1 Elmo R. Zumwalt Jr, *On Watch: A Memoir*, New York, Quadrangle, 1976, pp. 390–391.

2 For an account of the economic benefits to the Soviet Union which flowed from détente, see Sol Sanders, *Living Off the West: Gorbachev's Secret Agenda and Why It Will Fail*, New York and London, Madison, 1990, chapter 5.

3 Patrick Glynn, *Closing Pandora's Box: Arms Races, Arms Control and the History of the Cold War*, New York, Basic Books, 1992, p. 216.

4 Comprehension of the strategic geography of the Cold War is also missing from Raymond Garthoff's monumental works. See, for example, Raymond L. Garthoff, *Détente and Confrontation: American–Soviet Relations from Nixon to Reagan*, Washington D.C, Brookings, 1985.

5 Winston Lord, 'Memorandum for Henry A. Kissinger, Memcon of Your Conversation with Chou En-lai, 29 July 1971', p. 29, online at <www.gwu.edu/–nsarchiv/NSAEBB/NSAEBB/66> (accessed 12 July 2002). The Kissinger–Zhou conversations of October 1971 became available in May 2002. See online at <www.gwu.edu/–nsarchiv/NSAEBB/NSAEBB70/index2.html> (accessed 12 July 20020.

6 See Larry A. Niksch, 'Senkaku (Diaoyu) Islands Dispute: The U.S. Legal Relationship and Obligations', *Pacnet* (Pacific Forum CSIS), no. 45, 8 November 1996.

7 In his letter of 20 October 1971, Robert Starr, Acting Assistant Legal Adviser, said that 'The Governments of the Republic of China and Japan are in disagreement as to the sovereignty of the Senkaku Islands. You should know as well that the People's Republic of China has also claimed sovereignty over the islands. The United States believes that a return of Administrative rights over those islands to Japan, from which the rights were received, can in no way prejudice any underlying claims. The United States cannot add to the legal rights Japan possessed before it transferred administration of the islands to us, nor can the United States, by giving back what it received, diminish the rights of other claimants. The United States has made no claim to the Senkaku Islands and considers that any conflicting claims to the islands are a matter for resolution by the parties concerned'; Larry Niksch, 'Senkaku (Diaoyu) Islands Dispute'. For the Senkakus dispute, see also Erica Strecker Downs and Phillip C. Saunders, 'Legitimacy and the Limits of Nationalism: China and the Diaoyu islands', *International Security*, vol. 23, no. 3, Winter 1998/1999, pp. 114–146. The second Bush administration has quietly – but loudly enough for China and Japan to hear – reconfirmed the official US position that the islands come under the ambit of the US–Japan security treaty.

8 I am indebted to Professor Jim Auer for this point.

9 John Welfield, *An Empire in Eclipse: Japan in the Postwar American Alliance System*, London, Athlone, 1988, p. 251.

10 The four non-nuclear policies say that Japan will: adhere to the three non-nuclear principles; make efforts to promote nuclear disarmament; give high priority to the civilian nuclear programme; and depend on the American nuclear deterrent for protection against 'international nuclear threats'.

11 Richard C. Thornton, *The Nixon–Kissinger Years: The Reshaping of American Foreign Policy*, New York, Praeger, p. 132.

12 Even though Indonesia's neighbours averted their gaze, there were negatives for Suharto in invading East Timor. The invasion undermined the image that he had carefully cultivated of being much less adventurist than Sukarno. The Indonesians also behaved brutally, provoking a resistance that never died out. And even though they did much to develop the territory, where Portugal had done almost nothing in four hundred years, the Indonesians left the administration in the hands of the army, and that was a major error. Moreover, the Indonesians killed five Australian journalists during the invasion, which did much to upset Australian–Indonesian relations for the next two decades. Even though Portugal's colonial record did not bear scrutiny, Portugal was also able to maintain pressure on Indonesia via the EU. So the UN did not recognize the incorporation of East Timor into Indonesia.

13 See John W. Garver, 'China's Push Through the South China Sea: The Interaction of Bureaucratic and National Interests', *The China Quarterly*, December 1992, pp. 1001–1005.

14 The fudge went as follows. The White House would not volunteer information about continuing arms sales to Taiwan, but, if asked, it would say that the sale of

selected, defensive arms after the expiration of the defence treaty would continue in a way that did not endanger prospects for peace in the region. Patrick Tyler, *A Great Wall: Six Presidents and China*, New York, Century, 1999, p. 270.

15 For example, in 1979 foreign minister Sonoda Sunao held a meeting in New York with the Soviet foreign minister, Andrei Gromyko, the gist of which was widely publicized. In response to the rapid Soviet build-up, Sonoda said that 'although I would not approve of the build-up of the [Soviet] military strength, I can appreciate the Soviet position. I presume that in view of the state of US–Soviet relations, you are doing so in order to prevent a war. I do respect the efforts by Secretary Brezhnev because he is endeavouring to prevent wars'. Garrett N. Scalera, 'U.S. Policy Toward Asia: A Time for New Priorities', *Comparative Strategy*, vol. 2, no. 4, 1980, p. 311.

16 For the INF crisis, see Jonathan Haslam, *The Soviet Union and the Politics of Nuclear Weapons in Europe, 1969–87*, Ithaca, N.Y, Cornell University Press, 1990.

17 The seven-minute flight time of the Pershing IIA from West Germany to Moscow would have allowed the Soviet politburo insufficient time to head for their bunkers.

18 Similarly, the Soviet lodgement in Cuba complicated US reinforcement of Europe.

19 For an account of the importance of access routes in Southwest Asia, see Mahnaz Z. Ispahani, *Roads and Rivals: The Political Uses of Access in the Borderlands of Asia*, Ithaca, N.Y. and London, Cornell University Press, 1989.

20 See The Russian General Staff, *The Soviet–Afghan War: How a Superpower Fought and Lost*, trans. and ed. Lester W. Grau and Michael A. Gress, Kansas, University Press of Kansas, 2002.

21 Kenneth Adelman, 'Why is Europe Still Fighting "Star Wars"', *The Wall Street Journal*, 2 February 2001.

22 For the submarine 'war', see Sherry Sontag and Christopher Drew, *Blind Man's Bluff: The Untold Story of American Submarine Espionage*, New York, Public Affairs, 1998.

23 See Graham Spinaldi, 'Why the U.S. Navy Went for Hard-Target Counterforce in Trident II (And Why It Didn't Get There Sooner)', *International Security*, vol. 15, no. 2, Fall 1990, pp. 147–190.

24 John J. Holdridge, *Crossing the Divide: An Insider's Account of the Normalization of U.S.–China Relations*, Lanham, Md, Rowman and Littlefield, 1997, p. 232.

25 On the deficiencies of Japan's defence capability at the beginning of the Reagan era, see Taketsugu Tsurutani, 'Japan's Security, Defense Responsibilities, and Capabilities', *Orbis*, Spring 1981, pp. 89–106.

26 Calling each other 'Ron' and 'Yasu', Reagan and Nakasone met twelve times.

27 Aegis stands for 'Airborne Early warning/Ground Integration Segment'.

28 Officially, the *Midway* was not homeported in Yokosuka. Insisting on legal niceties, the Japanese government said the carrier was on 'extended deployment' to the Seventh Fleet, lest the term 'homeporting' be seen to violate the Cabinet Legislative Office's ruling that Japan could not engage in collective self-defence.

29 See Robyn Lim, 'Australian Security after the Cold War', *Orbis*, vol. 42, no. 1, Winter 1998, pp. 91–103.

30 Eric Heginbotham and Richard J. Samuels, 'Mercantile Realism and Japanese Foreign Policy', *International Security*, vol. 22, no. 4, Spring 1998, p. 176.

6. The quadrilateral continues

1 See Michael Green, *Japan's Reluctant Realism: Foreign Policy Challenges in an Era of Uncertain Power*, New York, Palgrave, Council on Foreign Relations, 2001.

2 Despite Japan's dependence on Gulf oil, few in Japan seemed to see an interest at stake when Iraq invaded Kuwait. Japan's instinct was to say that Iraq would keep pumping oil, and Japan had the money to buy it. The Bush administration did not push Japan to contribute offensive capabilities, but it did want Japan to send minesweepers, not least because of US deficiencies in minesweeping. But the Kaifu government dithered. In the end, it did send minesweepers, but only after hostilities ended. Japan contributed some $13 billion, but got little thanks, including from Kuwait. Had the war gone on longer, or if US casualties had been higher, the US–Japan alliance might have been at serious risk.

3 These were that the United States would not support Taiwan's independence, the creation of two Chinas, or the entry of Taiwan into any international body for which statehood was a requirement. The 'three noes' made their first appearance in a private letter that Clinton wrote to Jiang Zemin in the summer of 1995. James Mann, *About Face: A History of America's Curious Relationship with China, From Nixon to Clinton*, New York, Vintage, 2000, p. 355.

4 The Emperor expressed 'deep sorrow' and 'regret' for the 'great suffering' caused to the Chinese people.

5 But it should be noted that Japan's costs, including personnel costs, are high. Japan also manufactures most of its own arms and equipment, and is thus unable to achieve economies of scale because of the prohibition on arms exports.

6 Japan's lack of strategic depth is not necessarily an impediment to the acquisition of nuclear weapons. Similar problems did not prevent Britain from opting for an independent sea-based nuclear deterrent. True, lack of strategic depth did limit Britain's options during the Cold War. The British had the ability to threaten Moscow, but lacked the range of options available to the superpowers. Similarly, lack of strategic depth would limit Japan's options. But it does not rule it out of the game.

7 For an account of Japan's response to the North Korean nuclear crisis, see Funabashi Yoichi, *Alliance Adrift*, New York, Council on Foreign Relations, 1999, chapter 13. See also Michael Green, *Japan's Reluctant Realism*, pp. 120–123.

8 Michael J. Green and Katsuhika Furukawa, 'New Ambitions, Old Obstacles: Japan and its Search for an Arms Control Strategy', *Arms Control Today*, July/August 2000, p. 21.

9 Mann, *About Face*, p. 334.

10 This was one reason that India opted to test nuclear weapons in May 1998. India, confronted by a rising China, sought to make itself invulnerable to Chinese nuclear blackmail. But India then gave Pakistan little choice but to follow suit, thus providing Pakistan with an 'equalizer' that made up for its inferiority in the conventional balance. In the 1999 Kargil crisis, when Pakistan-backed forces occupied the high ground on the Line of Control and intruded into India-controlled Kashmir, Pakistan did not seem at all inhibited by India's possession of nuclear weapons. The next crisis, in mid-2002, occurred as a consequence of the war in Afghanistan. This crisis also subsided, though it required high-level attention from the United States, Britain and the European Union. But it was an illustration of one of the many paradoxes surrounding nuclear weapons. Just because they contributed to strategic stability during the Cold War, that does not mean that they will do so in all hands, and in all circumstances.

11 See Felix K. Chang, 'Beijing's Reach in the South China Sea', *Orbis*, Summer 1996, pp. 353–366; Jun Zhan, 'China Goes to the Blue Waters: The Navy, Seapower Mentality and the South China Sea', *The Journal of Strategic Studies*, vol. 17, no. 3, September 1994, pp. 180–208; John W. Garver, 'China's Push Through the South China Sea: The Interaction of Bureaucratic and National Interests', *The China Quarterly*, December 1992, pp. 999–1028.

12 John W. Garver, *Protracted Contest: Sino–Indian Rivalry in the Twentieth Century*, Seattle and London, University of Washington Press, 2001, p. 284.

13 The Chinese Navy began to show an interest in aircraft carriers in the early 1980s. In 1985, it purchased the retired Royal Australian Navy carrier, the *Melbourne*, apparently for scrap. After the collapse of the USSR, China also began to show an interest in acquiring the *Varyag*. The *Varyag* was one of two full-deck carriers that the USSR was building just before the end of the Cold War. In 1998, a Chinese firm bought the smaller antisubmarine carrier the *Minsk* from a South Korean scrapyard. It is now a museum piece in Guangzhou harbour. In 2000, China bought the sister ship to the *Minsk*, the *Kiev*, which became the centrepiece of an entertainment park in the port of Tianjin. By early 2002, the *Varyag* was in the Dalian shipyard, the Chinese government having prevailed upon Turkey to permit the tugs towing it to transit the dangerous narrows of the Bosphorous Strait. China claims that the *Varyag*, now little more than a floating hulk, will be used as a gambling casino in Macau. But some observers believe that China's shipyards could convert it to an operational carrier. Still, acquiring aircraft carriers would entail huge costs, including opportunity costs. To keep a single carrier on station requires at least three carriers, because of maintenance and deployment schedules. Moreover, China's acquisition of long-range maritime power projection capabilities would take a long time. It would also alarm Japan and the United States, thus strengthening their alliance and fostering moves towards a 'containment' strategy.

14 A. D. McLennan, 'Balance, Not Containment: A Geopolitical Take from Canberra', *The National Interest*, no. 49, Fall 1997, p. 56.

15 Some claim that nearly 20 per cent of the world's remaining recoverable oil lies beneath the South China Sea, while others dispute these estimates. Large reserves of natural gas are believed to be there. In addition, there are large resources of fish and other marine food sources.

16 The Philippine Navy, although one of the region's weakest, had rushed around tearing up Chinese reef markers in a transparent attempt to entangle the United States in the dispute. This has been a long-term objective of the Philippines.

17 In April 2002, Ichiro Ozawa, the Liberal Party leader and LDP renegade, said that if China did not stop bullying Japan, Japan could easily develop 'thousands of nuclear warheads'. Then, in May of that year, Abe Shinzo, grandson of Kishi Nobuske and current deputy chief cabinet secretary, told students at Waseda University that Japan's constitution does not rule out the possession of nuclear weapons. In the resulting furore when these comments leaked, Abe was backed up by the chief cabinet secretary Fukuda Yasuo, son of former prime minister Fukuda of the Kishi–Sato faction of the LDP. Fukuda and Abe should know. As we have seen, when he was prime minister, Kishi firmly rebuffed efforts to have any 'non-nuclear principles' attached to the constitution, which is difficult to amend. Nuclear weapons do not represent an attractive option for Japan. One reason is that the mere hint that Japan was really thinking of acquiring such weapons would trigger great tensions, both in the region and with the United States. Still, the fact that Fukuda and Abe were at no risk of losing their jobs showed that it was no longer taboo in Japan to discuss nuclear weapons, and that some Japanese were beginning to think that because of the growing threat to

Japan from Chinese and North Korean missiles, Japan's nuclear umbrella might be beginning to spring a leak.

18 On 1 April, a Chinese fighter aircraft crashed, killing the pilot, after it flew too close to an American EP-3 surveillance aircraft which was flying in international airspace off Hainan island. The EP-3 was forced to make an emergency landing on Hainan, and China detained the crew for eleven days. A stand-off ensued until the United States made an apology, and still the Chinese would not allow the aircraft to be repaired *in situ*. It was finally flown back to the US in crates. But it should be noted that the United States said it was 'very sorry' only for the loss of the Chinese pilot, and did not retract from its position that the pilot was at fault or that the US was entitled to use international airspace. The incident was notable because of the extent of Chinese nationalism that had been revealed, and because it seemed that the PLA had kept the truth from the political leadership for some time. The Chinese also tried to intimidate US allies, for example by challenging an Australian flotilla making a routine deployment through the Taiwan Strait, an international waterway. The Australians refuted China's alleged right to challenge them, and continued on their way.

19 For example, while repeating the mantra of 'one China', he did not mention the three communiqués, but referred repeatedly to the Taiwan Relations Act.

20 Most of the bombing was undertaken by B-1 and B-52 bombers operating from Diego Garcia.

21 J. Mohan Malik, 'Dragon on Terrorism: Assessing China's Tactical Gains and Strategic Losses Post 9–11', unpublished paper, June 2002, p. 28.

22 Still, Koizumi did not speak to Bush until two days after the attack, and was the last allied leader to do so. Moreover, initially Koizumi talked about Japan's constitutional limits, the usual Japanese code for doing nothing.

23 The others were Russia, North Korea, Iraq, Iran, Syria and Libya.

Conclusion: war without end?

1 See Robyn Lim, 'The ASEAN Regional Forum: Building on Sand', *Contemporary Southeast Asia*, vol. 2, no. 2, August 1998, pp. 115–136.

2 Cf. Benjamin Schwarz and Christopher Layne, 'A New Grand Strategy', *The Atlantic Monthly*, January 2002, pp. 36–42. See also Eugene Gholz, Daryl G. Press and Harvey M. Sapolsky, 'Come Home America: the Strategy of Restraint in the Face of Temptation', *International Security*, vol. 21, no. 4, Spring 1997, pp. 5–48.

3 Robert S. Ross, 'The Geography of the Peace: East Asia in the Twenty-first Century', *International Security*, vol. 23, no. 4, Spring 1999, pp. 97.

4 See, for example, W. Harrison Wagner, 'What was Bipolarity?', *International Organization*, vol. 47, no. 1, Winter 1993, pp. 77–106.

5 Zbigniew Brzezinski, *The Grand Chessboard: American Primacy and its Geostrategic Imperatives*, New York, BasicBooks, 1997, pp. 207–208.

6 See, for example, Edward Timberlake and William C. Triplett II, *Red Dragon Rising: Communist China's Military Threat to America*, Washington, D.C, Regney, 1999.

7 Cf. Selig S. Harrison, 'Time to Leave Korea', *Foreign Affairs*, vol. 80, no. 2, March/April 2001, pp. 62–78.

8 The clash, provoked by North Korea, was probably a result of the North's wishing to rain on Seoul's parade. It occurred on the same day as the final game in Yokohama of the International Football World Cup, co-hosted by Japan and South Korea.

Bibliography

Adelman, Kenneth L., *The Great Universal Embrace: Arms Control: A Skeptic's Account*, New York, Simon and Schuster, 1989.

——, 'Why is Europe Still Fighting "Star Wars?"', *The Wall Street Journal*, 2 February 2001.

Agawa, Hiroyuki, *The Reluctant Admiral: Yamamoto and the Imperial Navy*, Tokyo, Kodansha, 1979.

Baer, George W. A., *A Question of Trust: The Origins of U.S.–Soviet Diplomatic Relations: The Memoirs of Loy W. Henderson*, Stanford, Ca., Hoover Institution Press, 1986.

Beasley, W. G., *Japanese Imperialism 1894–1945*, Oxford, Oxford University Press, 1987.

Bix, Herbert P., *Hirohito and the Making of Modern Japan*, New York, Harper-Collins, 2000.

Brackman, Arnold C., *The Communist Collapse in Indonesia*, New York, Norton, 1969.

Brzezinsky, Zbigniew, *The Grand Chessboard: American Primacy and its Geostrategic Imperatives*, New York, Basic Books, 1997.

Cha, Victor, *Alignment Despite Antagonism: The United States–Korea–Japan Security Triangle*, Stanford, Ca., Stanford University Press, 1999.

Chang, Felix K., 'Beijing's Reach in the South China Sea', *Orbis*, vol. 40, no. 3, Summer 1996, pp. 353–366.

Chang, Gordon G., *The Coming Collapse of China*, New York, Random House, 2001.

Christensen, Thomas J., *Useful Adversaries: Grand Strategy, Domestic Mobilization, and Sino–American Conflict, 1947–1958*, Princeton, N.J., Princeton University Press, 1996.

Department of State, *Nazi-Soviet Relations 1939–1941*, Washington D.C., 1948.

Dickinson, Frederick R., *War and National Reinvention: Japan in the Great War, 1914–1919*, Cambridge, Ma., Harvard University Press, 1999.

Downs, Erica Strecker and Phillip C. Saunders, 'Legitimacy and the Limits of Nationalism: China and the Diaoyu Islands', *International Security*, vol. 23, no. 3, Winter 1998–1999, pp. 114–146.

Elleman, Bruce A., *Diplomacy and Deception: The Secret History of Sino–Soviet Diplomatic Relations, 1917–1927*, New York, Sharpe, 1997.

——, 'The 1907–1916 Russo–Japanese secret treaties: A reconsideration', *Journal of Cultural Studies*, no. 25, March 1999.

——, *Modern Chinese Warfare, 1795–1989*, London, Routledge, 2001.

Elleman, Bruce A., Michael R. Nichols and Matthew J. Ouimet, 'A Historical Reevaluation of America's Role in the Kuril Islands Dispute', *Pacific Affairs*, vol. 71, no. 4, Winter 1998–99.

Evans, David and Mark R. Peattie, *Kaigun: Strategy, Tactics, and Technology in the Imperial Japanese Navy, 1887–1941*, Annapolis, Md., Naval Institute Press, 1997.

Fox, John P., *Germany and the Far Eastern Crisis 1931–1938*, Oxford, Clarendon Press, 1982.

Funabashi, Yoichi, *Alliance Adrift*, New York, Council on Foreign Relations, 1999.

Garthoff, Raymond, *Détente and Confrontation: American–Soviet Relations from Nixon to Reagan*, Washington D.C., Brookings, 1985.

Garver, John, *Soviet–Chinese Relations 1937–1945: The Diplomacy of Chinese Nationalism*, Oxford, Oxford University Press, 1988.

——, 'China's Push through the South China Sea: The Interaction of Bureaucratic and National Interests', *The China Quarterly*, December 1992, pp. 998–1028.

——, *Protracted Contest: Sino–Indian Rivalry in the Twentieth Century*, Seattle and London, University of Washington Press, 2001.

Gholz, Eugene, Daryl L. Press and Harvey M. Sapolsky, 'Come Home America: the Strategy of Restraint in the Face of Temptation', *International Security*, vol. 21, no. 4, Spring 1997, pp. 5–38.

Glynn, Patrick, *Closing Pandora's Box: Arms Races, Arms Control, and the History of the Cold War*, New York, Basic Books, 1992.

Goncharov, Sergei N., John W. Lewis and Xue Litai, *Uncertain Partners: Stalin, Mao and the Korean War*, Stanford, Ca., Stanford University Press, 1993.

Gray, Colin S. and Geoffrey Sloan, eds, *Geopolitics: Geography and Strategy*, London, Cass, 1999.

Green, Michael, *Japan's Reluctant Realism: Foreign Policy Challenges in an Era of Uncertain Power*, New York, Palgrave, Council on Foreign Relations, 2001.

Green, Michael and Katsuhika Furukawa, 'New Ambitions, Old Obstacles: Japan and its Search for an Arms Control Strategy', *Arms Control Today*, July/August 2000.

Griswold, A. Whitney, *The Far Eastern Policy of the United States*, New Haven and London, Yale University Press, 1938.

Hall, Christopher, *Britain, America and Arms Control, 1921–1937*, New York, St Martins, 1987.

Hammer, Ellen J., *A Death in November: America in Vietnam, 1963*, New York, Dutton, 1987.

Harrison, Selig S., 'Time to Leave Korea', *Foreign Affairs*, vol. 80, no. 2, March/April 2001, pp. 62–78.

Haslam, Jonathan, *The Soviet Union and the Politics of Nuclear Weapons in Europe, 1969–87*, Ithaca, N.Y., Cornell University Press, 1990.

——, *The Soviet Union and the Threat from the East*, Pittsburg, University of Pennsylvania, 1992.

Hauner, Milan, *What is Asia to Us?: Russia's Asian Heartland Yesterday and Today*, London, Routledge, 1992.

Heginbotham, Eric and Richard J. Samuels, 'Mercantile Realism and Japanese Foreign Policy', *International Security*, vol. 22, no. 4, Spring 1998, pp. 178–203.

Heinrichs, Waldo, *Threshold of War: Franklin D. Roosevelt and American Entry into World War II*, New York and Oxford, Oxford University Press, 1988.

Hellmann, Donald, *Japanese Foreign Policy and Domestic Politics: The Peace Agreement with the Soviet Union*, Berkeley and Los Angeles, University of California Press, 1969.

Holdridge, John H., *Crossing the Divide: An Insider's Account of the Normalization of U.S.–China Relations*, Lanham, Md., Rowman and Littlefield, 1997.

Hosoya, Chihiro, 'The Japanese–Soviet Neutrality Pact', in James William Morley, ed., *The Fateful Choice: Japan's Advance into Southeast Asia, 1939–1941*, New York, Columbia University Press, 1980.

Huizenga, John, 'Yosuke Matsuoka and the Japanese–German Alliance', in Gordon Craig and Felix Gilbert, eds, *The Diplomats 1919–1939*, Princeton, N.J., Princeton University Press, 1953.

Iriye, Akira, *After Imperialism: The Search for a New Order in the Far East, 1921–1931*, Cambridge, Ma., Harvard University Press, 1965.

Ispahani, Mahnaz Z., *Roads and Rivals: The Political Uses of Access in the Borderlands of Asia*, Ithaca, N.Y. and London, Cornell University Press, 1989.

Jansen, Marius B., *The Making of Modern Japan*, Cambridge, Ma. and London, Belknap Press of Harvard University, 2000.

Johnson, Chalmers, *An Instance of Treason: Ozaki Hotsumi and the Sorge Spy Ring*, Stanford, Ca., Stanford University Press, 1964.

Kaufman, Robert Gordon, *Arms Control During the Pre-Nuclear Era: The United States and Naval Limitation Between the Two World Wars*, New York, Columbia University Press, 1990.

Le Donne, John P., *The Russian Empire and the World 1700–1917: The Geopolitics of Expansion and Containment*, New York, Oxford University Press, 1997.

Lensen, George Alexander, *Strange Neutrality: Soviet–Japanese Relations during the Second World War*, Tallahassee, Diplomatic Press, 1972.

Lewis, John Wilson and Xue Litai, *China Builds the Bomb*, Stanford, Ca., Stanford University Press, 1988.

Lim, Robyn, 'Australian Security after the Cold War', *Orbis*, vol. 42, no. 1, Winter 1998, pp. 91–103.

——, 'The ASEAN Regional Forum: Building on Sand', *Contemporary Southeast Asia*, vol. 2, no. 2, August 1998, pp.115–136.

Lord, Winston, 'Memorandum for Henry Kissinger, Memcom of Your Conversation with Chou En-lai, 29 July 1971. National Security Archives. Online at <www.gwu.edu/–nsarchiv/NSAEBB/NSAEBB/66> (accessed 12 July 2002).

McDougall, Walter A., *Let the Sea Make a Noise: Four Hundred Years of Cataclysm, Conquest, War and Folly in the North Pacific*, New York, Avon, 1993.

McLennan, A. D., 'Balance, Not Containment: A Geopolitical Take from Canberra', *The National Interest*, no. 49, Fall 1997, pp. 52–63.

Malik, J. Mohan, 'Dragon on Terrorism: Assessing China's Tactical Gains and Strategic Losses Post 9–11', unpublished paper, June 2002.

Mann, James, *About Face: A History of America's Curious Relationship with China, From Nixon to Clinton*, New York, Vintage, 2000.

Mayers, David Allen, *Cracking the Monolith: U.S. Policy Against the Sino–Soviet Alliance, 1949–1955*, Baton Rouge and London, Louisiana State University Press, 1986.

Mearsheimer, John J., *The Tragedy of Great Power Politics*, New York, Norton, 2001.

Millar, T. B., *Australia in Peace and War: External Relations Since 1788*, second edition, Botany, Maxwell Macmillan, Australian National University Press, 1991.

Morley, James W., 'Japan's Image of the Soviet Union 1952–1961', *Pacific Affairs*, vol. 35, no. 1, Spring 1962.

Myers, Ramon H., 'Japanese Imperialism in Manchuria: The South Manchuria Railway Company, 1906–1937', in Peter Duus, Ramon H. Myers, and Mark R. Peattie, *The Japanese Informal Empire in China, 1895–1937*, Princeton, N.J., Princeton University Press, 1989.

Niksch, Larry A., 'Senkaku (Diaoyu) Islands Dispute: The U.S. Legal Relationship and Obligations', *Pacnet*, Pacific Forum/CSIS, no. 45, 8 November 1996.

Okazaki, Hisahiko, *A Grand Strategy for Japanese Defense*, New York and London, Abt, 1986.

Peattie, Mark R., *Ishiwara Kanji and Japan's Confrontation with the West*, Princeton, N.J., Princeton University Press, 1975.

Pleshakov, Constantine, 'Nikita Khrushchev and Sino–Soviet Relations', in Odd Arne Westad, ed., *Brothers in Arms: The Rise and Fall of the Sino–Soviet Alliance, 1945–1963*, Washington D.C. and Stanford, Ca., Woodrow Wilson Center Press and Stanford University Press, Cold War International History Project Series, 1998.

——, *The Tsar's Last Armada: The Epic Voyage to the Battle of Tsushima*, New York, Basic Books, 2002.

Price, Ernest Batson, *The Russo–Japanese Treaties of 1907–1916 Concerning Manchuria and Mongolia*, Baltimore, Johns Hopkins Press, 1933.

Read, Anthony and David Fisher, *The Deadly Embrace: Hitler, Stalin and the Nazi–Soviet Pact 1939–1941*, New York, Norton, 1988.

Richelson, Jeffrey T., *America's Space Sentinels: DSP Satellites and National Security*, Kansas, University Press of Kansas, 1999.

Ross, Robert S., 'The Geography of the Peace: East Asia in the Twenty-First Century', *International Security*, vol. 23, no. 4, Spring 1999, pp. 81–118.

Sanders, Sol, *Living Off the West: Gorbachev's Secret Agenda and Why It Will Fail*, New York and London, Maddison, 1990.

Scalera, Garret N., 'U.S Policy Toward Asia: A Time for New Priorities', *Comparative Strategy*, vol. 2, no. 4, 1980.

Schmidt, Paul, *Hitler's Intepreter*, London, Heinemann, 1951.

Schorske, Carl, 'Two German Diplomats: Dirksen and Schulenburg', in Gordon Craig and Felix Gilbert, eds, *The Diplomats 1919–1939*, New York, Columbia University Press, 1980.

Schwarz, Benjamin and Christopher Layne, 'A New Grand Strategy', *The Atlantic Monthly*, January 2002, pp. 36–42.

Spykman, Nicholas John, *America's Strategy in World Politics: The United States and the Balance of Power*, New York, Harcourt Brace, 1942.

Sontag, Sherry and Christopher Drew, *Blind Man's Bluff: The Untold Story of American Submarine Espionage*, New York, Public Affairs, 1998.

Spinaldi, G.,'Why the US Navy Went for Hard-Target Counterforce in Trident II (And Why It Didn't Get There Sooner)', *International Security*, vol. 15, no. 2, Fall 1990.

Stephan, John J., *The Kuril Islands: Russo–Japanese Frontier in the Pacific*, Oxford, Clarendon Press, 1974.

Swain, Michael D. and Ashley J. Tellis, *Interpreting China's Grand Strategy: Past, Present and Future*, Santa Monica, Ca., RAND, 2000.

Taylor, Jay, *The Generalissimo's Son: Chiang Ching-kuo and the Revolutions in China and Taiwan*, Cambridge, Ma., and London, Harvard University Press, 2000.

The Russian General Staff, *The Soviet Afghan War: How a Superpower Fought and Lost*, Trans. and ed. by Lester W. Grau and Michael A. Gress, Kansas, University of Kansas Press, 2002.

Thornton, Richard C., *The Nixon–Kissinger Years: The Reshaping of American Foreign Policy*, New York, Paragon, 1989.

Timberlake, Edward and William C. Triplett II, *Red Dragon Rising: Communist China's Military Threat to America*, Washington D.C., Regney, 1999.

Toby, Ronald P., *State and Diplomacy in Early Modern Japan: Asia in the Development of the Tokugawa Bakufu*, Stanford, Ca., Stanford University Press, 1991.

Tsurutani, Taketsugu, 'Japan's Security, Defense Responsibilities and Capabilities', *Orbis*, vol. 25, no. 1, Spring 1981, pp. 89–106.

Tucker, Robert C., *Stalin in Power: The Revolution from Above, 1928–1941*, New York, Norton, 1990.

Tyler, Patrick, *A Great Wall: Six Presidents and China*, New York, Century Foundation, 1999.

Von Heywarth, Hans, *Against Two Evils*, New York, Rawson, Wade, 1981.

Wagner, W. Harrison, 'What was Bipolarity?', *International Organization*, vol. 47, no. 1, Winter 1993, pp. 77–106.

Waldron, Arthur, *How the Peace was Lost: The 1935 Memorandum, Developments Affecting American Policy in the Far East Prepared for the State Department by John Van Antwerp MacMurray*, Stanford, Ca., Hoover Institute Press, 1992.

Warner, Denis and Warner, Peggy, *The Tide at Sunrise: A History of the Russo–Japanese War, 1904–1905*, New York, Charterhouse, 1974.

Welfield, John, *An Empire in Eclipse: Japan in the Postwar American Alliance System*, London, Athlone Press, 1988.

Westad, Odd Arne, ed., *Brothers in Arms: The Rise and Fall of the Sino–Soviet Alliance, 1945–1963*, Washington D.C. and Stanford, Ca., Woodrow Wilson Center Press and Stanford University Press, Cold War International History Project Series, 1998.

Wetzler, Peter, *Hirohito and War: Imperial Tradition and Military Decision Making in Prewar Japan*, Honolulu, University of Hawaii Press, 1998.

Whymant, Robert, *Stalin's Spy: Richard Sorge and the Tokyo Espionage Ring*, London and New York, L. B. Tauris, 1996.

Wilmot, Chester, *The Struggle for Europe*, London, Collins, 1952.

Willmott, H. P., *Empires in the Balance: Japanese and Allied Pacific Strategies to April 1942*, Annapolis, Md., Naval Institute Press, 1982.

Zhan, Jun, 'China Goes to the Blue Waters: The Navy, Seapower Mentality and the South China Sea', *The Journal of Strategic Studies*, vol. 17, no. 3, September 1994, pp.180–208.

Zumwalt, Elmo R. Jr, *On Watch: A Memoir*, New York, Quadrangle, 1976.

Index